DESCRIPTIVE STATISTICAL TECHNIQUES FOR LIBRARIANS

Arthur W. Hafner

AMERICAN LIBRARY ASSOCIATION

Chicago and London 1989

Designed by Thomas J. Podsadecki and Arthur W. Hafner.
Composed by the author using Xerox Ventura Publisher Version
2.0 and the Professional Extension. Text was developed using
WordPerfect Version 5.0. All figures were created using
EasyCAD and Graph-in-the-Box Release 2. The typeface used
is Times Roman.

Printed on 50# Glatfelter B-16, a pH-neutral stock.

The paper used in this publication meets the minimum require-
ments of American National Standard for Information Sciences—
Permanence of Paper for Printed Library Materials,
ANSI Z39.48-1984. ⊚

Library of Congress Cataloging-in-Publication Data
Hafner, Arthur Wayne, 1943-
  Descriptive statistical techniques for librarians / Arthur W.
Hafner.
       p.   cm.
  Bibliography: p.
  Includes index.
  ISBN 0-8389-0510-2 (alk. paper)
  1. Library science — Statistical methods. 2. Library statistics.
I. Title.
Z669.8.H33 1989
020′.72—dc19   89-144

Contents

Preface

This book is the outgrowth of lecture notes from a general statistics course which I first taught at Northland College, Ashland, Wisconsin. Later, I expanded and modified these outlines for use in teaching a biostatistics course to first-year students of the University of Minnesota School of Medicine at Duluth. Many of the examples and problems are derived from lectures and seminars I have given over the past several years to librarians in health science and public libraries.

This book is intended to serve as a textbook for a first course in research methods for library and information science students. It is also designed as a reference manual to meet the needs of administrators, librarians, museum curators, archivists, resource center technicians, and managers working in information centers.

The book emphasizes descriptive statistics, the basis of statistical analysis. Understanding this discipline is essential for the application of the ideas and procedures that comprise more advanced statistics.

The book's objective is to show the reader how statistics is used and how to evaluate and interpret the meaning of the various statistical measures. No effort is made to train the reader to become a statistician.

In presenting statistical ideas, I have selected those that are most useful, most widely referenced in library journals, and most essential for further study. I have stressed an understanding of terminology. The focus of the text is on the analysis and interpretation of data. Some of the ideas may appear to be overexplained, but my experience has been that few readers of statistics believe that overexplaining is a danger. Examples are used throughout the book for clarification, and I have used common sense observations to appeal to the reader's intuition and experience. The reader will find no mathematical proofs. Even so, I have made every effort to ensure that the material is mathematically accurate.

I have assumed a familiarity with algebra but have limited the number of formulas and kept the notation simple, purposely including several problems that require considerable number-crunching. The objective of these exercises is to familiarize the student with the formulas introduced in the chapters and with the processes involved in arriving at a statistical measure.

I have deliberately eliminated material not used on the contemporary scene. Hence, techniques such as coding data are not shown since calculators and computers have made these routines obsolete. Grouped frequency distributions, however, are shown because they continue to appear in the literature despite the ease and wide availability of pocket calculators and computers for rapidly analyzing individual observations.

I believe that solving problems is an essential part of learning statistics. I have included problems from many areas of librarianship and the business side of information management. These problems are designed to stimulate the student's statistical thinking and to encourage recognition of other areas where statistical analysis can be applied. I recommend that the student attempt to solve all the exercises. As a check, detailed solutions for selected numerical exercises are shown in the appendix. When possible, I have selected real data. Sometimes tailored data ("hypothetical data") are used to simplify calculations, even though the situations described are real.

I hope that students and information service professionals enjoy using this book as much as I have enjoyed writing it. I encourage and welcome my readers' comments and suggestions for ways to improve this text and especially for problems to include in a future edition.

Acknowledgments

I want to thank Carol A. Doll, Ph.D., Graduate School of Library and Information Science, University of Washington, Seattle, for her constructive comments that helped me greatly in preparing this final version of the book. I am also appreciative to Herbert Bloom, Senior Editor, American Library Association, for his comments and encouragement throughout the preparation of my manuscript, and to ALA's Peter Broeksmit, Production Manager for Books, for his guidance and suggestions in the layout and design of this text.

I also want to thank my colleagues and students who have contributed in innumerable ways to my efforts in preparing it. I cannot name them all here, but the following deserve special thanks for making several significant suggestions based on practical experience: Brian G. Kibble-Smith, J.D., and William P. Whitely, whose comments and suggestions are reflected in the organization and presentation of the material; Thomas J. Podsadecki, for his critical views of the manuscript and for scrutinizing the tables and formulas and for verifying the solutions to the exercises; George Kruto for his technical advice and assistance with indexing; and C. Diane Holtz, for her encouragement, numerous thoughtful comments, and helpful criticisms of the manuscript from a nonmathematician's point of view and for her assistance in proofreading the manuscript.

I am indebted to Ralph J. Anderson, Elmer J. Franzman, and to the late James R. Lewinski, among others, who provided early encouragement for me to pursue undergraduate and graduate studies, and to M. Roy Schwarz, M.D., for his encouragement and support of my research and publishing interests, and to Menachem Mendel Schneerson, Shlita, who served to inspire me whenever my energy and enthusiasm waned.

I am grateful to the late Irma Bettina Austin and Dora Henrietta Lantz for their encouragement and unflagging support during the time that I knew them. I have greatly benefitted from their guidance and council and shall always be in their debt. I acknowledge the contribution of my wife Ruthie and family who understood when a certain grouchy writer was best left to himself and his deadlines.

Chapter One

Introduction to Statistics

Learning Objectives

After reading and understanding the contents of this chapter, you will be able to:

1. Differentiate descriptive from inferential statistics.
2. Define and give examples of often encountered statistical terms such as *data, population, parameter, sample, statistic, quantitative variable*, and *qualitative variable.*
3. Define and give examples of variables whose scales are nominal, ordinal, interval, and ratio.
4. Give examples of quantitative data that are discrete and that are continuous.

The library is both a user and producer of information. Circulation records, budgets, overdue fee records, and invoices are a few examples of information that is regularly and voluminously produced by a library. By understanding the implications of the numbers produced in these documents and by using them to the library's advantage, the librarian requires the help of statistics.

Uses and Misuses of Statistics

Statistics is a singular noun. It refers to a body of techniques employed to analyze information. These techniques are traditionally divided into two broad classes: descriptive and inferential statistics.

Descriptive statistics is a method for summarizing, organizing, and presenting information. By carefully organizing and summarizing information, descriptive statistics communicates trends and spares the end user the cumbersome task of looking at each piece of information individually.

For example, the National Weather Service monitors temperature continuously, but the newspapers report only the high and low temperatures of the day. These figures communicate the essence of the information and make it easier to identify warming and cooling trends. Moreover, these figures are more manageable than a long list of the succession of temperatures.

The other class of statistics is *inferential statistics*. Its methods go beyond information summary. It aims to predict new information and to make broad generalizations from results obtained from limited studies. Although the application of inferential statistics is an interesting topic, this book deals exclusively with descriptive statistics or information summary.

The tools used in descriptive statistics to summarize information include percents, graphs, and averages. By manipulating and summarizing information, these tools reveal trends, explore relationships, and suggest implications which may otherwise remain hidden. Thus descriptive statistics increases the level at which a situation can be approached, and it can ultimately help librarians in analyzing problems and in making decisions.

For example, a library that charges for its services discovers that many of the invoices go unpaid. The librarians apply a statistical analysis. They summarize information about paid and unpaid invoices in terms of *percents*. In so doing, they discover that bills for more than $10 are the real source of trouble. Invoices for more than $10 are paid much less often than invoices for under $10. As a result of this study, the librarians decide to require prepayment for all services that cost more than $10.

In the following sections, methods of data summary such as calculating percents will be shown. By providing well summarized and well organized information, these techniques can lay the groundwork for better decision-making.

While statistics has many useful applications, the evaluation of problems with statistics can be abused. On the negative side, a decision-maker may use excessive statistical evaluation to delay a decision. Another common misuse of statistics is creating numeric support for a decision already made on the basis of other criteria. The most egregious misuses of statistics, however, may be attempts to shield decision-makers from controversy by contriving figures.

Decision-makers, such as librarians, should be discriminating consumers of statistics and wary of their misuse. Knowledge of statistical techniques and methods helps the decision-maker conduct research and recognize intentional and unintentional statistical deception. The significance to librarians of the insights provided by statistics has grown with the increasing complexity of the day-to-day operation of the library.

Importance of Definitions

One of the purposes of this text is to provide an exposure to the common language of statistics. Another purpose is to explain the various techniques that are repeatedly used and encountered in the application of descriptive statistics.

An understanding of statistics begins with familiarity with the special terms employed in the field. The vocabulary of statistics is precise. Each term or symbol is a standardized abbreviation for a particular idea agreed upon by all parties concerned. In statistics, therefore, definitions are employed to make communication possible. The terms and systems of statistics are uniform, providing a common ground that cuts across field specialties.

Words used in statistics may have different common meanings, or different meanings in other contexts. Even so, they are specialized terms in statistics because of the specific concepts they express. Uniformity of conceptual understanding allows statistical investigators to communicate with precision while avoiding disputes over terminology. Such disputes occur in many fields. Philosophers debate the meaning of *time,* while physicians argue about what constitutes *health.* Librarians should be familiar with this problem. In librarianship, there continues to be severe conflict over the meaning, use, and differences between terms such as *serial* and *journal, standing order* and *subscription,* and *fiction* and *nonfiction* (among others).

Common Statistical Terms

In precise terms, descriptive statistics summarizes information called *data.* Data are measurements which are collected by observation. Data may be numerical or nonnumerical. In a library, the number of telephone calls received each hour is numerical data. On the other hand, the surnames of people who enter the library are nonnumerical data. Other examples of nonnumerical data are qualities, such as taste or color or gender, and demographic information such as place of birth or occupation. *Raw data* are information that have not yet been organized or summarized. Data remain "raw" until they are processed by statistical methods. (The singular of data is *datum*.)

Much of the data used in statistical studies is derived from *surveys*. A survey is a controlled mechanism for collecting data about a condition or event. The U.S. census, for example, is a survey in which most Americans have participated. More specifically, the census is a *statistical survey*. Its questions are carefully planned. Since participants must choose their responses from a limited list, the responses of many participants are easily tabulated, compared, and contrasted.

Statistical surveys are to be distinguished from *anecdotal surveys*, in which participants freely recount experiences or impressions. A diary, an astronaut's debriefing after a mission, and a grandparent's recollections of the "good old days" are examples of anecdotal surveys. The *anecdotal data* obtained through these surveys are important in explaining the nature of an event and the perceptions of the participants, even if they do not provide measurable information.

Most often, a library will rely on statistical surveys rather than anecdotal surveys. *User surveys*, for instance, are statistical surveys. They are carefully planned questionnaires or interviews designed to assess user satisfaction or dissatisfaction.

A *population* is the group of all items sharing at least one common characteristic. The items may be people, objects, units, observations, or measurements. They may be inanimate, as the population consisting of all English-language books. They may be animate, as the population of people whose age is divisible by 2. A population may be defined in terms of geography, such as all academic librarians in the state of Illinois. Occupation may be used as a characteristic to define a population, as in the population consisting of personnel employed in law libraries or of students enrolled in graduate programs of library science. An attribute or experience may be used to define a population, such as the collection (or *set* in mathematical terminology) of all people who have a library card and who have played at least one video game. Another example is the population of all people who have recently obtained relief from pain after taking a medication. A *target population* is the population about which one wishes to draw a conclusion. The complete enumeration of all the population's members is called a *census*.

While all members of a population share at least one characteristic, they may vary in other characteristics. For example, librarians as a population share the common characteristic of occupation. However, librarians vary with respect to income, age, gender, race, and location, among other characteristics. The characteristics of a population which can vary are called *variables*. The value of the variable is the *score*. For example, if a librarian is studying the ages of children who use the library, the variable is age and each child's age is a score.

Variables such as income and age are called *quantitative variables*. They tell how much of a given characteristic or attribute is contained in a member of the population. Variables such as gender, race, and location are *qualitative variables*. They place population members into categories. Qualitative variables are additionally divided into *dichotomous qualitative variables*, which are either-or categories, and *multinomial qualitative variables*, which classify elements into any one of three or more categories. In the librarian example, gender is a dichotomous variable: all librarians are either male or female. Location is a multinomial variable because librarians are located in many different cities and at many different institutions.

Often, practical considerations such as time or expense cause the investigator to conclude that a population is too large to be surveyed completely. In these circumstances, the population is *sampled*. A *sample* is part of a population. It consists of a subset or portion of a population. By definition, a sample is finite. For example, suppose the population consists of all cards in a library's shelflist. A selection of 500 cards from the shelflist constitutes a sample of all cards in the shelflist. A smaller selection, such as two or three cards, still constitutes a sample. From the population of all books in a library system's collections, the titles circulated on a particular day or over a period of time also constitute a sample.

Sampling is the process of selecting the group of population elements to constitute the sample. Ideally, samples are *representative*. That is to say, relevant characteristics occur in the sample population at the same frequency that they occur in the total population. For example, if the user population of a library consists of 30% graduate students, the ideal representative sample will consist of 30% graduate students.

Sampling is a technique that allows an investigator to make conclusions about a population, based upon the nature of the sample. Providing samples of cheese, meat, or ice cream is a common practice to entice consumers to make a purchase. Public opinion polls are based upon samples, as are television program ratings.

Sampling is a common technique because of its many advantages. It is less time consuming to study a sample than an entire population. When evaluation requires destruction of the sample, as in food or beverage tasting, automobile bumper impact studies, or the testing of explosives, sampling is preferred.

On the other hand, a sample may not represent the population. The use of small sample sizes, in particular, may lead to incorrect assumptions about the target population. This is a problem for inferential statistics and will not be considered in this book.

Whether the population is sampled or surveyed completely, the investigator will want to apply statistical methods, such as averaging or graphing, to the raw data. Statistical methods are based on techniques called *algorithms*. An algorithm is a set of instructions or operations for solving a problem. Algorithms can be anything from adding two numbers together to finding the mean of a set of numbers. Algorithms are not all numerical. Any set of steps that must be followed in sequence to produce a desired result is an algorithm. Brewing a cup of tea, playing a record, and dancing a waltz all require the successful completion of an algorithm. If any part of the procedure is omitted, or if the sequence of steps is not correct, the result is not obtained. Algorithms must also be finite. That is, each algorithm must end after a specific number of steps or operations has been executed.

Algorithms are the actual instructions that reorganize and summarize data. Whether the algorithm is applied to a sample or a population, the algorithm produces a numerical characteristic of that sample or population. The numerical characteristic of a sample is called a *statistic*. The numerical characteristic of a population is called a *parameter*.

There is an analogy between statistical algorithms and nonnumerical algorithms. Although it is important to understand *why* algorithms work and *how* they can be applied, real-life situations require human attention and intuition. That is, algorithms are not to be applied slavishly but with sensitivity. The same applies to statistics. Only thoughtful application of statistical theory will provide useful results and help the librarian to avoid the "garbage in, garbage out" trap, creating meaningless results from improperly chosen data.

In statistics, as in human perception, differences, distinctions, and changes are all perceived through our abilities to compare. Comparison, however, is impossible without a standard—a *point of reference*, or a *backdrop*—against which we can measure change. Time and location are familiar points of reference in literature and films.

Time is an extremely important point of reference. Changes in variables are often related to the passage of time. One such variable that changes over time is the growth of children. Usually a child's growth is so gradual that day-to-day changes escape notice. Visiting relatives, however, are able to apply accurately the exclamation all children have cursed, "My, how you've grown!" because the relatives can compare a child's size from one point in time to another without the intervening, gradual change that tends to blur differences over time. Many other variables are compared over time. Humidity and temperature in a rare book room or archive can be measured hourly, daily, or seasonally to provide information necessary for environmental control.

A population itself can serve as a backdrop for comparison. A census, for example, describes the number of people out of the total population that can be characterized as having a certain age, occupation, or income. Internal comparisons are possible as well. From the same census, we can, for example, compare the average income of one person to another. Many such standards and comparisons are possible.

Often, time-population comparisons are encountered in statistical analysis. A variable that can be compared against a time-population backdrop may be the number of books published in a certain category over a period of time. Time and population themselves, though they are useful backdrops, are often the variable under study.

Backdrops have the power to affect perceptions of change and to set standards for comparison. Accordingly, backdrops must be chosen carefully and scrutinized closely. Statistical illusions can be created, just like optical illusions. For example, an executive could assert that the revenues from his division doubled over the previous year while failing to mention that costs quadrupled and profits fell. In this case, profits would be a more realistic backdrop for comparison and for deciding whether the added revenues justified the costs necessary to generate them.

Measurement and Types of Scale

In previous discussions, variables were described as either qualitative or quantitative. In this section, the value of variables will be measured and compared to one another by the use of scales. For the purposes of comparison, four types of scale are used.

Nominal Scale Measurement

The *nominal scale measurement* is the simplest of the four. Nominal scale measures variables based on categories such as zip code, telephone number, eye color, religious affiliation, or blood type. In psychiatry, patients may be classified as psychotic, neurotic, manic depressive, or schizophrenic. The nominal scale shows only equality or inequality. The values of two variables are either in the same category and, therefore, equal or in different categories and not equal. For instance, users of a public library can be classified by zip code. This nominal scale measure will divide the users into groups that live in the same postal area, and it allows the librarian to distinguish between users that live in different postal areas.

Ordinal Scale Measurement

The values of some variables can be arranged in a series from lowest to highest or highest to lowest, according to a characteristic we wish to measure. This is *ordinal scale measurement.* In a marathon race, for example, the first runner to finish is identified as the winner because this is the characteristic chosen to measure victory. For measuring victory, no consideration is given to whether the winner is 1 second or 15 minutes ahead of the other runners. This is because the scale only ranks and does not compare. A committee is making a similar comparison if it ranks candidates for office by overall merit or voter popularity, or if it selects the year's 15 best books.

Additional examples of ordinal scale variables are street numbers on houses, attitude and opinion scales on a questionnaire, and the relevance of documents to queries. A final example is measures of social status, such as lower, middle, and upper class.

Ordinal scale measurement is useful since people can make valid judgments on comparisons even when they cannot make an accurate absolute judgment. A limitation to ordinal scale measurement, however, is that it does not state how far apart two people or things are. It ranks the finishers of a marathon race but does not say how far the first finisher was ahead of the second, or how far the second was in front of the third. An investigator can make these distinctions, however, by using interval scale measures.

Interval Scale Measurement

Interval scale measurement, the scale used to rank the values of variables, contains intervals of equal width. The degrees used in recording temperature, for example, are interval scale. This is because the distance between each degree is the same regardless of where it occurs on the scale.

Interval scale measurement gives more information than is available from nominal or ordinal scale measurement. It has a significant limitation, however. The origin, or zero point, of an interval scale must be arbitrarily selected. A score of zero on an IQ test, for example, probably does not mean that the person has *no* intelligence. A temperature of zero degree, except on the Kelvin temperature scale, does not mean that there is *no* temperature. The purpose of interval scales is to compare values, not to define the complete absence of the value.

Since interval scale measures have no exact zero point, they cannot be multiplied or divided. Clearly, a temperature of 100°F is not twice as hot as a temperature of 50°F. Interval measures, however, can be added or subtracted. For instance, 39°C is 2 degrees higher than 37°C. However, multiplication or division of temperatures, IQs, or other interval scale measurements yields meaningless results.

Sometimes, an ordinal scale is disguised to look like an interval scale. The ordinal classes may be placed on a line or graph so that the distances between them appear to be equal. The consumer of statistics must be aware of this type of statistical deception.

Ratio Scale

A *ratio scale* is a measurement on which an absolute zero point exists and which has equal intervals. The zero point represents a total absence of that which is being measured. Absolute zero points exist in scales for measuring physical units such as time, temperature, weight, area, volume, and capacity—among others. The absolute zero point for weight is the total absence of weight. For time, the zero point is the instant before which time is measured. Numbers on a ratio scale can be divided by others on the scale, compared, and analyzed, and a useful result obtained. A ratio scale allows us to make accurate comparisons, such as "twice as much," "half as tall," or "three times as fast." Assertions are often based on ratio scales. For example, 2 pounds of fish is twice as much as 1 pound. Similarly, a person who is 48 inches tall is two-thirds as tall as someone who is 72 inches tall. When ratio scale data are used, variables such as library floor space, collection size, collection costs, salaries, and circulation totals can be compared and expressed as ratios.

The ratio scale is the highest order of measure, and the nominal scale is the fundamental or first level of measure. Data which are expressed in terms of ratio scale measure automatically possess the characteristics of interval scale data. Likewise, interval scale data have the characteristics of nominal scale data. Variables measured at a higher level can also be analyzed by lower-level techniques. The reverse is not true.

Discrete vs. Continuous Measurement

An important characteristic of measurement which influences the way quantitative observations are analyzed is whether the measurements are *discrete* or *continuous*. A *discrete measurement* is one in which a variable can assume only whole-number values such as 0, 1, 2, or any other whole counting number. Discrete variable values are limited to these fixed numerical values, with no intermediate values permitted. A discrete variable is sometimes said to be *discontinuous*. Examples of discrete variables are the number of books on a library shelf or the number of children in a family. In both cases, the values are 0, 1, 2, 3, or some other whole counting numbers. Other examples of discrete variables are the number of gift books received by the library, the size of the library staff, or the number of clientele visits through the turnstiles per day. Discrete variables are counted rather than measured.

A variable which can theoretically assume any value between two given values is called *continuous*. For example, the age difference between two people can be a continuous variable because, in theory, the difference can be reduced by degrees. If a baby is born just before midnight on New Year's Eve and a second baby is born just after midnight, it can be said correctly that the first baby is a year, a month, a day, an hour, a minute, a second, or a millisecond older than the second baby, depending upon the accuracy of the measurement of time. If a statue in the entrance of a library is weighed, any particular measurement is approximate. This is because a measuring device of greater accuracy can always be imagined. If the weight is 2178 pounds, this means 2178 plus or minus 1 pound. If the scale is accurate to within 1 pound, a scale can be imagined that is accurate to within one-half, one-tenth, or one-hundredth of a pound. Measurement of a continuous variable, such as weight or length, is always approximate. Continuous variables may include the life expectancy of a lamp in a projector or the age of a document, either from the time of publication or from the time of ownership by the library.

Of course, most, if not all, observations are associated with some unavoidable finite error. Because measuring devices are of limited accuracy, and because practicality dictates that measurements are rounded off and grouped, most measurements in real life are probably discrete rather than continuous. This fact, however, should not deter the user from considering such variables as continuous.

Summary of Critical Concepts

1. *Statistics* is a body of techniques employed to analyze information. *Statistical analysis* is a scientific method of interpreting quantitative data.
2. *Descriptive statistics* summarizes data. *Inferential statistics* produces new data by making predictions and generalizations.
3. Measurements collected by observation are *data. Raw data* are information that have not been organized or summarized. *Anecdotal data* are the free-form recounting of experiences and impressions.
4. A *population* consists of all items that share a common characteristic. A population may be defined in terms of geography, occupation, or other attributes. A numerical measure of a population is called a *parameter.* A *sample* is part of a population. It is a subset of a population. A sample is finite. A *statistic* is a numerical measure computed from a sample. Because a sample's statistic is easier to compute than a population's parameter, a statistic is often used to estimate a parameter. Parameter estimation is part of inferential statistics and is not the focus of this book.
5. A measurable characteristic of a population or sample is a *variable.* The value of a particular variable is called a *score.* Variables are quantitative or qualitative. *Quantitative variables* tell how much of a given characteristic or attribute is present in an object, event, person, or phenomenon. Qualitative variables classify an object, event, person, or phenomenon into categories with respect to the attributes by which they differ.
6. *Nominal scale variables* classify observations into categories. Examples are variables such as marital status (single, married, divorced, widowed), political affiliation (Democratic, Republican, Libertarian), blood type (A, B, O, AB), or sex (male, female). No

mathematical properties such as "ranking" or "greater than" are associated with nominal scale variables. *Ordinal scale variables* classify observations into distinct classes *and* into rank. They also show a relation of the observations according to the degree or amount to which they represent a given characteristic. For example, human populations can be "ordered" by relations, such as being a descendant of, being older than, or having a higher job position. *Interval scale variables* classify, rank, *and* show the distance between classes. The distance in years between *classes* of father and son is not fixed. However, the distance in temperature between 78°F and 79°F is known and constant. *Ratio scale variables* classify, rank, distinguish distance, *and* provide a zero point. Length, weight, time, and income are example of ratio scale variables, and when these variables equal zero, there is no length, no weight, no time, and no money.

7. Quantitative data can be classified as being discrete or continuous.

Key Terms

Algorithm.   A set of rules or directions for obtaining a specific output from a specific input. Algorithms are procedure, process, routine, recipe, method, rigmarole, and rain dance. The term *algorithm* is usually used in connection with numerical calculations.

Census.   An enumeration of all the members of a population.

Continuous Data.   Data obtained by measuring, using centimeters, inches, liters, ounces, or similar units. The value of the measurement takes on an unlimited number of intermediate values, depending on the precision of the instrument used. Hence, height of a person may be recorded as 1.81m or 1.812m or 1.8123m, etc.

Data.   Facts collected as a result of observation. *Datum* is the singular of data. Examples of datum are height, weight, telephone number, and zip code. Nonstatistical data are arbitrary items. Examples are item order numbers in a sales catalog, telephone numbers in a directory, or physical measurements such as height or weight. Data may be numerical, such as the number of books checked out each hour in a library. They may be nonnumerical, such as occupation, political affiliation, or name. *Raw data* are unorganized statistical data. This information remains "raw" until it is processed by statistical methods.

Discontinuous Data.   Also called *discrete data.* Data obtained by counting or simple enumeration rather than by measuring against a scale. For example, we *count* the number of books on a shelf or the number of grains of sand in an hourglass. The counted units are indivisible. Hence, there may be 52 books on a shelf, but not 52.3. Unlike continuous data, the measurement of discrete data *must* produce a whole number.

Interval Scale Measure.   Measurement scale that groups observations in three ways: (1) by categorizing, as in nominal scale; (2) by ranking, as in ordinal scale; and (3) by illustrating, through the use of equal intervals, how much greater one case is on a given attribute or characteristic than another. Examples of interval scale measure are year and temperature. The interval scale measure lacks an absolute zero point.

Nominal Scale Measure.   Measurement scale characterized by either-or types of observations. Items are not ordered. The data summary used for nominal scale data is percents or proportions of observations that exhibit a specific attribute. Examples are sex (M, F), blood type (A, B, AB, O), religious affiliation (Catholic, Protestant, Jewish), and eye color (brown, blue, hazel).

Ordinal Scale Measure.   Measurement scale that classifies items into categories. The scale is arranged in ascending or descending order of the items according to some property. Examples are grouping people into low-, middle-, and high-income categories, or assigning people job titles, or evaluating employee performance from outstanding to poor, or by grouping according to rank (private through general).

Parameter.   A quantitative measure of a population.

Population.   The totality of all the items of interest. All the cases or items in a population have at least one specific attribute or characteristic. Since a population is an aggregate of *all* the items which have some specified characteristic, some populations are very small. Other populations can be infinite. The *target population* is the population about which an investigator wishes to draw a conclusion.

Ratio Scale Measure.   Measurement scale with an absolute zero point that groups observations in three ways: (1) by categorizing or classifying, as in nominal scale; (2) by ranking, as in ordinal scale; and (3) by illustrating, through the use of equal intervals, how much greater one case is on a given attribute or characteristic than another. Examples of ratio scale measure are time, height, distance, weight, and altitude.

Sample.   A subset, portion, or segment of a population. A sample is used to make inferences about the population from which it is drawn. A *representative sample* contains a population's characteristics in the same proportion that they occur in the population. *Sampling* is the selection process of identifying the population elements that will constitute a sample. A sample is finite.

Statistic.   A quantitative measure of a sample. A statistic is a sample summary such as mode, median, mean, or standard deviation.

Statistics.   Techniques for the graphic and tabular presentation of data. The term also refers to the methods used to summarize a body of data with useful measures. *Descriptive statistics* is the organization, presentation, and summarization of data. *Inferential statistics* concerns the basis by which conclusions regarding a population are drawn from results obtained in a sample.

Variable.   A property with respect to which people or objects in a sample or population differ in some ascertainable way. A *continuous variable* can assume any number of possible values between an upper and lower limit. Values for continuous variables are usually obtained through measurements. A *discrete variable* (also called a *discontinuous variable*) can assume only whole-number values, such as 0, 1, 2, or any other whole counting number. Fractions or decimal values are *not* examples of discrete variable data values. Values for discrete variables are usually obtained through counting. *Quantitative variables* classify objects into categories by how much they differ. Examples are number of books, staff size, or daily circulation. *Qualitative variables* classify cases with respect to the attribute by which they differ. Examples are product models, animal species, and color. *Dichotomous variables* are qualitative variables which classify cases into either-or categories, such as pass-fail courses, paid and unpaid invoices, or items that have circulated or not circulated. *Multinomial variables* classify cases into more than two categories. An example is religious affiliation (Catholic, Jewish, Protestant) or employee status (salaried, hourly, contract, or agency temporary).

Self-Assessment Quiz

True or False 1.   Descriptive statistics is the orderly collection and summarization of data.

True or False 2.   The name of a river is a quantitative variable.

True or False 3.   Distance is a qualitative variable.

True or False 4.   An example of a discrete measurement is the number of books in a library collection.

True or False 5.   An example of a continuous measurement is the count of reference-desk questions received in a 2-hour period.

True or False 6. A variable may take on different values.

True or False 7. A population is a set of all objects that have one or more characteristics in common.

True or False 8. A parameter is a characteristic of a sample that is almost always known or that can be computed.

True or False 9. If a library task force were made up of 5 men and 5 women, it would be representative of the library's full-time staff of 66 females and 34 males.

Answers

1. True. Descriptive statistics summarize and eliminate the need to look at each piece of data.
2. False. A name cannot be counted or quantified. A river's name is a qualitative variable.
3. False. A distance has a definite value (inch, yard, mile) and can be measured. Distance is a quantitative variable.
4. True. The number of books has to be a whole number.
5. False. Counts yield discrete measurement. Continuous measurement examples are height, weight, temperature, and distance (among others).
6. True. The variable is an idea or class, such as height, weight, age, or sex. A variable may have any of a variety of values, depending on what is being observed.
7. True. A population can also represent a set of measurements that characterize some phenomenon of interest.
8. False. A parameter refers to a population. A statistic is a characteristic of a sample.
9. False. To be representative, the task force should have the same composition of men and women as in the population. Hence, it should consist of 7 women and 3 men. The sample percents should equal the population percents.

Discussion Questions and Problems

1. It is not unusual for two or more people to have different definitions of the same topic. What incidents in your professional or personal life can you identify as misunderstandings caused by differing definitions?

2. Go to the library and find at least three major statistical periodicals or abstracts. Discuss the subject focus of each.

3. Find the following works and discuss their purposes:
   a. *World Almanac and Book of Facts*
   b. most recent U. S. census
   c. *Baseball Abstract*
   d. *Science Citation Index*.

4. Several examples were given in this chapter to show that a sample can be more efficient than a population census. Identify three additional examples in which a sample is more effective.

5. Distinguish the terms *statistics*, *statistic*, *parameter*, and *variable*.

6. Consider the scales of measurement discussed in this chapter: ordinal, interval, and ratio. Identify examples of each that you have encountered in your personal life, work, and hobbies.

7. Identify the type of measurement scale used in each of the following:
   a. "four-star" rating system used by a movie reviewer
   b. survey in which males are coded by 1 ($M=1$) and females are coded by 2 ($F=2$)
   c. Standard and Poor's bond rating system
   d. ranking of sports teams in a league, conference, or division
   e. Kelvin temperature measures (for the Kelvin scale, an absolute zero point exists)
   f. survey question on state of residence
   g. Celsius temperature measures.

8. Identify the following measures as discrete or continuous:
   a. number of hamburgers sold annually by a fast-food chain
   b. aggregate cooked weight of the hamburger meat (above)
   c. volume registered on an applause meter
   d. light intensity as measured by a photographer's light meter
   e. quantity of photons in a beam of light
   f. number of dinosaurs now roaming the earth.

Chapter Two

Basic Methods of Data Summary

Learning Objectives

After reading and understanding the contents of this chapter, you will be able to:

1. Explain and apply the rules for rounding numbers.
2. Define *ratio* and calculate ratios, proportions, percents, and percentage changes.
3. Explain and calculate comparison measures such as component percents, dollar and percent change, ratio, and benefit-cost.
4. Identify and describe the usefulness of comparison measures in analyzing library situations.
5. Apply ratio analysis in library situations for calculating output measures.
6. Identify and list the dangers and deceptions inherent in the incorrect use of percents.
7. Explain how to label data points.
8. Explain how summation notation helps simplify long equations.

In this chapter, several basic techniques of data summary are introduced. One technique, *rounding* or *rounding off*, shortens numbers to bring them within a desired accuracy. Another technique, *summation notation*, shortens addition. Three other techniques, *ratios*, *proportions*, and *percents*, are used to compare and contrast numbers.

Rounding

Rounding is an important and common technique for abbreviating data. The idea of rounding is very familiar. Anyone who has filled out an income tax return or an application for academic financial aid has "rounded" actual income to the nearest dollar. However, in statistics, to guarantee that rounding is accurate and uniform, there are certain conventions.

Many occasions arise when it is necessary to round off data values. The problem of how many places to carry in the final answer occurs when one number is divided by another and a long or infinitely repeating decimal, such as $2/3 = .666...$, is obtained. Using too many decimal places lends a false sense of precision to the data. Hence, at some point, the decimal must be ended and a value assigned to the last number in the series that best reflects the remainder. The same is true if there are dollar amounts such as $87.4995, which might represent the weekly wage of an hourly employee who is paid $5.8333 per hour for 15 hours' work. It is not unusual to find the hourly wage expressed to four decimal places. However, there is no unit of money equaling .4995 dollars. Instead, this number, $87.4995, is rounded off to $87.50. Rounding is also convenient when data provide more detail than is required. For example, if a library contains 38,292 volumes, it may be enough to say there are approximately 40,000 volumes. Variables, such as temperature, weight, or height, which can always be measured more exactly, are also rounded.

A useful guideline in making calculations is to carry out the operation to two places more than are in the original data. Then round off by one place. Therefore, if the original data consist of whole numbers, the calculations are made to hundredths, then rounded to tenths. If data are recorded to the nearest hundredth, one expresses the result of the rounding in thousandths, after calculating to ten-thousandths.

After the number of places to express results is decided, guidelines are useful for rounding. For example, assume that calculations are to be expressed to two decimal places:

1. If the third digit is less than 5, the second digit is left *unchanged* and the third digit is dropped.
2. If the third digit is more than 5, the second digit is increased by 1.

3. If the third digit is *exactly* 5, with a remainder, the second digit is *increased* by 1.
4. If the third digit is *exactly* 5, with no remainder, and the second digit is odd, the second digit is rounded up to the nearest even integer.
5. If the third digit is *exactly* 5, with no remainder, and the second digit is even, the second digit is left unchanged and the third digit is dropped.

Example 2-1. Rounding

Round each of the following to the nearest hundredth.

1.	3.141	becomes 3.14	Guideline 1
2.	2.718	becomes 2.72	Guideline 2
3.	87.4995	becomes 87.50	Guideline 2
4.	0.01501	becomes 0.02	Guideline 3
5.	0.0050	becomes 0.00	Guideline 5

Round each of the following to the nearest thousandth.

6.	3.4852	becomes 3.485	Guideline 1
7.	3.4856	becomes 3.486	Guideline 2
8.	3.1415002	becomes 3.142	Guideline 3
9.	3.1415000	becomes 3.142	Guideline 4
10.	3.1425000	becomes 3.142	Guideline 5

It is important to understand how to apply these conventions. Special attention is called to problems 8, 9, and 10 in Example 2-1:

8. Rounded to three places, 3.1415002 becomes 3.142. Guideline 3 applies. The fourth digit is exactly 5 and there is a remainder, 5002. Thus, the third digit is increased by 1.
9. Rounded to three places, 3.1415000 becomes 3.142. Guideline 4 applies. The fourth place is exactly 5 and there is no remainder. Because it is odd, the third digit, 1, is rounded up to the nearest even integer, 2.
10. Rounded to three places, 3.1425000 becomes 3.142. Guideline 5 applies. The fourth digit is exactly 5 and

there is no remainder. Since the third digit is even, it remains unchanged. This convention is widely accepted.

Ratio, Proportion, and Percents

Ratio and Proportion

A *ratio* is a mathematical relationship between two quantities. A device for comparing one amount to another, a ratio is obtained by dividing one number by a second number.

For example, the ratio of 200 to 100 is expressed as the fraction 200/100, which equals 2. Ratios can also be symbolized with a colon. For example, the ratio 200 to 100 can be represented as 200 : 100, or 2 : 1. When a ratio is expressed as a fraction, the upper number is the *numerator* and the lower number is the *denominator* or *base*. The numerator of this ratio is 200. The denominator or base is 100. The computation of a ratio involves a simple arithmetical operation, but its interpretation is more complex.

$$\text{Ratio} = \frac{\text{Numerator}}{\text{Denominator}} \qquad\qquad (2\text{--}1)$$

$$\text{Ratio} = \text{Numerator} : \text{Denominator} \qquad\qquad (2\text{--}2)$$

To illustrate the idea of ratio, one might examine qualities of life, such as happiness. When the Greek philosopher Aristotle used the word *happiness,* he defined it as meaning a whole human life, well lived. He and other philosophers have written at length about what happiness is and how it is achieved in terms of the relationship between satisfied and unsatisfied desires. These philosophers might have conceived of happiness, expressed as a ratio, in the following way:

$$\text{Happiness} = \frac{\text{Satisfied Desires}}{\text{Desires}} \qquad\qquad (2\text{--}1\text{A})$$

Any ratio can be altered in three ways. This is accomplished by varying the numerator, changing the denominator, or varying both at different rates. In the example above, happiness, as expressed by the ratio of satisfied desires to desires, can be augmented as follows:

1. The number of satisfied desires can be increased.
2. The number of desires can be decreased.
3. Both satisfied desires *and* desires can be increased, so long as satisfied desires are increased faster.
4. Both can decrease, so long as desires decrease faster.

To be useful, a ratio must express a relationship that has significance. Table 2-1 compares the acquisition expenditures of the public libraries in two counties. County A and County B expenditures are calculated and reported. Each of these ratios, such as Book Expenditures County A : Book Expenditures County B, summarizes a significant relationship and allows direct comparisons of the relative expenditure allocations between the counties. Because the ratio Microfilm Expenditures County B : Book Expenditures County A, would be meaningless and would not allow such direct comparisons, it has not been calculated.

Sometimes the relevance of a relationship is more difficult to determine. For example, a municipality, starting an equal-pay-for-equal-work policy, could evaluate salary parity through ratios. It could compare the salary of its public librarians to the salary of other, similarly qualified municipal workers. A ratio of 1 : 1 would signify equal salaries for two positions, and any deviation from this ratio would show inequality.

The difficulty in applying ratios to salary parity is in deciding which public servants are "similarly qualified." The recurring debate in assessing salary parity is whether the compared positions are similar. If a municipality chooses to evaluate pay through statistical comparison, it is reasonable to compare a librarian's salary to the salary of other information workers, such as computer programmers or accountants. Of course, this comparison depends upon the complexity of the particular librarian's role. It makes little sense to compare a librarian's salary to a file clerk's, or to a fire fighter's or a bus driver's salary. The

Table 2-1. County Comparison of Library Acquisition's Expenditures			
	County A	County B	Ratio
Audiovisuals	$ 628,710	$ 122,508	5.13
Books	10,338,933	1,438,938	7.19
Microfilms	208,793	12,525	16.67
Periodicals	1,733,935	164,148	10.56
Total	$ 12,910,371	$ 1,738,119	7.43

meaning of a ratio is in part determined by the assumption of a relationship between the compared data. Comparing unrelated numbers, such as the librarian's salary and the number of municipal parking spaces, produces ratios that are meaningless.

Another important consideration is the quality of the numbers in the computation. If the numbers are suspect, the ratios based on such figures are also suspect. The data from which ratios or other calculations have been derived need to be shown whenever possible. The decision-maker is rightly skeptical of ratios that cannot be verified.

Ratios, like many other calculations discussed throughout this book, are most illuminating when they are related to other information. When interpreted with past ratios of the same activity, or with ratios of similar libraries, or with some other predetermined standard or objective, ratios can provide valuable insights about trends and activities.

Percent

In Latin, *percent* means "per hundred" or "out of each hundred." Accordingly, 100% effort is maximum effort and 100% support is complete support. Percents shows the relative size of two or more numbers. Like a ratio, a percent is calculated by dividing a numerator by a denominator. Unlike ratios, percents are then converted to a scale based on 100. Example 2-2 illustrates changing a percent to a decimal and a decimal to a percent. Another difference between percents and ratios is that the numerator and denominator of a ratio can be vastly different numbers, such as linear feet of library shelf space and the number of full-time catalogers. The numerator and denominator of a percent, however, must be numbers that are expressed in the same units. If the numerator is expressed in linear feet, the denominator must also be expressed in linear feet. If the numerator is a dollar figure, the denominator must be a dollar figure as well.

The three types of percent problems that the librarian often encounters are illustrated in Example 2-3. They are finding what percent one number is of another; finding a specific percent of a given number; and finding a denominator when given a number that is a specified percent of that denominator. Each of these problems involves three quantities: the numerator, the denominator, and the percent. In each type of problem, two of the quantities are known.

$$\text{Percent} = \frac{\text{Numerator}}{\text{Denominator}} \times 100 \qquad\qquad (2\text{--}3)$$

Example 2-2. How to Change a Percent to a Decimal

Procedure: Move the decimal point 2 places to the *left* and
remove the percent sign.

1.   .3% = .03   5.   135% = 1.35
2.   17% = .17   6.   1000% = 10.0
3.   7 1/2% = 7.5% or .075   7.   .1% = .001
4.   100% = 1.00   8.   1/2% = .5% or .005

How to Change a Decimal to a Percent

Procedure: Move the decimal point 2 places to the *right* and
add a percent sign.

1.   .01 = 1%   5.   7.5 = 750%
2.   .33 = 33%   6.   .003 = .3%
3.   .125 = 12.5% or 12 1/2%   7.   1.15 = 115%
4.   2 = 200%   8.   11.5 = 1150%

In each type of problem, the answers may extend many places after the decimal point. However, expressing 79/215 as 36.744186% gives a false sense of precision. Such figures are also difficult to manipulate, do not promote easy comparison, and look silly. It is more appropriate to round percents to whole numbers or to tenths. Thus 36.744186% is best expressed as 36.7% or 37%.

It is one thing to answer questions about percent but another to calculate percents from original raw data. Three useful techniques for establishing relationships and trends with percents are (1) component percent analysis, (2) dollar and percent change analysis, and (3) ratio analysis.

Comparison Measure Analyses

Component Percent Analysis

The first technique, component percent analysis, focuses on the percent relationship between a component part and the whole. To calculate component percents, the whole is used as the denominator and the part is used as the numerator.

Example 2-3. Three Common Types of Percent Problems

1.   What percent of 5 is 3?

Equation: $\dfrac{\text{Numerator}}{\text{Denominator}} \times 100 = \text{Percentage}$

Calculation: $\dfrac{3}{5} \times 100 = 60\%$

2.   What is 75% of 800?

Equation: $\dfrac{\text{Percentage} \times \text{Denominator}}{100} = \text{Numerator}$

Calculation: $\dfrac{75\% \times 800}{100} = 600$

3.   30 is 12% of what number?

Equation: $\dfrac{\text{Numerator}}{\text{Percentage}} \times 100 = \text{Denominator}$

Calculation: $\dfrac{30}{12\%} \times 100 = 250$

$$\text{Component Percent} = \dfrac{\text{Part}}{\text{Whole}} \times 100 \qquad\qquad (2-4)$$

Component percent analysis, often applied to library budgets, helps to identify the relative importance of an item or group of items. Example 2-4 shows component percents determined for public library acquisition expenditures introduced in Table 2-1. For County A, audiovisual expenditures represent 4.9% of the total expenditures for the county. This amount is determined by dividing audiovisual expenditures by total expenditures, \$628,710/\$12,910,371, which yields .0487 or 4.9%. The interpretation of the component percent data is that, for both counties, book expenditures represent the largest proportion of budgeted dollars, followed by expenditures for periodicals, audiovisual materials, and microfilms. The component percent analysis, in turn,

Example 2-4. Public Library Acquisitions Expenditures by Component Percents	County A	County B
Audiovisuals	4.9	7.1
Books	80.1	82.8
Microfilms	1.6	0.7
Periodicals	13.4	9.4
Total	100.0	100.0
(Dollars)	($12,910,371)	($1,738,119)
Source: Hypothetical data		

helps to focus on the relative importance of acquisition items to the overall budget.

Table 2-2 depicts a hypothetical public library's program. Its activities can be structured into three broad categories: education, individualized services, and research services. Although only revenue-producing services are identified in this example, a complete chart would identify and place all the library's activities and services in one of these three categories.

The revenue statement by product line of the hypothetical library program described in Table 2-2 is shown in Table 2-3, together with a component percent analysis. In this analysis, all items are expressed as a percent of revenue. The term *operating expenses* means only that share of expenses due to the listed service items. For example, "Advertising" represents only the costs of promoting the listed services; it is not the library's total advertising budget. Some minor discrepancies in percent sums are due to rounding to whole percents. At a glance, the component percents show the contribution of each component to the total. Again, the percents bring perspective to the dollar amounts in each column.

In analyzing the component percents, we see that gross profits increased from 35% in Year 1 to 40% in Year 2. By the end of Year 3, they declined to 30%. Successful cost-cutting measures are reflected in a steady decline of operating expenses over the three-year period. The costs of the goods and services provided fell from 65% of revenue in Year 1 to 60% in Year 2. This significantly influenced net income (the *bottom line*), which increased from 8% in Year 1 to 15% in Year 2. Costs of goods and services increased, however, from Year 2 to Year 3. Even with decreasing operating expenses, this resulted in a decline in net income from 15% in Year 2 to 10% in Year 3.

Table 2-2. A Library's Product Mix and Listing of Billable
Items Which Generate Revenue through Fees,
Registration, and Other Charges

Education Service	Individualized	Research
Communication Access	Book Delivery	Facilities Rental
AV Presentations	Books by Mail	Locker Rental
Cable Television	Bookmobile	Study Carrels
Computer Networks	Homebound Services	
Satellite Networks	Nursing Home	Online Literature
Teleconferences		
Meeting Room Rental	Book Reserves	Reference Research
Conference Rooms		Genealogy
Auditorium	Circulation Rentals	Info & Referral
	Art, Sculpture	Ref Info Services
Seminars/Mini Courses	Books	Telephone Info Serv
Concerts for Children	Discs, Records	
CPR Training	Tools	Selective Dissemin-
Financial Planning	Toys	ation of Information
How-to Classes	Videotapes	
Parenting Seminars		
Puppet Construction	Fines	
Reader's Advisory		
Reading Programs	Interlibrary Loans	
Résumé Preparation		
Tax Classes	Sale of Discarded/Gift Books	
Travelog Series		
	Usage Fees	
Story Hour	CD-ROM Database Access	
	FAX Sending/Receiving	
	Personal Computer Time	
	Photocopy Exposures	
	Typewriter Rental	

Analysis of the dollar amounts yields additional useful information. For example, net income improved significantly, from $1545 in Year 2 to $3682 in Year 3, an increase of 2.4 times. However, revenue has increased faster than net income. This means that the library had to earn more from its services in Year 3 for every dollar it retained as net income than it earned in Year 2. This shortcoming cannot be discerned from the component percents. It illustrates that changes in component

Table 2-3. Revenue and Component Percentage Analysis*

	Dollars			Component Percent		
	Year 3	Year 2	Year 1	Year 3	Year 2	Year 1
REVENUE	$ 32620	24545	19305	100%	100%	100%
Education	3670	2630	1430	11	11	7
Communications	1000	750	200	3	3	1
Meeting room rental	2250	1500	900	7	6	5
Mini courses	300	280	250	1	1	1
Story hour	120	100	80	0	0	0
Individualized Services	16100	12190	10575	49	50	55
Book delivery services	2650	2200	1800	8	9	9
Book reserves	120	90	75	0	0	0
Collection rentals	4200	3100	2700	13	13	14
Fines	580	400	450	2	2	2
Interlibrary loans	4900	3500	3150	15	14	16
Sales discard/gift books	500	300	200	2	1	1
Usage Fees	3100	2800	2200	10	11	11
Research	12850	9725	7300	40	39	38
Facilities rental	3700	2600	1800	11	11	9
Online services	4950	3625	2500	15	15	13
Reference research	4200	3500	3000	13	14	16
COST OF GOODS/SERVICES	22800	14750	12600	70	60	65
GROSS PROFIT	9820	9795	6705	30	40	35
OPERATING EXPENSES	6558	6113	5160	20	25	27
Advertising	700	500	125	2	2	1
Depreciation	425	400	400	1	2	2
Insurance	250	225	210	1	1	1
Interest	125	210	180	0	1	1
Salaries	4330	3500	3100	13	14	16
Telephone	600	540	900	2	2	5
Other	128	738	245	0	3	1
NET INCOME	$ 3262	3682	1545	10%	15%	8%

*Percentage sum discrepancies are due to rounding.
Source: Hypothetical data

percents can result from changes in the component, in the total, or in both. Hence, using a combination of these methods gives a more complete picture.

Component percent analysis produces insights in addition to identifying changes and making comparisons. A percent analysis can be used for classification as well. Institutions, for example, often use a percent of time analysis as a performance guideline. The jobs of everyone, from technicians to directors, are described in terms of the percent of time they spend shelving, ordering, planning, organizing, directing, supervising, or any other tasks.

Dollar and Percent Change Analysis

The second technique, dollar and percent change analysis, compares dollar or percent changes over time. Identifying the percent of change adds perspective to the dollar amounts. For example, the significance of a $5000 budget increase is different, depending on whether the amount is an increase of 10% over last year's budget of $50,000 or an increase of 1% over a budget of $500,000. A percent change analysis relates a base number to a comparison number. To calculate percent change, find the difference between the comparison and base numbers, then divide by the base number. Of course, the quotient must be multiplied by 100 to convert the quotient to a percent. Mathematically, this can be shown by Equation (2-5):

$$\text{Percent Change} = \frac{(\text{Comparison Number} - \text{Base Number})}{\text{Base Number}} \times 100 \quad (2-5)$$

Table 2-4 depicts both the historical expenditure data for a small library and a corresponding percent analysis. The dollar amount of change is the difference between the amount for the base year and for a comparison year. The percent change is computed by dividing the amount of change by the base number. For example, the difference between Year 3 and Year 2 salary and wage expenditures in the table is $(103 - 88)/88$. This is 15/88, or a 17% increase in Year 3 over Year 2.

There are also several points to notice about the way data are shown in the table. First, a common business practice is to round financial data to thousands or millions of dollars, but the table must show when this is done. Rounding should not be assumed. Second, a decrease or loss is shown by placing the quantity in parentheses. Third, a percent sign is placed after the first percent in a column of percents. Although this practice appears to be redundant since the column is labeled "percent," the percent sign reminds the reader that percents are being reported. Since most readers do not closely study a table, this important convention helps to reduce data misinterpretation. Last, a percent rounded

Table 2-4. Expenditures and Dollar/Percentage Change Analysis*

| Category | Expenditures in Thousands | | | Increase / (Decrease) | | | |
| | | | | Year 3 over Year 2 | | Year 2 over Year 1 | |
	Year 3	Year 2	Year 1	Amount	%	Amount	%
Salaries and wages	$ 103	88	81	15	17%	7	9%
Fringe benefits (19%)	20	17	15	3	18	2	13
Acquisitions:	30	26	10	4	15	16	260
Books	23	21	7	2	10	14	200
Magazines	4	3	2	1	33	1	50
Media	3	2	1	1	50	1	100
Binding	1	1	1	0	0	0	0
Supplies & small equip.	2	2	2	0	0	0	0
Online Services	7	6	6	1	17	0	0
Travel	2	1	2	1	100	(1)	(50)
Repair & maintenance	3	3	2	0	0	1	50
Other	3	2	2	1	50	0	0
Total	$ 171	146	121	25	17	25	21

*Percentage sum discrepancies are due to rounding.
Source: Hypothetical data

down to zero should not be shown by a dash, which may imply noncalculated or unavailable figures.

Further, although the library's budgeted expenditures increased by $25,000 in both Year 2 and Year 3, the percent change differs. This is because the base year amount shifts from Year 1 to Year 2. Later years can also be compared with a previous base year. For example, Year 1 can be used as a base year for comparison with Year 2, Year 3, and Year 4. A dollar and percent change analysis can be made on many types of data, as long as the data represent a positive quantity. If the base-year amount is negative or zero, no percent change can be computed.

Example 2-5 provides additional percent change problems using Formula 2-5.

Ratio Analysis

In addition to percent change and component percents, the third technique for measuring trends is *ratio analysis*. Ratio analysis quantifies the performance of an institution, a person, or a product. Ratio

Example 2-5. Finding the percent of increase or decrease of a number from an original base amount.

1. In mid-year the library subscribed to 250 magazines. By the end of the year, the subscription list had grown to 290 titles. Find the percent of increase.

a. Let P = the percent of increase

b. Amount of increase: 290 - 250 = 40 titles

c. 40 is *what percent* of 250? (250 is the base.)

$40 = P \times 250$

$40/250 = P$

$.16 = P$ Thus the percent of increase is 16%.

2. In the early part of the year, a special library provided low-cost copy machines in the journal area of the collection. Over the year, journal circulation dropped from 24,000 to 21,000 volumes. Find the percent of decrease.

a. Let D = the percent of decrease

b. Amount of decrease: 24,000 - 21,000 = 3,000 volumes

c. 3000 is *what per cent* of 24,000? (24,000 is the base.)

$3000 = D \times 24,000$

$3000/24,000 = D$

$.125 = D$ Thus the percent of decrease is 12.5%.

analysis uses a variety of statistical techniques, including ratios, percents, and *per capita* analyses.

In the library, ratio analyses help to evaluate library performance. The ratios, percents, and per capita calculations are known as *output measures*.

In their book (published in 1984), *Research for Decision Making: Methods for Librarians*, Swisher and McClure classified output measures into four broad areas. First is *community penetration*. Measures in this area are designed to evaluate the extent of community awareness of library services. The base for measuring community penetration is the number of people in the community who identify themselves as library users. Community penetration is calculated in terms of circulation *per capita* ("per person"), a comparison of the quantity of a variable to the size of a defined population. The per capita income of a nation is the total amount of money earned by the national population, divided by the number of people in the population. In library services, *per capita* refers to the comparison of some variable to the number of members in the community or clientele served by the library.

Circulation per capita is obtained by comparing annual circulation of all library materials to the population of the community that the library serves. The resulting ratio represents the number of items each person in the community borrowed. That is, the number of items if every person in the community borrowed an equal number of materials during the year. For example, in a library with an annual circulation of 200,000 items and a user population of 40,000, the circulation per capita is 200,000/40,000, or 5. The interpretation of this statistic is that each member of the user population, on average, borrows five items per year.

A second broad area of output measure is *user services*. Services from special programs to general reference can be quantified. This is because program attendance, reference transactions, and library visits can be evaluated on a per capita basis. For example, the library may host, sponsor, or cosponsor activities such as book talks, lectures, classes, dramas, puppet shows, film showings, travelogs, or tours. Program attendance per capita is the ratio of annual attendance at all such programs to the population of the community that the library serves. Hence, if program attendance is 6000 and the population is 40,000, program attendance per capita is 6000/40,000, or 0.15. The interpretation of this statistic is that each member of the user population, on average, attends 0.15 program per year. In other words, about one out of every seven members of the population attends a library program.

Resource management is a third area that can be appropriately evaluated through output measures. The goal of resource management is to make effective use of the funds, materials, facilities, and staff that are available to the library. A measure related to resource management is collection turnover rate, or the number of times the materials are checked out over a given period of time. This measure is determined by dividing the total circulation of all library materials for one year by the total number of cataloged and noncataloged library holdings. If the annual circulation is 200,000 items, and if there is a total of 50,000 cataloged and noncataloged items in the collection, the collection turn-over rate is 200,000/50,000, or 4. This means that, on average, there are four circulations per item in one year. In applying this measure, the reader should note that not all items in the collection enjoy an equal amount of circulation. In most libraries, recently published items circulate more often than older materials and current or popular novels generate more circulation than older fiction. Turnover rates may be separately calculated for these higher-use items. Multiple copies of books and shorter circulation periods will increase circulation opportunity and will affect the ratio.

A fourth area, *administration and finance*, reflects library administrative performance. Measures such as library financial support per capita, materials as a percent of total expenditures, and library funds as a percent of the total community or institutional budget are ways to measure library financial administration performance over varying periods of time. This area, however, is more sensitive to circumstances that are out of the direct control of the library administrator.

Benefit-Cost Analysis

Benefit-cost analysis is an application of the techniques used in ratio analysis. It is a technique to compare the cost of initiating or continuing an activity to the economic benefits which result from providing that activity.

Benefit-cost analysis can be applied to proposals as diverse as modification of equipment for the library's computer system, the purchase of a new phone system, collection development in a specific field, staff travel for an annual meeting, or even to the postage necessary for promotion of a program series.

In a benefit-cost analysis, the dollar value of an activity's benefits is the sum of both tangible and intangible benefits derived from that activity. Tangible benefits tend to be easier to quantify in monetary terms than intangible benefits. Examples of resource savings due to tangible benefits are lower costs through increased operating efficiency; reduced supply expenses through volume purchase discounts; decreased salary expenses due to personnel reduction achieved through staff re-assignment or through the increased use of non-professional personnel or of part-time personnel who are not paid fringe benefits; and savings from modifications in library service hours or reductions in staffing levels during off-peak periods of use.

Intangible benefits are of two types: those which have a quantifiable economic or monetary value and those which cannot be assigned a dollar value. Examples of quantifiable intangible benefits are rights including copyrights on materials produced by the library (pamphlets, books, published bibliographies), licenses (on software produced by library personnel), and patents and trademarks which can be registered by library personnel or owned by the library through purchase or donation. Examples of intangibles which cannot be assigned a dollar value are the pleasure children receive from attending story hour; improvement in the quality of living brought to a community through its library's programs (adult literacy, film series, gardening seminars); and the number of lives saved as a result of library-sponsored programs on topics such as drug abuse, first aid and CPR, or home safety, among others.

The underlying principle in benefit-cost analysis is that the library's financial resources are best allocated to those activities which hold the most promise for helping the library to achieve its mission. The basic decision criterion in benefit-cost ratio analysis is to accept or reject a proposed new activity or even the continuation of a current activity, based on whether costs for the activity exceed its benefits. When several worthy activities, all of which have benefits that exceed their costs, are considered, the activities are rank ordered and then selected.

Although additional factors may be considered, if the ratio of the total benefits (B) of an activity divided by the activity's total costs (C) is greater than 1, then the benefits from the activity exceed its costs and the library could reasonably accept the activity. If the ratio of benefits divided by costs is less than 1, then costs exceed benefits and the allocation of scarce library resources to activities of only marginal benefit would be inefficient.

Table 2-5 illustrates benefit-cost comparisons for five hypothetical library activities. In interpreting the table, the reader's attention is drawn to the use of the designation ($000s). This shorthand notation alerts the reader that data values are recorded in thousands and means that the entry $210 represents $210,000. Further, the reader should recognize that it is not within the scope of this book to detail how the dollar value for either benefits or costs is estimated, a determination that often presents a formidable challenge to the practitioner. The application of the benefit-cost algorithm is the simple part of the analysis.

The usefulness of benefit-cost analysis, for example, is in determining whether it would be efficient for the library to purchase its own

Table 2-5. Benefit-Cost Ratios for Proposed Library Activities ($000s)						
			Net	Benefit-Cost		
Project	Benefit	Cost	Benefit	Ratio	Rank	Rank
	(B)	(C)	(B – C)	(B/C)	(B/C)	Net B
1	$ 210	$ 147	$ 63	1.4	3	1
2	90	30	60	3.0	1	2
3	27	30	- 3	0.9	5	5
4	3	2.5	0.5	1.2	4	3
5	0.3	0.2	0.1	1.5	2	4
Source: Hypothetical data						

telephone system rather than continuing to lease equipment. A second example is whether the library should purchase pay telephones on which the library would receive revenue. In the first case, the library would purchase equipment outright to avoid the recurring costs of the lease. The costs of the new equipment and the benefits of owning that equipment must be weighed against the costs of the lease agreement. In the second case, the library would receive revenue from the pay telephones that might balance or offset the costs of purchasing the new pay phones. Other proposals for which a benefit-cost analysis might be helpful in decision-making include the expansion of a service which requires additional staff, collections, or equipment, or the contraction of a service to contain its cost. In these cases the benefits of added (or reduced) services must be weighed against the additional (reduced) costs of staff, collections, or equipment.

The results of this analysis on Table 2-5 shows that the benefits exceed the costs for all activities except for the third activity. The benefit-cost ratio of the third activity is $27,000/30,0000 = 0.9$. Assuming there are not other valid reasons to retain this activity, its costs exceed its benefits and it should be discontinued. If the activities where benefits exceed costs are ranked from the highest to lowest benefit-cost ratio, the ranking of projects is 2, 5, 1, and 4. That is, the second project has the highest benefit to cost ratio of all the projects and the fourth project has the lowest. However if the projects are ranked by *net benefit,* the difference between benefit and cost *(B – C),* then the order of choice is 1, 2, 4, and 5.

In reality, the final projects selected and the resource allocation preferred may depend on the amount of funds available to the library. If the library has ample resources, a choice based either on net benefit or the benefit-cost ratio is acceptable. In cases of capital rationing, the ranking based on benefit-cost ratio is compelling since this is the direct ratio of per-dollar return from an activity. That is, an investment of $30,000 in the second activity will yield three times the benefit per dollar of cost. This is an important factor in justifying new or existing activities particularly in times of a budget reduction.

Quantity and Quality

Output measures are designed to evaluate the quantity of service provided by the library. Quantity, however, is not always an effective indicator of library performance. More activity does not necessarily mean better activity. Analyses of library services based entirely on quantity are becoming less persuasive to administrators. Difficult financial choices can no longer be made on the strength of increases in absolute numbers alone. Public and institutional financial planners are looking beyond performance records to scrutinize the merit of the activities themselves.

The application of output measures, therefore, must be modified if these measures are to be used effectively in the organizational climate. Output measures cannot be used to gather statistics for their own sake. The numbers must be placed in a context that communicates the significance of the numbers to decision-makers and administrators.

The best way to place output measures in a useful context is to relate them to the *quality* of library services. The delivery of high-quality services or products is a universal objective among successful organizations. Because of the growing appeal of quality products and services to consumers and clienteles, many organizations are finding new ways to assess quality through output measures.

Progress toward quality can only be assessed by comparison of output measures to some standard. Standards, however, are often criticized. A common objection to externally imposed standards, such as those developed by an association or consultant, is that they may be unrealistic or nonrepresentative of the historic goals of the institution. On the other hand, internally created standards can be self-serving and deceptive.

Library managers are finding that realistic standards for their particular library are those that are demonstrably supportive of the *mission* of the organization. The mission, summarized in a broad statement of purpose called a *mission statement*, expresses the conceptual goals that motivate the organization to exist and to achieve. The mission for the U.S. democratic system, for example, is summarized in the Constitution, particularly in the Preamble and the Bill of Rights. The precepts of this document are broad. For generations the Constitution has served as the standard against which every law of the land is evaluated.

Defining the mission of the library is very difficult. A mission statement expresses the library's purpose or reason for existence. It must be a long-range commitment of all library resources toward a stated goal. Often, articulation of the statement requires input from, or approval by, library trustees, regents, or other boards of directors. The mission statement for a public library may be "To work as an agent and partner within the community to promote the quality of society, individual self-development, and the enrichment of the citizenry through the provision of services for the dissemination of knowledge and cultural information." The successful library manager realizes that all decisions on strategy, marketing, services, priorities, and every other management choice—from recruitment and staff promotion to organization developments that affect the library—are made with the furtherance of the mission in mind. Informed decision-making requires output measures that can be related to advancement of the mission.

For example, a library might define its mission as above, to promote the quality of society through self-development. To this end, the library institutes an adult literacy program to teach illiterate adults to read. Output goals have been determined with measures of service usage as a proxy for the total population served. In addition, to monitor the *quality* of the program, the library will assess the dropout ratio (number of dropouts/total number of participants). Thus, progress toward achieving the goals of the library and fulfilling its mission can be monitored both quantitatively and qualitatively.

Dangers and Deceptions of Percents

The user and producer of percents should be aware of several liabilities of percents. First, the denominator must be large enough to be meaningful. Percent change analyses, for instance, are particularly susceptible to distortions caused by small base numbers. This is because low initial values make a change seem greater than high initial values.

If the denominator is small, it is better to use actual numerical values rather than percents. For example, in a survey of three people, we may find that 33% of those surveyed are frequent library users. To avoid deception, we should say that of three people surveyed, one is a frequent library user.

A similar distortion occurs when the base and percent are disguised or not given, as in "I have a single share." Only two shares may exist. The listener, however, supplies missing information and assumes there are many shares. Although the statement is accurate, if there are only two shares, the statement conceals the true ownership percent, which is equal to 50%.

There are many ways to express a relationship that best supports a desired result. This is an important point for the consumer of statistics to consider. Most likely, the method chosen to express the relationship will be the one that best seems to support the desired result. It is therefore up to the consumer to scrutinize data summaries. The consumer must ensure that the summary accurately reflects the situation or circumstance under study. The consumer must also confirm that the resulting conclusions are appropriate and reasonable.

Data Point Labeling and Summation Notation

An unavoidable fact is that statistics deals with numbers and calculations. Many librarians have a difficult time appreciating the relevance of the linear, problematic thinking associated with statistics to the humanistic profession of librarianship. Statistical techniques, however, can provide a system for understanding the environment in which the library functions to promote its mission and achieve its goals.

To use statistics effectively, the librarian must acquire skills which may seem unrelated to library experiences. Acquiring these new skills, however, is not difficult. Two very important techniques that can be quickly learned and almost immediately appreciated are *labeling of data points* and *summation notation*. Understanding these methods is no more difficult than understanding William Shakespeare's or Geoffrey Chaucer's rhyme schemes.

Data point labeling and summation notation are examples of mathematical shorthand to communicate ideas, methods, and operations efficiently and symbolically. These techniques simplify long equations. This is a significant advantage in dealing with formulas and expressions that are both necessary and, in their nonsimplified forms, cumbersome. Also, if the student of basic statistics has any interest in pursuing additional statistics training, understanding summation notation and data point labeling is essential.

Data Point Labeling

The first technique, data point labeling, establishes a general procedure for analyzing a set of data. Labeling is simplified if the data points are considered as a set of X's (Y's, P's, Q's, ...) or a sequence of points, each of which is identified or "tagged" by a number. This principle is similar to taking a number while waiting in line at the bakery. In the labeling process, the value of each data point is ignored. The first data point is labeled X_1 (read as "X sub-one"), the second is labeled X_2, the third is X_3, and so on. The X is called a *dummy variable*. Any letter may be used as a dummy variable ($X, Y, P, Q, ...$). The small number to the right of and below the X is a *subscript*. The subscript is intended strictly for identification and is not used for computational purposes.

After all the observations have been labeled, the data set can be pictured in this way:

X_1 = first data point
X_2 = second data point
X_3 = third data point, and so on.

The last data point is conventionally represented by X_N (read as "X sub-N"), because the N is understood as representing the total number of data points in the set. The elements of the above set can be expressed as $\{X_1, X_2, X_3, ... , X_N\}$.

Assume that Example 2-6 is a list of new videotapes, added each month (over 6 months) to a library's videotape rental collection.

Example 2-6. Number of Videotapes Added Monthly	
Month	Number of Tapes
July	27
August	18
September	32
October	19
November	20
December	24

In this example, the dummy variable, X, is used to denote the month. The first number, 27, is tagged or labeled X_1, so $X_1 = 27$. The second number, 18, is labeled X_2, so $X_2 = 18$. The last number, 24, is labeled X_6, so $X_6 = 24$. Because there are 6 data points, N is equal to 6.

Summation Notation

Understanding the basic rules of data point labeling is central to understanding *summation notation*, which is a symbolic way to represent the sum of a series of numbers. Summation notation allows for the brief expression of long equations. Summation notation will be used throughout this book to simplify the many algorithms presented.

Suppose, for example, that a librarian wishes to add the ages of all children present during a story hour. Such a sum can be useful in any number of statistical operations, described later in this text. For now, however, the task is to find a simple way to represent the addition of the ages.

If the children are asked in a random order for their ages, the ages reported are a series of observations or data points. These may be reported as $\{9, 9, 6, 7, 8, 6, 5, 9, 7\}$. Note that several of the ages, or data values, repeat and that there is no particular order to the listing of the ages. An equation adding the ages together would look like this:

$$9 + 9 + 6 + 7 + 8 + 6 + 5 + 9 + 7 = 66$$

Summation notation shortens this equation. The first step in converting this equation to summation notation is to tag or label each data point. We will use A as the dummy variable to represent age. Then, A_1 stands for the age in the first observation, 9, so that $A_1 = 9$. Likewise, A_2 stands for the second observation, also 9, so that $A_2 = 9$. The third observation, 6, is represented by A_3, 7 by A_4, and so on, until the final observation, 7, is represented by A_9. After the data points have been labeled, the equation becomes

$$\text{Sum} = A_1 + A_2 + A_3 + A_4 + A_5 + A_6 + A_7 + A_8 + A_9$$

The only feature in this equation that changes is the value of the subscript. It begins with 1 and increments by 1 with each observation, through the ninth observation. This pattern makes it possible to represent the equation symbolically. If a symbol is used for the operation, addition, and a symbol is used to show a constantly increasing subscript, this equation—and others like it—can be simplified. The symbol mathematicians have selected to represent addition is a Greek letter, capital Sigma, or Σ . Lowercase i represents the subscript and is the *summation index*. Therefore, this equation can be written:

$$\sum_{i=1}^{9} A_i = A_1 + A_2 + A_3 + A_4 + A_5 + A_6 + A_7 + A_8 + A_9$$

This construction is mathematical shorthand. It means: "In a series of 9 observations, each observation, A beginning with A_1 and continuing consecutively through A_9, will be added to find the sum total of all the observations."

Note that if the *summation index*, i, is changed from 1 to another number, such as 4, summation will begin with the fourth observation and continue through the ninth observation. A summation index of 5 directs summing to begin with the fifth observation, and so on. An important convention in summation notation is that, if the summation index is not specified, its range is understood to be between 1 and N, where N is the number of data points in the set. So, the following expressions represent the same operation:

$$\sum_{i=1}^{N} A_i \text{ is the same as } \sum A_i$$

The student must remember that, in data point labeling and in summation notation, the order and actual values of the subscripted variables are irrelevant. The examples are valuable for developing a facility for applying this technique. They also assist the student in understanding formulas more complicated than those in this book. Once the basic rules of summation notation are understood, many applications become apparent.

Summary of Critical Concepts

1. *Rounding* numbers is necessary when data are to be expressed to a certain number of decimal places, as in 0.66666, which may be expressed as 0.67. Rounding is also used in summary tables where

usually only three or four digits are shown, such as 2,347,218 volumes, which may be expressed as 2.347 million volumes. To minimize rounding error, some consistent method for rounding numbers must be followed.

2. A *ratio* is a relationship between two numbers expressed by division. The first quantity is called the *numerator* and the second is the *denominator*. The denominator is also called the *base*.

3. *Percent* is a frequently used statistic because of its wide acceptance and ease of computation. It is often used for expressing change in measurement or frequency, in comparison with a base number. The *base number* is the key to evaluating a ratio or percent. If the base is not representative, data distortion is possible.

4. *Data analysis* is concerned with identifying significant relationships between and among quantities. Data analysis is also concerned with identifying the amount and direction of change that has occurred since a previous date. Common techniques such as *dollar and percent change, component, component percents, ratio analysis*, and *benefit-cost analysis* are useful analytic techniques.

5. Library *output measures* are quantitative terms for evaluating the performance of a library. They identify the success with which services are provided and resources are made available. In this way, they provide the librarian with objective evidence of the relationships between library activities and resource allocation.

6. *Output measures* are usually compared with some *standard,* or identified level of achievement. However, because each library has different clientele needs and capabilities to finance library services, externally developed standards may be of little value. Increasingly, administrators question the authority on which standards are based. Use of absolute numbers to justify increases are also meeting with resistance. This is because the relevance of absolute numbers to quality of services is not objectively clear.

7. A *mission statement* is a broad statement of purpose toward which a library strives. It expresses a long-term commitment of library resources. It is possible for libraries to have similar mission statements. For example, all public libraries may express their mission as "To work as an agent and partner within the community to promote the quality of society, self-development, and the enrichment of the citizenry through providing services for the dissemination of knowledge and cultural information."

8. *Data point* labeling is a form of mathematical shorthand. Its usefulness is in being able to convey thoughts about data in a concise manner. In this technique, data points are thought of as forming a sequence. Each point is assigned a number or tag, as when a person

takes a number in the bakery shop. The value of the data point is not considered. The first data point becomes the first value in the sequence. It is labeled with a *subscript*, as in X_1 (read "X sub 1") and so on. If there are N data points, the set is written $\{X_1, \ldots, X_N\}$. If there are 8 data points, the set is written $\{X_1, \ldots, X_8\}$, and N is understood to equal 8.

9. *Summation notation* is a useful technique for shortening equations that use both labeled data points *and* addition. If the data points are labeled into a sequence such as $X_1, X_2, \ldots, X_N$, then their sum, $X_1 + X_2 + \ldots + X_N$, can be written, using summation notation, as ΣX_i.

Key Terms

Benefit-Cost Analysis. A technique to compare the costs of initiating or continuing a project or activity to the economic benefits which result from providing that project or activity.

Component Percent Analysis. A technique for using percents to focus on the relationships between component parts and a whole. Component percent analysis is frequently used in relation to budgeting for determining relative importance of particular budgetary items (expenses).

Data Point Labeling. The use of dummy variables $(X, Y, P, Q, \ldots)$ to tag data points and simplify long equations. In data point labeling, the value of the individual data points is ignored.

Dollar and Percent Change Analysis. Techniques for comparing monetary values and percentages over time. The analysis compares the change in dollars or percents between two periods relative to some arbitrarily chosen base figure.

Mission Statement. A statement which expresses a long-range commitment of all library resources toward a stated goal. All decisions on strategy, marketing, services, priorities, and other management choices that affect the library are made with furtherance of the mission in mind.

Output Measures. Also known as performance measures, these are quantitative measures of library performance. They serve as markers of the success with which services are provided and resources made available. Their purpose is to provide managers with objective evidence of the relationships among library activities and resource allocation toward accomplishing the library's goals.

Percent. A quantity expressed in hundredths. (Percent means "per hundred" or "out of each hundred.") Percents show the relative size of two or more numbers, and they are usually smaller than 100.

Ratio. A mathematical relationship between two quantities, indicated by division. The ratio of 700 to 500 is expressed as 7 : 5, or as 1.4. The validity of a ratio depends on the validity of the numbers entering into its computation. Ratios are useful for disclosing relationships. They help to identify conditions, trends, and comparisons that are not easily detected by review of the individual quantities of the ratio.

Ratio Analysis. The use of a variety of statistical techniques such as ratios, percents, and per capita analyses for measuring and quantifying the performance of a person, product, or institution. Ratio analysis is useful in comparing performance and in identifying trends in data.

Rounding. A method for shortening numbers to bring them within a desired accuracy. Rounding, or "rounding off," is an important technique for simplifying, summarizing, and abbreviating data.

Summation Notation. A symbolic means for representing the sum of a series of numbers. Summation notation allows for the brief expression of long equations and is used to simplify statistical algorithms.

Self-Assessment Quiz

True or False 1. Rounded to two decimal places, the number 27.745001 is 27.75, but 27.745000 rounded to two decimal places is 27.74.

True or False 2. The percent is a useful statistic, because it is familiar and meaningful even to people who have little training in statistics.

True or False 3. A number expressed as a percent of something large may give the impression that the number is small. Similarly, the same number expressed as a percent of something small will make the number appear to be large.

True or False 4. When two or more things are being compared, it is better to compare actual numerical values than to compare percents, particularly if the base value of any of the percents is small.

True or False 5. A raise of 100% offsets a pay cut of 50%.

True or False 6. Last month, 60 compact discs were checked out.

		This month, 45 were checked out. The percent decrease was 15%.
True or False	7.	Benefit-cost ratio analysis is a technique for choosing activities to initiate, expand, or contract.
True or False	8.	Library performance is too intangible to be gauged by output measures.
True or False	9.	Effectiveness measures for collection development may be the number of reserves for particular books and clientele complaints.
True or False	10.	Data may be summarized in different ways for different purposes.
True or False	11.	Using your best judgment, but without making calculations, 87.3% of 22.80 is more than 22.8% of 87.3.

Answers

1. True. If the third digit is 5 and there is a remainder, the second digit is increased by 1. If the third digit is exactly 5, with no remainder, and the second digit is even, the second digit is unchanged.
2. True. A percent is a familiar expression and puts ratios and fractions into a convenient format.
3. True. The percent can be deceptive if some source data are not also shown.
4. True. When the bases are small, slight differences in the numerator cause radical changes in the percents.
5. True. If a quantity is reduced by 50% (halved), the new quantity must be increased by 100% (doubled) to get the old quantity again.
6. False. The percent decrease is the numerical difference divided by the original number, $(60 - 45)/60 = 25\%$, and is not the numerical difference alone, $(60 - 45 = 15)$.
7. True. Benefit-cost ratio analysis is a managerial tool used to determine the most efficient allocation of resources among competing projects or activities. It helps the   librarian to decide which new projects to initiate and which existing projects to expand or contract.
8. False. Output measures help to determine how the library is successfully meeting its objectives.
9. True. If reserves and complaints fall, effectiveness has probably increased.
10. True. The way data are organized or presented can emphasize certain points.

11. False. The two quantities are equal since $X\%$ of Y will always equal $Y\%$ of X. This is true because the former equals $X/100$ times Y (or $XY/100$), and the latter equals X times $Y/100$ (also $XY/100$).

Discussion Questions and Problems

1. Given the examples below, determine whether rounding would be appropriate, and if so, to what extent.
   a. population of your home town
   b. results of a merchandise inventory in a nationwide retail chain
   c. results of a merchandise inventory in a local jewelry store
   d. your gross taxable income on a tax return.
2. Objects in a classroom can be grouped into many populations, such as students, instructors, furniture, and books. Use these objects to calculate various useful ratios. (Hint: the ratio of students to faculty or tables to chairs)
3. A soap was once advertised as "99.44% pure." *Pure,* however, was never defined. Discuss examples, besides those in the book, of the possible misleading use of percents.
4. Gather population data about the size of the community that is served by each of the following types of libraries:
   a. college or university library
   b. local hospital library
   c. corporate library
   d. local public library.
5. A criticism of output measures is that they unnecessarily focus on performance of current library activities. Some argue that use of output measures in library program development benefits current library clientele at the expense of potential new activities or users. Discuss this point of view.
6. One disadvantage to output measures is that their accuracy depends upon the integrity of the recorder of the statistics. Identify and discuss the merit of various steps that can be taken to ensure that data are not "faked."
7. Discuss whether the value of an output measure as an indicator of performance is outweighed by the disadvantages identified in Question 6. Give examples from other fields where reported activity or accuracy depends on the good faith of the reporter of the observations.
8. Quantitative measures are at best approximations of the quality of the item under study. In manufacturing, the quality of a product is often

measured by tolerances. Tolerance measurement has, as an objective, an ideal product containing zero defects. Because tolerance is measurable, and defects are countable, discuss whether this approach represents a measure of quality or quantity.

9. One measurement of quality in education may be to identify the number of university graduates employed soon after graduation in their chosen fields. What other standards may be applied to measure the quality of education or training? How can these standards be expressed as ratios?

10. List and comment on considerations for evaluation when setting objectives for a new library activity.

11. The *immediacy index*, an important ratio in scientific publishing, is a measure of the currency of reference citations in the average research article. A high immediacy index is desirable because it shows that the research upon which a journal's articles is based is current information. The immediacy index is calculated by first counting the number of bibliography or footnote citations at the end of all articles published by a journal during the year to articles (including those of the journal itself) published that same year. The second step is to divide the number of citations to current year articles by the number of articles ("source items") published by the journal that year. In other words,

$$\text{Immediacy Index} = \frac{\text{Citations in Current Year to Articles Published in Current Year}}{\text{Total Number of Source Items in Current Year}}$$

Suppose that the editorial board of a monthly scientific research periodical compiled the following data for Year X:

Total articles published in Year X:	246
Total citations from articles:	3962
Citations to Year X works:	102

a. Determine the immediacy index for this journal.

b. Discuss the relevancy of the immediacy ratio to the objective of this journal.

c. Assume the editorial board wishes to increase its journal's immediacy index. Discuss the possible effects of its decision to place more emphasis on current literature references when making manuscript acceptance decisions.

d. A review article summarizes much of the current research about a topic, and its bibliography contains citations to the most recent works available. Discuss how the acceptance and publication of more review articles might increase a journal's immediacy index. If this strategy were followed, speculate when in the calendar year it would be most advantageous to publish such articles.

e. Discuss the effect on a journal's immediacy index of an editorial decision to publish fewer, but longer, articles, or to publish more short articles. Keep in mind that the total number of journal pages remains fixed under either decision.

f. Are the methods discussed in c, d, and e to manipulate this ratio expansionist or contractionist? (Hint: Look for ways to manipulate the numerator and the denominator.)

12. Circulation data are shown below for videotapes and compact discs over the past 6 months. Compute the identified sums.

Month	Videotape Circulation V_i	Disc Circulation D_i
1	240	29
2	252	46
3	238	41
4	244	45
5	255	40
6	225	36

a. What is the value of V_3? What is the value of D_5?

b. Express $V_1 + \ldots + V_6$ in summation notation. Find this value.

c. Express $D_1 + \ldots + D_6$ in summation notation. Find this value.

d. Express in summation notation and find the value of
$$\frac{(V_1 + \ldots + V_6)}{6}$$

e. Express in summation notation and find the value of
$$\frac{(D_1 + \ldots + D_6)}{6}$$

13. Express in summation notation:

a. $M_1 + M_2 + M_3 + \ldots + M_8$

b. $X_3 + X_4 + X_5 + \ldots + X_{15}$

c. $X_0 + \ldots + X_9$

d. $f_1 + f_2 + f_3 + \ldots + f_9 + 4.5$

e. $1 + 2 + 3 + \ldots + 12$ (Hint: Let n represent the integers.)

Chapter Three

Communicating Data

Learning Objectives

After reading and understanding the contents of this chapter, you will be able to:

1. Define a data array and sort data numerically in ascending or descending order.
2. Define a frequency distribution for ungrouped or grouped data and discuss the advantages of each for displaying data descriptively and economically.
3. Show the process of building a frequency distribution, a histogram, and a frequency polygon, and explain the advantage of each.
4. Depict data by plotting it on the *X-Y* coordinate plane.
5. Discuss the advantages and uses of histograms compared with a frequency polygon and explain and show how to construct each.
6. Construct and explain the usefulness of graphs such as horizontal bar, vertical column, pie, and line graphs to illustrate quantitative and qualitative comparisons.

If library services are to grow and flourish in the environment of increasing budget restrictions, librarians must be adept at making persuasive financial arguments. Librarians must become very skilled in data analysis and presentation. The librarian can begin the process of analysis by organizing and describing data economically.

Table 3-1. 20th Century Year of Copyright $(n = 93)$

56	66	69	61	76	62	71	60	74	68
74	77	80	84	59	61	78	64	68	67
72	67	56	59	57	70	57	67	60	71
71	65	84	67	68	65	81	73	76	73
65	79	72	74	84	63	78	69	60	66
77	72	73	69	61	62	76	79	80	70
58	82	63	82	76	70	55	64	62	74
64	58	80	70	77	83	57	83	85	86
72	77	63	74	73	61	81	59	68	64
65	66	68							

Describing Data Economically

One useful technique for organizing data is to sort them numerically in either ascending or descending order. This sorting produces a *data array*. Arranging data in an array can be accomplished manually or by a computer.

The advantages of organizing data into an array can be seen in the example of a study to determine the age of the books in a particular area of the library's collection. The variable is age of the books. The value of the variable, or score, varies from one observed book to another. In this study, a particular range of call numbers is selected which contains 93 books. The copyright year of each book is recorded. Table 3-1 shows the raw data in the order in which they were collected. The data are not organized and do not convey any meaning or trend.

Table 3-2 is an ascending-order array of these data. It allows one to observe immediately the lowest and highest values in the data set, to divide the data into sections, and to observe if particular values occur more than once in the array. The distance between successive values can also be observed from the array.

The years in the data array in Table 3-2 range from 1955 to 1986. It is possible to divide this data listing in many ways. For example, the first half of the data occurs between 1955 and 1970 and the second half between 1971 and 1986. Similarly, the lower one-third of the observations is between 1955 and 1964. The middle third is between 1965 and 1973, and the most recent third occurs between 1974 and 1986. Years 1955, 1985, and 1986 appear only once. Notice that 1975 does not appear at all. The table also shows that the years increment by 1 from

Table 3-2. Data Array of 20th Century Copyright Year $(n = 93)$									
55	56	56	57	57	57	58	58	59	59
59	60	60	60	61	61	61	61	62	62
62	63	63	63	64	64	64	64	65	65
65	65	66	66	66	67	67	67	67	68
68	68	68	68	69	69	69	70	70	70
70	71	71	71	72	72	72	72	73	73
73	73	74	74	74	74	74	76	76	76
76	77	77	77	77	78	78	79	79	80
80	80	81	81	82	82	83	83	84	84
84	85	86							

Source: Table 3-1

1955 through 1986, except for the jump from 1974 to 1976. The array in Table 3-2 is decidedly an improvement over a simple raw data listing. An array, however, is still cumbersome, particularly for showing large amounts of data. A frequency distribution can display these data more descriptively and economically.

A *frequency distribution* is a tabular display of data that shows the number of observations from the data set that fall into classes or intervals. The advantage of a frequency distribution is that it classifies, condenses, and greatly simplifies data for presentation, analysis, and interpretation. In a frequency distribution, *frequency* refers to how often an observation or score occurs. *Distribution* refers to how the occurrences are spread across different locations. A frequency distribution compresses the data by eliminating the repetition of equal values. There are two types of frequency distributions: one accommodates ungrouped data and one accommodates grouped data.

Ungrouped Frequency Distributions

A frequency distribution for ungrouped data shows the distribution of each data point in the set. It is constructed by listing the scores in an array from lowest to highest value. A notation is made each time a score occurs. The number of marks represents the frequency of occurrence of each score. The marks are then tallied. Table 3-3 is a frequency distribution that illustrates this construction. Each data point in the set is summarized in the distribution. There are frequencies for 93 values that occur at 32 separate observation levels, beginning with 1955 and ending with 1986. Each observation level increments by 1. Even observa-

Table 3-3. 20th Century Copyright Years ($n = 93$)

X	f	Tally	X	f	Tally
55	/	1	71	///	3
56	//	2	72	////	4
57	///	3	73	////	4
58	//	2	74	/////	5
59	///	3	75		0
60	///	3	76	////	4
61	////	4	77	////	4
62	///	3	78	//	2
63	///	3	79	//	2
64	////	4	80	///	3
65	////	4	81	//	2
66	///	3	82	//	2
67	////	4	83	//	2
68	/////	5	84	///	3
69	///	3	85	/	1
70	////	4	86	/	1

Source: Table 3-2

tion levels that have a zero score — for example 1975 — are included in the distribution. The frequency distribution in Table 3-3 is more efficient and useful than are Table 3-1 data. It is also more descriptive of the data than is the array in Table 3-2.

Data in this type of frequency distribution are ungrouped. A grouped frequency distribution is obtained by dividing the data into similar groupings or categories, called *classes*. Classes have *limits*, the upper and lower boundaries. The data from Table 3-3 are reorganized into eight classes in Table 3-4. The *class limits* for the first class, 1955–58, are 1955 (the lower limit) and 1958 (the upper limit). In the second class, 1959 is the lower limit and 1962 is the upper limit. The purpose of class limits is to establish a gap between classes so that every observation can be unambiguously assigned to just one class. If, for example, the classes were 1955–58 and 1958–61, it would be unclear where to count the observations for 1958. The gap makes the classes *mutually exclusive*. Mutual exclusivity eliminates overlap and is an essential aspect of a well-constructed frequency distribution.

Class width is the term given to the standard size of each class. A

Table 3-4. 20th Century Copyright Dates ($n = 93$)

Classes	Frequencies
55-58	8 1+2+3+2= 8)
59-62	13 (3+3+4+3=13)
63-66	14 (3+4+4+3=14)
67-70	16 (4+5+3+4=16)
71-74	16 (3+4+4+5=16)
75-78	10 (0+4+4+2=10)
79-82	9 (2+3+2+2= 9)
83-86	7 (2+3+1+1= 7)
	$n = \overline{93}$

Source: Table 3-2

class with a width of 4, for example, means that 4 observation levels are included in the class. For the most accurate data presentation, the frequency distribution's classes should have equal widths. Class width and the number of classes are chosen with several concerns in mind. Customarily, there are between 6 and 15 classes, regardless of the number of data points. Most effectively drawn frequency distributions contain only 7, 8, or 9 classes.

Table 3-5 provides a heuristic or rule of thumb for choosing an appropriate number of classes. It translates the number of data points into a number of classes. For example, Table 3-3 contains 93 data points. According to Table 3-5, at least 8 classes should be used in the frequency distribution. If the 32 observation levels of Table 3-3 are divided into 8 classes, each class will contain 32/8 or 4 observation levels. That is, each of the 8 classes will have a class width of 4.

Grouped Frequency Distributions

For several reasons it is ideal to divide Table 3-3 into 8 classes with a uniform class width of 4. First, the number of classes falls in the customary 6–15 range. Second, each and every class has the same width. The frequency distribution that results from these divisions is shown in Table 3-4. The first class of 1955–58 includes the frequencies recorded for the years 1955, 1956, 1957, and 1958. These frequencies, respectively, are 1, 2, 3, and 2. They sum to 8. This sum, 8, is called the *class frequency*. The second class consists of observation frequencies for years 1959 through 1962. These frequencies, 3, 3, 4, and 3, sum to

Table 3-5. Minimum Number of Classes for Various Size Data Sets of Continuous Scale Observations

Number of Data Points	Minimum Number of Classes
10-15	5
16-31	6
32-63	7
64-127	8
128-255	9
256-511	10
512-1023	11
1024-2047	12
2048-4095	13
4096 +	14

the class frequency of 13. When we continue this process to the last class, which spans the years 1983 through 1986, the respective frequencies are 2, 3, 1, and 1. These sum to 7. The resulting frequency distribution is shown in Table 3-4, which illustrates the number of observations from the data set that falls into each of the eight classes. In constructing a grouped frequency distribution, it is not necessary to show the sum of the frequencies for each individual point. Instead, only the class frequencies need to be recorded. Hence, the sums in Table 3-4, such as (1 + 2 + 3 + 2 = 8), are shown only for illustrative purposes.

Although 4 and 8 are excellent choices for class width and number respectively, other combinations are possible. In fact, depending upon the intentions of the producer, other combinations may be more desirable. The producer of statistical graphs should be aware that they can be used as tools of persuasion. Depending upon the point the producer wishes to make, a graph can be constructed in a variety of ways.

Table 3-6 portrays several frequency distributions, illustrating the effect of using a varying number of class intervals. These are derived from the data in Table 3-3. Comparison of these frequency distributions reveals several interesting points. As the width of the class interval increases from 1, the number of classes decreases. This is because more scores are lumped together into fewer classes. The effect of fewer classes is that the numerical value of each score becomes obscured.

Table 3-6. Frequency Distributions Illustrating the Effect of a Varying Number of Class Intervals

Class	f	Class	f	Class	f
55-70	51	55-65	32	55-62	21
71-86	42	66-76	39	63-70	30
		77-87	22	71-78	26
				79-86	16
Class Intervals:	2	Class Intervals:	3	Class Intervals:	4
Class Width:	16	Class Width:	11	Class Width:	8

Class	f	Class	f	Class	f
53-59	11	53-58	8	53-57	6
60-66	24	59-64	20	58-62	15
67-73	27	65-70	23	63-67	18
74-80	20	71-76	20	68-72	19
81-87	11	77-82	15	73-77	17
		83-88	7	78-82	11
				83-87	7
Class Intervals:	5	Class Intervals:	6	Class Intervals:	7
Class Width:	7	Class Width:	6	Class Width:	5

Class	f	Class	f	Class	f
55-58	8	54-56	3	55-56	3
59-62	13	57-59	8	57-58	5
63-66	14	60-62	10	59-60	6
67-70	16	63-65	11	61-62	7
71-74	16	66-68	12	63-64	7
75-78	10	69-71	10	65-66	7
79-82	9	72-74	13	67-68	9
83-86	7	75-77	8	69-70	7
		78-80	7	71-72	7
		81-83	6	73-74	9
		84-86	5	75-76	4
				77-78	6
				79-80	5
				81-82	4
				83-84	5
				85-86	2
Class Intervals:	8	Class Intervals:	11	Class Intervals:	16
Class Width:	4	Class Width:	3	Class Width:	2

Source: Table 3-3

This overcondensing of the distribution compromises its usefulness. The distribution in Table 3-6 is

Class width	1	2	3	4	5	6	7	8	11	16	32
Number of classes	32	16	11	8	7	6	5	4	3	2	1

Notice from Table 3-6 that once data are grouped, the identity of each single score is lost. Accordingly, it is better to begin with a larger number of classes and then determine whether fewer, broader classes are desirable. A large number of classes can be combined into fewer, broader classes. However, once data are grouped, it may be impossible to reconstitute the individual values.

The calculation of class size and class limits is more complicated when the represented data are continuous scale data. Theoretically, continuous scale data such as height, weight, and time can assume any fractional value along a continuous scale. Yet, in practice, continuous scale data are rounded and the values reported are uncertain by a factor of plus or minus one- half of the last decimal place.

This means that the *real limits* of continuous scale data are plus or minus one half unit beyond the stated limits. For example, the real limits for the interval 12.0–17.9 are 11.95–17.95. The real limits for 12.00–17.90 are 11.995–17.905. If height is measured to the nearest inch and the class limits are 48–50, the real or true limits are 47.5 to 50.5. If noise level is measured to the nearest 0.01 decibel and if the class limits are 60.00 to 64.90 decibels, the real or true limits are 59.995 to 64.905 decibels. In other words, the real limits of the classes include values slightly higher and lower than the class limits show. However, for discrete variables, no distinction is made between class limits and real limits. If the interval is 55–58, then 55 and 58 are both the class limits and the real limits.

Class midpoint refers to the exact middle of the class. To find the class midpoint, apply the following formula:

$$\text{Class Midpoint} = \frac{\text{Lower Class Limit} + \text{Upper Class Limit}}{2} \qquad (3-1)$$

For example, in a public library that provides users with access to computer equipment, suppose printing is done with an impact printer. A study determines that the noise level for the impact printers falls within the interval 60.0–64.9. To calculate the class midpoint for this interval, use Formula 3-1:

$$\text{Class Midpoint} = \frac{\text{Lower Class Limit} + \text{Upper Class Limit}}{2}$$

$$= \frac{60.0 + 64.9}{2}$$

$$= \frac{124.9}{2}$$

$$= 62.45$$

As discussed in the next section, the class midpoint is often used in graphing.

Frequency Distribution Graphs

A *graph* is the visual representation of statistical data. A well-constructed graph distills complicated data into trends or relationships that can be understood at a glance. The value of a good graph lies in its ability to communicate concepts to the user without cumbersome details. A graph that is accurate and easily interpretable commands attention. Because graphs appeal directly to the user's visual sense and to the user's intellect, they can help to stimulate imaginative analysis.

Graphs present data in a gridlike pattern of columns and rows. The columns and rows are established by two number lines which are perpendicular to one another. The horizontal number line, shown in Figure 3-1, is the *X-axis*. The vertical number line is the *Y-axis*. Except for being at right angles, or perpendicular to each other, the X-axis and Y-axis are identical. Each is like a scale that extends endlessly in both directions from zero. Each contains a continuous set of *coordinates.* The coordinates are a continuous scale of numbers which define the *coordinate plane.*

The point of intersection of the two axes is the *origin.* Measurement on the X-axis to the right, of the origin is positive and is recorded in positive numbers. Measurement to the left of the origin on the X-axis is negative and is recorded in negative numbers. Similarly, positive measure and positive numbers on the Y-axis occur above the origin.

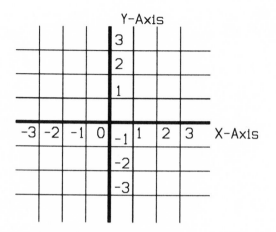

Figure 3-1. The Rectangular Coordinate Plane

Below the origin, values and measures on the Y-axis are negative. Values recorded above, or to the right of the origin are *positive numbers. Negative numbers* are those recorded to the left or below the origin.

An example of a negative number is a temperature reading such as –5 degrees. This number means that the recorded temperature is 5 units less than the zero point on the temperature scale. On the horizontal or X-axis, this reading is located 5 units to the left of the origin. On the vertical scale or Y-axis, it lies 5 units below the origin. Negative numbers are often encountered when discussing variables such as temperatures, sea level readings, and yard penalties in football. In a library, the number of books removed from the shelves by collection weeding is reported as a negative value.

As shown in Figure 3-2, the axes separate the coordinate plane into four distinct regions or quadrants. The axes themselves, however, are regarded as not contained in any quadrant. Note the manner in which the quadrants are numbered. To graph a point, *P*, in the coordinate plane, an *ordered pair* of coordinates (*x,y*) is used. The first number of the ordered pair, *x*, refers to the location of the point with respect to the X-axis. The second number, *y*, refers to the location of the point with respect to the Y-axis. Thus, the point (4,3) is located on the plane 4 units to the right of the Y-axis and 3 units above the X-axis. This is illustrated in Figure 3-3. This ordered pair (*x,y*) is sometimes called, ungrammatically, the coordinates of point P. The origin has coordinates

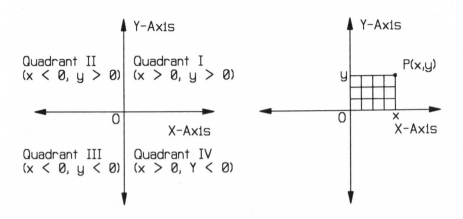

Figures 3-2 (left) and 3-3 (right). Coordinate Plane Showing Quadrants and Plotting of an Ordered Pair on the Coordinate Plane *P(4,3)*

represented by the ordered pair *(0,0)*. Most statistical charts use only Quadrant I because studies usually generate positive numbers.

When data points are plotted on a graph, the values of the characteristic being measured are conventionally shown on the horizontal axis (X-axis). This may be age, distance, income, library collections, time, population, or any other variable. On the Y-axis, the frequencies, relative frequency percents, or index numbers associated with the variable's classes are shown. For example, year of publication may be graphed on the X-axis, with the number of books published in that year (frequency) on the Y-axis.

Histogram

A data set may be represented by a *histogram*. This is a graph composed of a series of rectangles with their bases on the horizontal axis (X-axis). The centers are at the class marks or class midpoints. The histogram's widths are equal to the class interval sizes. A histogram provides more information about a data set than could be learned from casual inspection of its frequency distribution. Figure 3-4, for example, is a histogram of the copyright dates of books from Table 3-4. Notice that there seems to be a clustering and possible symmetry about some central value near 1970. The graph also conveys the frequency of the intervals in their relation to each other. In addition, it provides a sense of the concentration of items between 1967 and 1974. Notice also that the histogram in Figure 3-4 has a discontinuous or broken X-axis. This is designated by –ᐯ–, because none of the copyright data collected in this study precedes 1955. Rather than have a very wide graph with no bars between 0 and 1955, the X-axis is shown as "broken."

In a histogram, the *areas* of the rectangles represent the class frequencies. As you recall, area is equal to height times width. If all the classes have equal widths, all the rectangles of the histogram will have equal widths. In this case, *height* alone can represent the class frequencies. When the class widths are equal, the common practice is to set the heights numerically equal to the class frequencies.

An *open-ended interval* is a class that allows either the upper or lower end of a quantitative classification to be limitless. For example, in a frequency distribution of book costs, an open class interval might be "Under $10" or "Over $100." Distributions that contain open-ended intervals require special handling. A practical guideline is that open-ended intervals should be avoided whenever possible. Such intervals impose calculation limitations and present problems in graphing.

Table 3-7 illustrates an open-ended interval. The frequency distribution represents the age of library clientele of a hypothetical community with a population of 40,000. The histogram for this distribution is illustrated in Figure 3-5. There are seven class intervals. The first six classes are limited to certain ages. The last interval is an open-ended interval. In this interval, all the community's citizens who are age 60 and over are grouped together. A high frequency count in this interval is not surprising. This imprecision is a serious limitation with open-

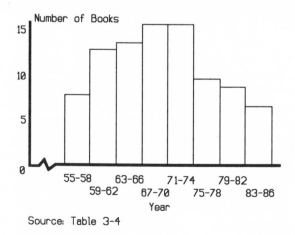

Source: Table 3-4

Figure 3-4. 20th Century Copyright Year

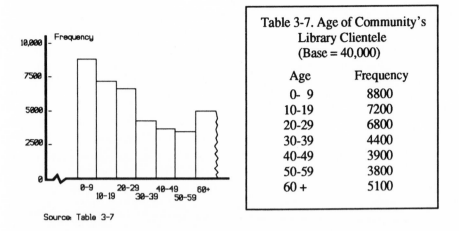

Table 3-7. Age of Community's Library Clientele (Base = 40,000)

Age	Frequency
0- 9	8800
10-19	7200
20-29	6800
30-39	4400
40-49	3900
50-59	3800
60 +	5100

Source: Table 3-7

Figure 3-5. Age of Clientele

ended intervals. The citizens in the last category could be age 60, 70, 80, or older.

In constructing a histogram, the following guidelines are useful to insure uniformity:

1. Classes are plotted on the horizontal axis (X-axis) with centers at the class marks. Frequencies are plotted on the vertical axis (Y-axis).
2. The areas of the rectangles represent class frequencies.
3. If the classes are of equal width, the bars selected to represent the classes should be of equal width. The rectangle height represents class frequency.
4. The rectangles or bars of a histogram are contiguous, touching each other. When the chart is constructed, the practice is to leave a space between the origin and the first bar.
5. Frequencies always start at zero on the vertical scale (Y-axis). However, they do not necessarily start at zero on the horizontal axis (X-axis). The vertical axis (Y-axis) should not be broken, because a false impression of the data almost always results.
6. In plotting the frequencies, the height of the point representing the score with the highest frequency should be approximately equal to three-fourths the length of the horizontal axis. The point of highest frequency is also known as the mode and will be discussed in detail in Chapter Four.

The consumer of statistics must be aware of the importance of the fifth and sixth statements in the above guidelines. These elements of the guidelines promote uniformity in the scaling of data to minimize data distortion. Graphs are suspect if part of the vertical scale is removed or if scale units are inappropriate.

Frequency Polygon

A *frequency polygon* is a closed-figure graph of class frequency plotted against class midpoint. It may be used in place of a histogram to illustrate the pictorial nature of a frequency distribution. In a frequency polygon, the scores or midpoints of class intervals are shown on the horizontal axis (X-axis). The frequencies are shown on the vertical axis (Y-axis). The frequency associated with each score or class interval is shown by a point which is connected to adjacent points by a straight line. After the midpoints are connected, the polygon is formed by connecting the first class midpoint to the next lower class midpoint and then connecting the last class midpoint to the next higher class midpoint on the horizontal axis. Since both of these class midpoints have a frequency of zero, this allows the polygon to be closed.

A frequency polygon includes the same information as a histogram and can be built by connecting the midpoints of the tops of the rectangles in the histogram, as illustrated in Figure 3-6. As shown in the figure, there is a distinction between a frequency polygon and a his-

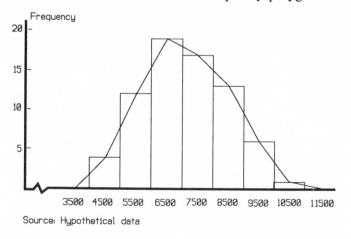

Source: Hypothetical data

Figure 3-6. Number of Photocopy Exposures (n=73)

togram. In the frequency polygon, the number of observations in each interval is assumed to be concentrated at the midpoint of the interval. In the histogram, the observations are assumed to be distributed uniformly within each interval. Each graph offers its own advantages*. The advantages of the histogram are

- Each bar represents the exact number of frequencies for a class interval, whereas the corresponding area under the polygon does not.

- In discrete distributions, separated bars can be employed to emphasize data gaps.

- Particular classes stand out more distinctly than in a frequency polygon.

The advantages of the frequency polygon are

- It is superior in illustrating two or more data sets in the same chart since multiple polygons make fewer, less confusing intersections.

- It consists of fewer lines and appears more streamlined than a histogram.

- The shape of the polygon more closely resembles the curve of the population than does the shape of the histogram.

Relative and Cumulative Distributions

Most of the tabular summaries presented thus far have been of frequency distributions showing only the frequency for the individual classes. In addition to this information, it is useful to know the fraction or percent of the total number of observations that fall into each of the mutually exclusive classes. The ratio used for this statistic is the *relative frequency* of each class interval. This measure is the number of observations which occur in each class interval divided by the total number of observations in the data set. Expressed as an equation,

---

* Portions of this text were derived from *Business and Economic Statistics* by W.A. Spurr, L.S. Kellogg, and J.H. Smith. ©1961, Richard D. Irwin, Inc., pages 166-167. Used by permission of the publisher.

$$\text{Relative Frequency} = \frac{\text{Frequency of a Single Class}}{\text{Sum of All Class Frequencies}} \qquad (3-2)$$

For an example illustrating relative frequency computation, refer to Table 3-8. This table presents the relative frequency distribution for the copyright dates of the 93 books illustrated earlier in Table 3-1. The relative frequency of the interval 1955-58 is calculated by dividing the number of observations that occur in the interval, 8, by the total number of observations in the data set, 93. Hence, the relative frequency for the first interval is the fraction 8/93 or .086. Rounded off and expressed as a percent, this is 9%. The relative frequency of the second class, 1959–62, is 13/93, or .140. Rounded off and expressed as a percent, this is 14%. If the relative frequencies are expressed as percents, they must sum to a total of 100%. If they are expressed as decimals, they must sum to 1.00. (Note: Small errors may occur due to rounding of either percents or decimals.) When the table is built, it is not necessary to show all calculations. Only the relative frequency percents need to be shown.

Relative Frequency Distribution

When relative frequency information is included as part of the fre-

---

Table 3-8. Relative Frequency Distribution of 20th Century
Copyright Dates of Books (n = 93)

Class	Frequency			Relative Frequency (Percent)
55–58	8	8/93	=	.09 (9%)
59–62	13	13/93	=	.14 (14%)
63–66	14	14/93	=	.15 (15%)
67–70	16	16/93	=	.17 (17%)
71–74	16	16/93	=	.17 (17%)
75–78	10	10/93	=	.11 (11%)
79–82	9	9/93	=	.10 (10%)
83–86	7	7/93	=	.08 (8%)
	n = 93			101%*

*Percentage sum discrepancies due to rounding.
Source: Table 3-4

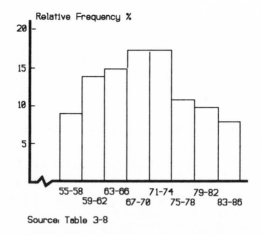

Source: Table 3-8

Figure 3-7. 20th Century Copyright Year

quency distribution, the distribution is called a *relative frequency distribution*. The frequencies may be presented in terms of fractions, decimals, or percents, but percents are most commonly used.

A graph of a relative frequency distribution can be obtained from the histogram or frequency polygon by changing the vertical scale (Y-axis) from frequency to relative frequency. The resulting graphs are called *relative frequency histograms* or *percent histograms*. The polygons are called *relative frequency polygons* or *percent polygons*. An example of a relative frequency histogram is illustrated in Figure 3-7, with copyright year shown on the X-axis and relative frequency percent on the Y-axis. Relative frequency graphs provide the user with a comparison of the part to its whole. The part/whole relationship, or component percent, can help to express the relative importance or significance of different data.

Cumulative Frequency Distribution

A distribution that is especially useful to librarians is the *cumulative frequency distribution*. This distribution is constructed by adding the distribution frequencies of successive classes together. Arranging distribution data cumulatively allows analysis of the data that lie above or below certain target levels of interest.

A "less than" cumulative frequency distribution provides the total of all distribution frequencies that are less than or equal to a stated value. This technique is useful in answering planning questions, such as "How many books purchased last year cost less than $15.00?" or "What proportion of libraries serves a population less than 25,000?" or "What is the percent of library books that circulated for less than ten days?"

A "more than" provides the total of all the frequencies values that are greater than a stated value. A "more than" cumulative frequency distribution is useful in answering strategy development questions. Examples of such questions are "How many users borrowed more than seven items at one time?" or "What proportion of the collection's journal titles is included by more than five major abstracting and indexing services?"

Table 3-9 illustrates construction of a "less than" cumulative frequency distribution. This table is a frequency distribution of contributions made by the Friends of the Library for developing special collections. The "less than" distribution is built by accumulating the frequencies, beginning with the lowest class. In this way, the cumulative frequency for each class reflects the number of observations that fall below the lower limit of the succeeding class. In this example, each class interval represents an increment of $50. From the table, one sees that no contributions (observations) are less than zero dollars. Since

Table 3-9. Cumulative Frequency Distributions (n = 200)

Class ($)	Frequency	"Less Than" Cumulative Frequency		"More Than" Cumulative Frequency	
$0	0		0		200
Up to $50	24	(0+24) =	24	(200-24) =	176
$50.01–$100	17	(24+17) =	41	(176-17) =	159
$100.01–$150	20	(41+20) =	61	(159-20) =	139
$150.01–$200	25	(61+25) =	86	(139-25) =	114
$200.01–$250	28	(86+28) =	114	(114-28) =	86
$250.01–$300	26	(114+26) =	140	(86-26) =	60
$300.01–$350	23	(140+23) =	163	(60-23) =	37
$350.01–$400	18	(163+18) =	181	(37-18) =	19
$400.01–$450	14	(181+14) =	195	(19-14) =	5
$450.01–$500	5	(195+5) =	200	(5-0) =	0
TOTAL	200				

Source: Hypothetical data

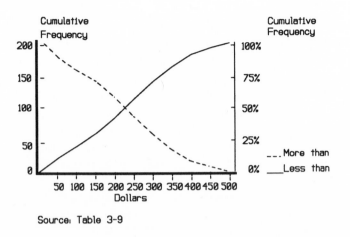

Source: Table 3-9

Figure 3-8. Friends of the Library Financial Contributions (n=200)

there are 24 occurrences in the interval "Up to $ 50," there is a cumulative total of 24 observations before the interval "$50.01–$100." Since there are 17 observations in the interval "$50.01–$100," there is a cumulative total of 41, or 24+17, occurrences before the interval "$100.01–$150." In constructing the "less than" frequency distribution, it is not necessary to show all calculations. The calculations shown in the text are for illustrative purposes only.

The "less than" cumulative distribution graph is formed by plotting the cumulative frequencies on the vertical axis (Y-axis) against the upper limits of the corresponding class interval values on the horizontal axis (X-axis). The points are then joined by straight lines to form a *cumulative frequency polygon,* as illustrated in Figure 3-8.

In this figure, notice that cumulative frequency can also be translated into a cumulative percent. This is shown on the right-hand column of the graph of the cumulative distribution. Hence, the curve can be read in a glance in terms of frequencies or percents. Also, the number of cases either above or below a given point can be determined by inspection of the curve, regardless of the sizes of the class intervals.

The "more than" cumulative frequency distribution, illustrated in Table 3-9, is constructed by beginning with the highest class and summing the frequencies to the lowest class. The graph is constructed by plotting the lower class interval limits opposite their corresponding frequencies and then joining the points by straight lines. Figure 3-8 also illustrates the graph of the "more than" cumulative frequency distribution.

Common Types of Graphs

Various types of graphs, such as horizontal bar, vertical column, pie graphs, and line graphs, can be used to illustrate quantitative and qualitative comparisons. These various types of graphs are illustrated in Figure 3-9. The main types of graphs used by librarians are

- bar graphs, composed of horizontal or vertical columns
- pie graphs, also called *circle graphs*, formed by representing parts of a whole by wedge-shape sectors of the circle
- line graphs, formed by using straight lines to connect a series of graphed points
- diagrams, such as organizational charts, pedigrees, genealogical trees
- combinations of the above types of graphs.

In selecting a graph to portray data, the designer must be aware that

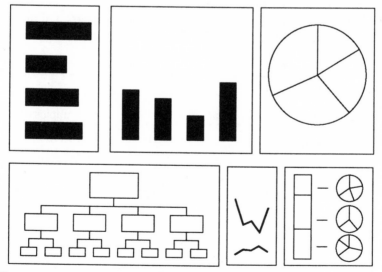

Figure 3-9. Common Types of Graphs

all illustrations are not equally successful in their ability to convey different types of information. Hence, the decision to use a particular type of graph must be carefully made. The first step in selecting an appropriate graph is to identify clearly the aspects of the data that are most important. Determining a title for the graph before it is created is one way to ensure that the relationships or purposes for the graph are kept in mind. The next step is to choose the graph that best illustrates the intended message.

Each type of graphs is particularly adept at communicating certain messages. Table 3-10 summarizes these capabilities.

Horizontal Bar Graph

An appropriate graph for comparing related items is the *horizontal bar graph*. The data in the graph may be classified by either quantitative or qualitative variables. Figure 3-10 shows average weekly circulation comparisons of groupings of books categorized by Dewey classification for a hypothetical library.

In a horizontal bar graph, the bars originate from a common base line such as the vertical axis (Y-axis). The bar graph has one scale that extends horizontally along the length of the bars. Grid lines run from top to bottom of the graph but are not drawn through the bars. The length of each bar is determined by the value it represents and is measured by the horizontal scale. This scale may be written at the top or the bottom of the graph, or both. The width of the bars and intervening spaces provide balance and make the graph readable. Spacing between the bars is one-half the width of a bar.

Table 3-10. Types of Charts		
Type of Graph	Usual Uses	Examples
Horizontal Bar	Comparisons between related items	Budgets of public libraries by state
Vertical Bar	Change of 1 item across 1–5 time periods	Dow Jones index, Monday–Friday
Circle	Component percents	Percent-of-time analyses
Line	Change of 1 item across 5 or more periods	Library's budget from 1980–1990

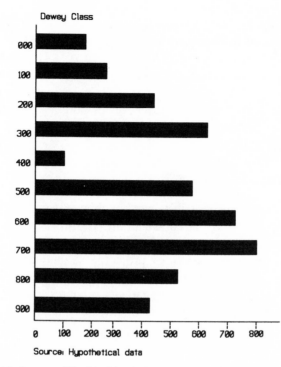

Figure 3-10. Average Weekly Circulation

An advantage of the bar graph is that it can accommodate many bars in one graph. When several bars are used, their arrangement should be in some logical order. Examples of logical arrangement are alphabetical, chronological, geographical, progressive (in order of decreasing length from top to bottom), qualitative, or numerical. A typical practice in a series of bars is to place "catch-all" categories such as "other," "miscellaneous," or "unclassified" at the bottom. Bars are usually shown in solid black or with cross-hatching. In any graph, patterns that create distractions should be avoided, because they decrease the data's impact. When shading variations are used in a horizontal bar graph, the progression in shade patterns should be from bottom to top, with the dark shading on the bottom of the graph. Lighter shading should be shown toward the top of the graph. Figure 3-11 illustrates three common variations of the horizontal bar graph.

Viewing the figure from left to right, the first panel is a subdivided bar graph. It shows the components that make up the total such as volumes on hand and titles on hand. The second panel is a deviant bar

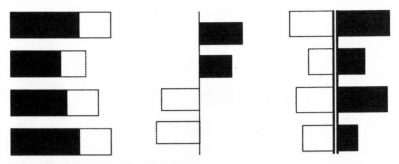

Figure 3-11. Horizontal Bar Graphs

chart. It shows differences such as percent change in circulation by type of media. The last is a paired bar chart. It shows two information elements about a component, such as expenditure for books by classification and their circulation, or project costs and project revenue. Figure 3-12 shows two additional types of bar charts. Reading from left to right, the first is a grouped bar chart. It compares various aspects of the same item, such as the number of titles available and number of times titles are borrowed. The second panel is a range bar chart. It shows spread, such as difference between amounts, status, or phasing of projects or activities, or range in values.

In a bar graph, the bar should be continuous, not broken. A permissible exception is when the length of the longest bar is not essential to the graph. The numeral that shows the value of the category is then placed in the broken portion, even if a scale is not shown.

Vertical Column Graph

The *vertical column graph* is effective for comparing a single variable over five or fewer time periods. For example, a column graph

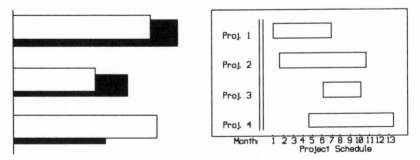

Figure 3-12. Additional Examples of Horizontal Bar Graphs

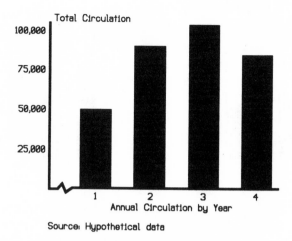

Figure 3-13. Annual Circulation of Your Town Library, Years 1-4

would be a good choice with which to show annual circulation over a four-year period, as in Figure 3-13. It would also be an effective vehicle to illustrate total dollar amounts, such as revenue or expenditure over several months or years. Column graphs are especially effective for portraying size comparisons or large changes from one period to the next.

The column graph has two scales, one measuring horizontally across the graph and one measuring vertically. The horizontal scale usually represents time and the vertical scale usually represents quantity. Columns start from a base line, drawn horizontally, and values are represented by the height of the columns. As in the horizontal bar graph, spacing between the columns is one-half the width of a column. The columns, which emphasize individual amounts, are effective for illustrating data that are confined to a specific period. This suggests a beginning for each period.

As in horizontal bar graphs, the practice is not to break a column— except when the bar illustrates an erratic point. The column may then be broken at the top, with the amount shown directly over it. Figure 3-14 illustrates four common variations of the vertical column graph.

Viewing the figure from left to right, the first panel is a subdivided column graph. It shows component parts. The second panel is a grouped column graph. It compares two items or shows relationships between them. The third is a deviation column graph. It shows differences. The final panel is a range column chart. It shows spread or range.

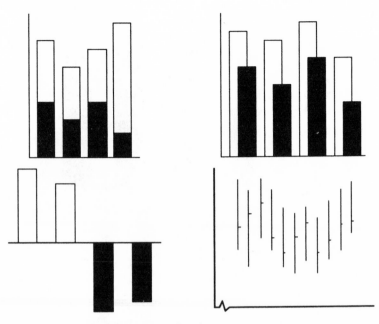

Figure 3-14. Common Vertical Bar Graphs

This type of graph is popularly used in newspapers to chart the Dow Jones averages.

Pie or Circle Graphs

A *pie graph* is also known as a *circle graph*. It is effective for showing components of a whole, such as budgets, assets, liabilities, or time distributions. In the pie graph, the total, or 100%, is represented by the size of the circle. Each portion of the whole is represented by a wedge-shape part of the circle. Each wedge is the so-called slice of the pie, representing a percent of the whole. The construction of a pie graph can be illustrated by graphing the distribution of a hypothetical librarian's time (see Table 3-11 and Figure 3-15).

The first step is to determine the component percent represented by each of the librarian's five activities. Since 15 hours of the librarian's 37.5 hour week are spent in general reference services, the component percent is 15/37.5 or 0.40, which is 40%. The component percent for online reference services is 7/37.5 or 0.19, which is 19%.

The second step is to determine the number of degrees in each wedge or angle of the circle. Since a circle has 360°, 1% of the total can be represented by a wedge of 3.6° (.01 x 360). To determine the number of

Table 3-11. Distribution of Librarian's Time

Activity	Hours Per Week	Percent of Time	Degrees (Rounded Off)
General reference service	15.0	40%	40x3.6 =144°
Online reference service	7.0	19	19x3.6 = 68
Bibliographic instruction	6.0	16	16x3.6 = 58
Collection development	4.5	12	12x3.6 = 43
Other	5.0	13	13x3.6 = 47

degrees a category should occupy, multiply 3.6 by the component percent. Since the first activity is 40%, the wedge or angle is 0.40 x 360° (40 x 3.6), or 144°. The wedge or angle of the second activity is .19 x 360°, or 68°.

The third step is to draw a circle with a compass. Circles may be of any convenient diameter, although a diameter of 2 inches or more is suggested. A protractor and straight edge are then used to plot the angle required for each wedge. Sectors are usually plotted in a clockwise direction. Figure 3-15 illustrates the finished project.

The final step is to identify each sector by placing a label inside or adjacent to the sector. If a sector is small, the label should be placed adjacent to the graph with an arrow pointing directly toward the sector

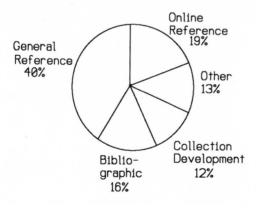

Figure 3-15. Pie or Circle Graph of Librarian's Time Distribution by Activity

to avoid confusion. Coloring or cross-hatching the sectors may be helpful to emphasize differences. It is not unusual for a distribution or study to contain more categories than can easily be accommodated in a sector graph. Usually, pie graphs contain no more than five sectors. Because more than five sectors make a graph difficult to construct and confusing to the reader, categories such as "Other" and "Miscellaneous" can be used to consolidate multiple, small components of the whole. For the librarian in the example, the category "Other" is composed of the following activities:

Specialized filing	1.0 hour
Client callbacks	0.3 hour
Current awareness	0.2 hour
Unclassifiable	3.5 hours
Total	5.0 hours

The librarian's complete time distribution can be shown by using the pie graph in combination with a vertical column graph. In Figure 3-16, the graph of the librarian's time has been slightly rearranged. Lines from the "Other" sector focus attention on the sector and show that the column graph more accurately describes the category. This combination of graphing methods conveys more information than does the pie or circle graph alone.

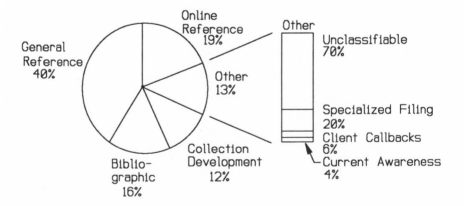

Figure 3-16. Librarian's Time Distribution by Activity

A disadvantage to this approach is the size of the column graph compared to the pie graph, and the resulting risk of conveying a false impression. For example, the category "Unclassifiable" includes time expenditures such as telephone interruptions, drop-in visitors, and meetings. While this is a very small component of the total weekly time, it occupies a disproportionate amount of page space. It must be made clear in the graphs that the 100% in the column graph refers to 100% of the "Other" category. This category, in turn, is only 13% of the total.

Figure 3-17, an "exploded" pie graph, emphasizes a particular segment of the time distribution shown in the preceding figure. This example illustrates the percent of time the librarian spends doing a specialized reference service such as online literature searching. This emphasis is accomplished by shading and setting this segment off from the remainder of the pie. This technique highlights the comparison between one segment and the total activities. Because the graph's emphasis is exclusively on online searching, every activity not in this category becomes a part of the category "Other."

Pie graphs are an excellent visual medium for communication of comparisons. Their strength is in their impact on the consumer, although they are one of the simplest graphs to read. Pie graphs work best when the type of relationship being portrayed is uncomplicated, such as percent-of-time distribution or how the budget dollar is segmented.

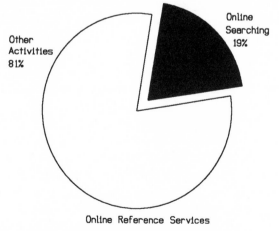

Online Searching 19%

Other Activities 81%

Online Reference Services

Figure 3-17. Exploded Pie Chart to Emphasize a Segment

Although a pie graph very successfully illustrates component comparisons, it is not without its shortcomings. Some find the computations difficult and the use of compass, protractor, and straight edge awkward. Others find it difficult to divide the circle into correct proportions. Readers often are not able to estimate sector percents accurately in unmarked graphs. These barriers are overcome through practice and attention to detail in construction. Checks for errors must be made in construction of the circle's segments and in plotting the wedges.

Of course, many computer packages now offer sophisticated graphics software that greatly simplify the process of constructing pie graphs. These systems allow the manager to enjoy the benefits of pie graphs with less labor.

Line Graph

The *line graph* is a simple graph, effective for showing data trends over five or more periods of observation. Thus the usefulness of the line graph begins where the usefulness of the vertical bar graph ends. In many respects, the more data points in a line graph, the more descriptive the graph in portraying a trend. Line graphs are excellent vehicles for illustrating whether a variable is increasing, decreasing, fluctuating, or remaining constant.

Figure 3-18 is a line graph that depicts the annual circulation of medical books categorized by Dewey 610–619 classification. Figure 3-19 shows two line graphs that compare the circulation of both medical and business books categorized by Dewey 610–619 and 650–659. This figure might represent the circulation data for a hypothetical high school library. In this example, in 1986 the librarian and classroom teachers for the life sciences developed a model curriculum for college-bound students. This program was extended to business students in 1988. The line chart is effective in showing the circulation results following implementation of the new programs.

In Figure 3-20, another example of a line graph, a manager has compared the performance of an employee to a standard or performance expectation, both before and following a training program. Prior to the training program (the left portion of the graph), the employee's performance was below the manager's expectations. Following the training program, the performance of the employee was much improved, and clustered near the expectations set by the manager. This chart provides an excellent depiction of the employee's performance and highlights positive or negative changes in performance over time.

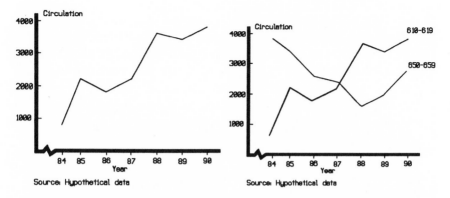

Figures 3-18 (left) and 3-19 (right). Line Graphs of Annual Circulation

This method is especially effective if the employee's duties translate well into quantitative measurements. For example, the manager may decide that 200 work units per week is an acceptable level of output for this position. The units may represent answering reference questions, processing invoices, filing cards in a catalog, or other outputs.

Line graphs are able to illustrate several different patterns of change. Figure 3-21 (A–F) depicts six typical patterns. In these six graphs, the value of the variable (vertical axis) is plotted against time (horizontal axis). The figure illustrates how a variable can increase and decrease in

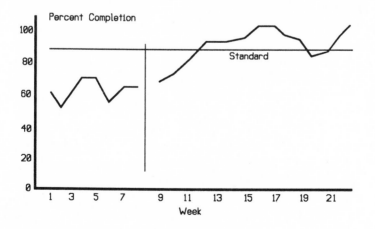

Figure 3-20. Line Graph of Performance Standards

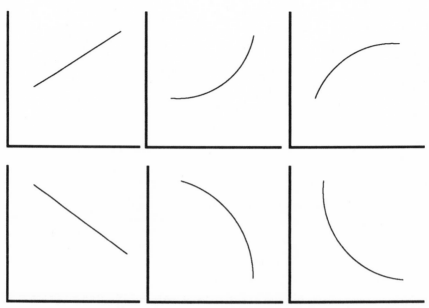

Figure 3-21. Line Graphs Illustrating Patterns of Rate Change

three ways. These patterns convey important information regarding trends in data and for the correct interpretation of graphs.

Viewing this graph from left to right, the first three panels show that a variable can *increase* at constant, increasing, and decreasing rates, respectively. The last three panels show how a variable can *decrease* at constant, increasing and decreasing rates.

Avoiding Deception

Understanding graphs can help alert the librarian to misuses of graphs and displays. It is best to assume that data are presented to support a point and to influence the audience. Librarians and other statistical consumers should be wary of presentations that select a graph that is inappropriate to the subject. An example is a bar or column graph presentation, instead of a line graph, to show trends. Comparing too many elements on a single graph is a poor graphing technique; however, it is an effective way to disguise unfavorable information. The alert consumer studies graphic displays for items that are highlighted or deemphasized. Similarly, displays are particularly scrutinized when complicated graphing techniques are employed, when a simple graph (such as a pie or bar graph) would be adequate. Failure to use a graph to

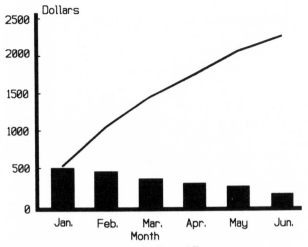

Figure 3-22. Graphs of Videocassette Rental Revenue

display data appropriate for graphing may be motivated by a desire to conceal poor performance or a negative result. While graphs are an excellent means of visual communication, they can be skillfully used to mislead the consumer.

Figure 3-22, for example, is an overlay of two graphs, a line graph and a vertical bar graph. Each graph presents information about revenue generated through videotape circulation. However, the line graph, which is a cumulative total like a cumulative distribution, distorts the data. Careful review of the figure reveals that video cassette rental revenue per month is decreasing. Yet the curve, because it is cumulative, tends to mask this fact. As in Figure 3-21C, total rental revenue is increasing, but the rate of increase is less in each successive month. The consumer of statistics must be attentive to such details.

It is helpful to watch newspapers, magazines, professional journals, reports, and other materials for graphs that are especially successful in conveying information. These examples should be clipped and tucked away and referred to periodically to stimulate ideas for describing data. Live presentations are another source of ideas for graphs. Presentations also allow you to evaluate the graph's effect upon the audience. This author's informal observation reveals that speakers delivering presentations most often use line graphs. Other graphs, in order of popularity, are vertical and horizontal bar graphs followed, by pie graphs.

Guidelines for Designing Graphs

There are several important considerations in creating a graph. The following guidelines, though not exhaustive, are useful:

1. The graph's title is most effective when brief and descriptive.
2. The horizontal (X-axis) and vertical (Y-axis) axes should be shown and labeled horizontally.
3. The scale should be provided for the horizontal (X-axis) and vertical axis.
4. Scale figures should be shown on the axis, usually supplemented with scale points or "ticks" between scale figures. Axis numbers should be large enough to read easily. Grid lines should be shown, but not be drawn through columns or bars.
5. A break in the horizontal or vertical axis (X or Y axis) should be shown with a symbol such as $-\bigwedge-$. A break in the vertical axis (Y-axis) should be avoided when possible, since a false impression of the data almost always results. (See Guideline 4 for histogram construction.)
6. Data sources should be shown at the bottom of the graph.
7. When a line graph is used to show one trend line, make the trend line bolder than the grid lines.
8. When a line graph is used to compare the performance of two items, single out one of the lines for emphasis by using a bold solid line and a thinner or patterned line (of short or long dashes) for the other.
9. Avoid logarithmic or ratio scale graphs unless the audience is familiar with them. Librarians are most familiar with arithmetic horizontal and vertical scales.

The task of constructing graphs can be simplified by the use of personal computers and graphics software. The computer allows for the convenient comparison of data in different types of displays. Computer-aided design (CAD) and graphics packages permit flexibility in use of labels, text, legends, color, size, scale, side-by-side comparison, and other graphic manipulations.

Computer graphics are very helpful to the librarian in creating and comparing graphs. However, they are no substitute for understanding graphing techniques.

Summary of Critical Concepts

1. Organizing data by arranging them from low to high or high to low is a useful technique for presenting and analyzing information. The resulting sort is called a *data array*. In an array, one can immediately see the largest and smallest values of the data set.

2. Data can be sorted into categories and displayed in a tabular manner. The resulting *frequency distribution* shows the number of observations from the data set that fall into the various categories. This technique classifies, condenses, and greatly simplifies data for presentation, analysis, and interpretation.

3. The categories into which frequency distribution data are sorted are called *classes*. Each class has a standard size, called *class width*. It is preferable that the class widths be equal, because *intervals of equal width* make computation easier and help to prevent data distortion.

4. A frequency distribution should be composed of between 6 and 15 classes. Too many classes make the information difficult to use. Too few classes overcondense the information, and useful information about the data is lost.

5. The choice of class width and the number of classes influences the way a frequency distribution appears. The usual practice, therefore, is to compute several distributions using a different number of class intervals. The librarian can then select the distribution which best fits the data.

6. Class intervals must be *mutually exclusive*. That is, they must be defined so that each data point can be sorted into only one class interval.

7. *Class limits* establish the lower and upper boundaries for discrete data. *Real limits* set the boundaries for continuous scale data.

8. Graphs are visual representations of statistical data that classify data and show trends and relationships not readily apparent in tabular data.

9. Graphs are presented in a two-dimensional picture in the *rectangular coordinate plane*. This plane is formed by the perpendicular intersection of two *real-number lines* that form the axes. The two number lines are called the *horizontal (X-axis)* and the *vertical (Y-axis) axes*.

10. A *histogram* illustrates a data set by using a series of rectangles with their bases on the horizontal axis (X-axis), centers at the class midpoints, and widths equal to the class interval scales. A histogram shows rectangles with areas that are proportional to class frequencies. If the class intervals are of unequal size, the heights of the rectangles are made proportional to the size of the class frequencies.

11. A *frequency polygon* includes much of the same information as a histogram. It is a closed-figure graph of class frequency plotted against class midpoint. This graph can be constructed easily from the histogram by connecting the midpoints of the tops of the histogram's rectangles.
12. All illustrations are not equally successful in conveying information. The librarian should be sensitive to selecting the type of graph that best illustrates the data. Several useful graphs are the *horizontal bar graph*, the *pie* or *circle graph*, the *vertical column graph*, and the *line graph*.
13. The *horizontal bar graph* is effective for showing item comparisons. It has one scale, extending horizontally along the length of the bars. The *vertical column graph* is effective for showing time and size comparisons. It has two scales. The horizontal scale usually represents time and the vertical scale represents quantity. A difference between horizontal and vertical bar graphs is that the bars are usually horizontal in qualitative and geographic comparisons and vertical in time and size distributions. *Circle graphs* are effective for showing components of a whole. They work best when picturing a maximum of five items. The *line graph* is effective for illustrating whether a variable is increasing, decreasing, fluctuating, or remaining constant.

Key Terms

Array. A group of numbers organized in an increasing or decreasing order. A *data array* is the arrangement of raw data in increasing or decreasing order.

Class. A group of scores in a data set. A *class interval* is a grouping of scores with a range of values. For example, the class interval 1–4 contains scores for 1, 2, 3, and 4. The intervals in a frequency distribution are *classes*.

Class Limits. The smallest and largest values that go into any given class.

Class Midpoint. The score value midway between the upper and lower limit of a class. The midpoint of a class interval in a frequency distribution is calculated by summing the upper and lower class limits and dividing by 2.

Class Width. For discrete data, the number of integer score units is the score interval. For continuous data, class width is the difference between the class interval's upper and lower real limits.

Coordinate Plane. Plane that is formed by the intersection of two perpendicular number lines. The *X-axis* is horizontal and the *Y-axis* is vertical. The point of intersection is the *origin*. A gridlike pattern of intersecting columns and rows results, forming a two-dimensional picture. Points on the plane are identified by coordinates. The convention is to identify the *X*-coordinate, then the *Y*-coordinate. The (x,y) coordinates of a point are called an *ordered pair*. This is because the order in which they are written is significant in locating the point on the coordinate plane.

Cumulative Frequency. The sum of the frequencies of all values. This measure shows how many observations lie above or below certain values.

Frequency. The number of times a score or group of scores (class) occurs in a sample or population. The terms *class frequency* and *interval frequency* are used interchangeably. In place of frequencies, proportions or relative frequencies are often used.

Frequency Distribution. A tabulation of data showing the number of times a score or group of scores appears. The tabulation lists all possible score values, from the lowest to highest, and the number of cases receiving each of these scores. A *grouped frequency distribution* is a tabular listing showing scores grouped into class intervals of equal width and the number of cases falling into each class interval. The graph of this distribution is called an *ogive*.

Frequency Polygon. A closed geometric figure used to represent a frequency distribution. It is a line graph formed by connecting the midpoints of each class in a data set, plotted at a height corresponding to the frequency of the class.

Graph. A pictorial representation of a data set.

Heuristic. A rule-of-thumb or short-cut methodology consisting of various simplifying judgment rules for arriving at a decision. An example of a heuristic in the game of chess is for the player to try to dominate the board's center squares or to develop slower moving pieces such as the knights and pawns before faster ones such as the bishops or castles. In direct mail advertising, a heuristic is that long copy sells. Evidence of this bedrock principle is the absence of short direct-mail advertising delivered to our mailboxes daily.

Histogram. A vertical bar graph representation of a frequency distribution. Scores or midpoints of class intervals are shown on the horizontal axis (X-axis) and frequencies are shown on the vertical axis (Y-axis). Areas of the vertical bars are proportional to class frequencies. The rectangles or bars of a histogram are contiguous, touching each other. A histogram contains the same information as a frequency polygon.

Mutually Exclusive. Separate and distinct, with no overlap. Two events are mutually exclusive if they cannot occur simultaneously. Class intervals are mutually exclusive if no overlap is permitted. The intervals 1–3 and 4–6 are mutually exclusive, but 1–3 and 3–5 are not since a data value of 3 might be inconsistently counted in the interval 1–3 or 3–5, or perhaps be counted in both.

Ogive. A graph of the cumulative relative frequency distribution.

Open-Ended Interval. A class interval that allows either the upper or lower end to be limitless.

Relative Frequency. The frequency (*f*) of one score or group of scores divided by the total frequency of all the observations (*n*). Hence, relative frequency (*rf*) = *f/n*. The result is usually expressed as a percent. For example, if the class interval 1–4 occurs with a frequency of 5 and if there are 50 observations, the relative frequency is 5/50 = 0.1 or 10%. The relative frequencies of all classes sum to 100%.

Score. An expression for the number assigned to a case consisting of people, items, or objects. A score represents the amount of some property or attribute that the case exhibits.

Self-Assessment Quiz

True or False   1.   In an array, data are arranged from high to low or from low to high.

True or False   2.   *Class width* is the term given to the standard size of each class.

True or False   3.   All classes should be of equal width.

True or False   4.   Mutually exclusive classes do not solve the problem of requiring that class intervals be defined such that data points can be sorted into only one class.

True or False   5.   As a rule, grouped data should be organized into between 10 and 20 classes.

True or False   6.   Graphs make it possible to show trends and comparisons more vividly than by a tabular display.

True or False   7.   The vertical axis is called the X-axis and the horizontal axis is called the Y-axis.

True or False   8.   Vertical bar graphs are effective for showing change in a single variable over time.

True or False   9.   Pie graphs are effective in emphasizing the size of a component relative to the total.

True or False 10.   The true limits of the class interval 3–5 (for continuous data) are 2.9–5.1.

True or False 11.   The width of the interval 3–5 (for continuous data) is 2.

True or False 12.   An advantage of the histogram over the frequency polygon is in using it to illustrate two or more data sets on the same graph.

True or False 13.   It is always possible to construct a histogram from a frequency polygon.

True or False 14.   In a frequency distribution, classes need not be mutually exclusive.

Answers

1. True. An array is a list that is arranged in ascending or descending numerical order.
2. True. Width corresponds to the number of observation levels in each class.
3. True. Classes of equal width help to reduce data distortion.
4. False. By definition, mutually exclusive classes are constructed so that overlap between or among them is not possible.
5. False. Between 6 and 15 classes.
6. True. A person can more easily glance at a graph and discern a trend.
7. False. The horizontal axis is the X-axis and the vertical axis is the Y-axis.
8. True. Vertical bar graphs are best when used to compare a variable at 5 or fewer time periods.
9. True. Pie graphs provide an excellent visual image of component percents.
10. False. The true limits are 2.5–5.5.
11. False. The true limits are 2.5–5.5, so the class width is 3.
12. False. Frequency polygons are superior to histograms for this purpose since multiple polygons make fewer, less confusing intersections.
13. True. The frequency polygon shows the midpoint and frequency for each class. The width of the classes can be inferred from the location of the midpoints. Midpoint, frequency, and width can then be used to construct a histogram.
14. False. Classes in a frequency distribution must be defined so that each data point is assigned to one and only one interval. This is mutual exclusivity between classes.

Discussion Questions and Problems

1. Discuss how information can be "lost" when observations are classified and data are condensed in constructing a frequency distribution.
2. Discuss how statistical investigation may be affected by the nature of the anticipated audience for a report.
3. Suppose you are reading a report that classifies data in four categories: 10–30, 30–60, 60–120, and 120+. These categories illustrate at least 3 classification practices to avoid. Identify each and discuss.
4. Construct separate histograms of the data in Table 3-6, using the following number of classes: 16, 7, 4, and 2. Compare the resulting histograms and discuss the effect upon the graph of using fewer classes.
5. A library consortium canvassed its members to learn the number of days each member's computer system was down during the previous 90 days. Prepare a histogram for the following distribution:

Days of Downtime	0	1	2	3	4	5	6	7
Frequency	6	7	10	14	7	3	2	1

6. A large library has 55 full-time employees, 80% of whom are female. Staff ages are follows:

48	18	51	32	56	52	54	60	44	30
50	29	53	23	51	46	19	52	45	23
50	26	53	40	53	59	52	19	37	54
33	19	55	44	60	24	20	30	39	35
25	44	47	65	65	61	50	49	47	51
65	28	63	60	48					

   a. Prepare a data array.
   b. Prepare grouped and ungrouped frequency distributions.
   c. Using the class intervals from your grouped frequency distribution in (b), prepare and graph "less than" and "more than" cumulative frequency distributions.
   d. Construct a histogram of the data.
   e. Construct a frequency polygon of the data.
   f. Construct a vertical column graph and a pie graph showing
      (1) the respective number of male and female employees and
      (2) the respective percent of male and female employees.

Discuss the advantages and limitations of each graphic technique and of numbers vs. percent displays.

7. A circulation librarian conducted a study of staffing and equipment needs at the circulation desk. Over one week, 2-hour time periods were sampled. A record was made of the time (to the nearest tenth of a minute) required for a library user to check out materials. Data for a representative 2-hour period ($n = 100$) are shown below. Prepare a frequency distribution, beginning with class interval 0.4–0.6, and ending with interval 2.2–2.4. Make graphs, such as a histogram and a "less than" cumulative percent distribution, to assess the circulation desk area. Identify what additional information, if any, might be helpful in deciding questions about additional staffing and equipment.

2.3	1.6	1.2	1.7	1.3	1.8	2.2	1.4	2.1	1.3
2.3	2.2	2.2	1.8	1.8	1.7	1.8	2.2	2.1	1.9
2.2	2.2	1.4	0.9	1.5	1.9	1.7	0.8	2.3	2.0
2.1	1.4	2.3	0.8	1.6	1.9	1.6	2.0	1.2	1.9
2.2	1.4	1.9	2.2	1.6	1.3	1.7	1.3	2.4	1.9
1.8	0.9	2.2	1.3	1.4	0.5	1.1	1.6	1.1	2.0
1.8	0.9	1.6	1.3	0.9	0.4	1.3	1.5	1.0	1.9
2.3	1.5	2.2	0.9	2.3	1.9	1.6	1.4	1.8	1.2
1.5	2.3	0.9	1.9	0.9	1.2	1.5	1.4	1.7	1.1
1.5	1.4	1.7	1.8	1.9	0.8	1.5	1.0	1.5	1.8

8. A public library, serving a community of 30,000, circulates videocassettes for a 2-day loan period. Revenue from the $1 fee is used to acquire additional cassettes. The following data show the number of videocassettes owned and circulated.

Month	Videocassettes Owned	Videocassettes Circulated
January	161	1633
February	205	2358
March	238	2521
April	260	2371
May	298	2407
June	341	2178
July	381	2531

For the following questions, use the horizontal axis to show months.

a. Prepare separate line graphs illustrating the number of videocassettes owned, one with a broken vertical axis, beginning at 140 through 380, and the other with an unbroken scale, 0–450. Discuss the visual impact of each graph.

 b. Prepare separate line graphs illustrating the number of videocassettes circulated, one with a broken vertical axis, beginning at 1600 through 2550, and the other with an unbroken scale, 0–3000. Discuss the visual impact of each graph.

 c. Prepare two vertical column graphs, one showing videocassettes owned and the other showing videocassettes circulated. Do not break the vertical scale. Contrast the column graph with the line graphs prepared above. Discuss impact and advantages of each graph.

 d. Prepare a single graph showing the number of videocassettes both owned and circulated. The subdivided column graph or the grouped vertical column graph are two of several possible appropriate graphs.

9. An academic and public library microcomputer user group conducted a survey of its 100 members. Results showed that 45% used the equipment for budget and bookkeeping activities, 30% for database activities such as specialty indexes, 20% for electronic mail, 40% for graphics, 13% for invoice preparation, 75% for spreadsheet analysis, and 65% for word processing. Prepare a graph that best illustrates these data.

10. A recently promoted staff member participated in a job study of department directors. As a part of this study, the librarian categorized job activities by percent of time into three areas: ideas, people, and things. "Idea" activities, or those associated with department planning, accounted for 20% of the staff member's time. Activities about "things," or those associated with department administration, accounted for 35%. "People" activities, or those associated with personal contact and relationships, accounted for 45% of the librarian's time. Within "People" activities were the tasks of assigning and coordinating duties (50%), monitoring conformance of outputs to established performance standards (30%), and staff development and training (20%).

 a. Illustrate the three major activities of the librarian's time profile with a pie graph.

 b. Illustrate the "People" component with a 100% column graph.

11. The River Town Public Library serves a community of 25,000. The library obtains its operating budget through collection of a maximum 0.15% (0.0015) tax levy on the value of all taxable property within its community boundary. The library trustees have not requested an increase in the tax rate for the past 10 years. The recently hired librarian, wishing to introduce several new activities and acting in

consultation with the board of trustees, is preparing a presentation for the River Town Council to request a referendum to increase the library's levy rate to 0.40%, the maximum allowed by state law.

Some library trustees are concerned since a large number of River Town property owners are senior citizens. As a part of the presentation, the librarian must discuss the economic impact of the levy upon this group. On a single graph, the director wants to show the economic position of persons 65 years of age or older, together with that of the younger population. Unfortunately, no economic study has ever been conducted exclusively on River Town residents. Even so, the librarian will use the *Current Population Survey*, published by the U.S. Bureau of the Census, since River Town is roughly representative of the U.S. population at large.

Prepare this graph showing two line graphs: one of seniors and the other of nonseniors. Show the trend of the past 20 years, using the horizontal axis for time and the vertical axis for percent. Interpret the graph.

12. A librarian has decided to purchase a home computer system. The system will be used primarily for word processing and for freelance indexing. The librarian financed $1090 of the purchase price with a 12-month, 10% installment loan.

Interest is $109.00 (principal $1090 x interest rate 0.10 x time in years, 1.0 = $109.00) and each monthly payment is approximately $100.00 (($1090 + $109)/12). There is no interest penalty for early repayment of the loan. Interest is computed according to the "Rule of 78s," in which each month is assigned a number. The last month of the loan is assigned the number 1, the next-to-last month is 2, and so on, up to the first month, which is given a number equal to the total months of the loan. In this problem, the number is 12. The amount of interest paid in any month is equal to the number assigned to the month divided by the total of the numbers (in a 1-year loan, 12 + 11 + 10 + ... + 2 + 1 = 78). In this loan, the interest due in the first month is 12/78 x $109, or $16.77. In the second month, the interest due is 11/78 x $109, or $15.37.

a. Calculate the interest due in each month and prepare a subdivided 100% column graph and a line graph illustrating your findings. Discuss the strengths of each graphing technique and which graph is better to illustrate these data.

b. Based upon the graphs in (a), discuss whether "no interest penalty for early payment" is actually a financial incentive, especially in regard to later payments.

13. A minimum security prison recently contracted with the local public library for library services. A leisure reading collection of ap-

proximately 1200 paperback books was developed. After 6 months of operation, inmates inventoried the collection. They also tallied the number of circulations for each item according to the circulation slip in each book.

Results of the data survey were forwarded to the librarian to determine the types of materials that circulated best.

	No. of Titles	Total No. of Circulations
Fiction		
Adventure	105	1869
Mystery	66	1958
Romance	135	5154
Science Fiction/Fantasy	132	6220
Western	91	2021
Other	138	2315
Total	667	19,537
Nonfiction		
Biography	134	1392
History/Travel	255	2699
Humor	37	748
Literature	52	1247
Local interest	6	15
Self-help	35	627
Other	16	64
Total	535	6792
Grand Total	1202	26,329

a. Extend the table with two columns. The first column should show the circulation per title, and the second column should show what percent each type of book represents of the total collection of books.
b. Prepare a pie chart showing the types of books that make up the fiction books and another for the nonfiction books. You may wish to combine some categories, if necessary.
c. Analyze the data and determine those types of books with the highest and lowest circulation for fiction and non-fiction.
d. If the collection size cannot grow, what collection change recommendations would you make to stimulate an increase in circulation?
e. If the current loan period is 10 days, speculate on the effect of changing it to 5 calendar days.

14. A college librarian tabulated survey results from 90 faculty members who responded to questions about their information searching habits. The table below shows the librarian's findings for the question, "When you come to the library to find a specific article, how often do you find reference to the article by consulting... ?"

	Usually	Occasionally	Rarely
Abstracting journals	62	21	7
Bibliographies/book footnotes	46	35	9
Bibliographies/journal footnotes	15	34	41
Colleagues	11	34	45
Librarians/library staff	13	50	27
Subject bibliographies	13	17	60
Other	2	12	76

Construct a table showing the percent of faculty members using each source by the frequency of such use.

15. In the survey cited in the question above, slightly more than 56% of faculty acknowledged it would be helpful to have professional librarians help them to identify useful articles for their research. In light of the above data, comment on this finding.

16. For the past several weeks, the librarian has collected data on the use of corporate annual reports to study the effects of collection size on circulation. Plot the data and discuss the curve, referring to Figure 3-21. (Hint: plot week on the horizontal axis).

   a. Each week, 25 new titles are added. The weekly circulation is {500, 550, 600, 650, 700, 750}.

   b. Each week, 50 old titles are removed from the collection and no new titles are added. The weekly circulation is {900, 875, 850, 825, 800, 775}.

17. A media center librarian has observed that vocational items circulate differently, depending on the time of the year. Plot the data and discuss the curve, referring to Figure 3-21. (Hint: plot week on the horizontal axis).

   a. Toward the end of the academic year, the librarian recorded the following weekly circulation data: {60, 75, 100, 150, 250, 450}.

   b. At the beginning of the fall semester, the circulation of vocational materials was {300, 330, 350, 360, 368, 370}.

18. Due to budgetary limitations, the librarian has not purchased any new fiction titles for the past year. To analyze the effect of collections on circulation, the following data were collected over a six-week period: {500, 475, 430, 360, 260, 135}. Plot the data and discuss the curve, referring to Figure 3-21. (Hint: plot week on the horizontal axis).

19. A librarian conducted a citation analysis for a specific scientific

discipline. The bibliometric analysis consisted of drawing citations from five primary research journals that are well known for reporting research findings in this scientific field. Journal issues for the first quarter of the current and previous year were data sources. Citations to personal communications, book reviews, news, bibliographical notes, and similar items were not included in the study.

The librarian collected 28,714 serial citations and 2955 citations to books. Citations to serials spanned 909 serial titles and citations to books referenced 1894 unique titles. The serial citation data is summarized in the table below.

Cumulative Number of Journal	Cumulative Percent Titles Citations
1	10.9%
2	20.7
3	24.6
4	28.5
5	31.5
6	34.2
7	36.9
8	39.5
9	42.0
10	44.1
13	49.4
23	60.0
32	65.1
45	70.3
62	75.1
85	80.1
117	85.0
168	90.0
909	100.0

    a. Identify the percent of citations to books and to serials.

    b. Draw a cumulative percent graph. Interpret the graph by commenting on the number of titles required to increase collection coverage by 5 percent increments.

20. The librarian of a special library decided to review the circulation records for all nonreference titles in the collection. Believing that a book's past use is a valuable predictor of its future use, the librarian wanted to identify the core collection of materials that satisfy 90 percent of the library's demands.

Applying a technique first described by R. W. Trueswell (1966), the librarian collected data from each book when it was about to be circulated. At checkout time, the librarian noted the last date on which the book was borrowed and then constructed a distribution of the current circulation against a scale that showed the number of months since the item was last borrowed.

When this distribution is grouped, the X-axis represents the number of months since the item was last borrowed, and the Y-axis shows the percent of circulation.

Number of Months Since Last Circulated	Percent of Circulation
1	26.6%
2	35.5
3	43.8
4	50.3
5	56.3
6	61.7
7	66.1
8	69.8
9	73.0
10	76.0
11	82.5
12	90.1
13	93.4
18	97.5
23	99.1
28	100.0

Graph these data and interpret your graph.

21. The acquisitions librarian at a medium-size college decided to review recently completed book order transactions. The purpose of the study was to evaluate the success of ordering items. The study examined orders sent directly to the publisher as well as to two vendors. The first vendor maintained a large inventory of items, and the second maintained only a small inventory but made extensive use of drop-shipping (shipping directly from the publisher).

A review of book order cards revealed that about 125 orders had been placed with each of the sources. Using these cards, the librarian determined the number of days between when the items were ordered via electronic mail and the date of the invoice when the items were shipped.

a. Draw each supplier's distribution. Discuss the general shape of each curve and determine the point where the curves peak.
b. Speculate on reasons for each distribution's shape.

Calendar Days	Vendor I Cumulative %	Vendor II Cumulative %	Direct Orders Cumulative %
7	0%	0%	0%
14	33	0	35
21	66	10	72
28	70	50	84
35	72	75	87
42	74	84	90
49	75	89	94
56	80	91	99
63	85	93	100
70	90	97	
77	92	100	
84	100		

Measures of Central Tendency

Learning Objectives

After reading and understanding the contents of this chapter, you will be able to:
1. Identify and discuss the differences and advantages among the mode, median, and mean.
2. Calculate the value of the mode, median, and mean for both ungrouped and grouped data.

S tatistics is not a management technique but a powerful management tool. Its usefulness as a tool is in providing a means to analyze data. Statistics provides rational support for decisions under any applied method of management. Statistics helps the manager isolate issues, identify and assess opportunities, target areas of vulnerability for improvement, fine tune operations, and provide concrete information to confirm intuition.

Often, the results of applied statistical measures and techniques are too abstract or detailed to allow a manager to comprehend the essence of a problem or situation. What the manager often needs are a few methods to "boil down" data into a single, explanatory number.

Numerical Summaries

In the previous chapter, for example, raw data were organized by using data arrays, frequency distributions, and graphs. Although these techniques help to display data in useful ways, they do not provide quantitative statements about the data. This shortcoming is apparent in comparing two or more frequency distributions. Suppose, for example, that a librarian is analyzing the outputs of several competing models of equipment for purchase. It would be difficult to draw conclusions about the comparative outputs of the models by using frequency distributions or charts. This limitation is solved by computing measures of selected characteristics using the elements of a grouped or ungrouped data set. These quantitative measures are *summary statistics*. One such summary statistic is the *measure of central tendency*, or *measure of location*.

Measures of Central Tendency

There are three measures of central tendency: mode, median, and arithmetic mean. Each of these measures describes a data set in summary fashion by showing the data's location, tendency, or trend in terms of their central or middle value. These measures are related, but they also differ. Each measure is built on its own definition of "central" or "middle." For the *mode*, the center point is the distribution's most often occurring data point or score. The mode identifies the most prevalent score or scores in the distribution. For the *median*, the center point of the data set defines the distribution's middle. The median evenly divides the distribution. It is the score below (or above) which 50% of the observations fall. For the *mean*, the size or weight of each data point defines the "middle" of the distribution. The mean represents the "balance point" of the distribution.

Under certain conditions, these three measurements can be the same. Most often, however, they are not. Each has its own advantages and disadvantages as a measure of central tendency.

The Mode

The *mode* of a data set is the value(s) which occurs most often. The mode is the simplest measure of central tendency. Technically, it can be applied to nominal, ordinal, interval, and ratio scale data. Table 4-1 illustrates appropriate central tendency measures by measurement scales.

The mode is calculated in different ways, depending upon how the data are presented. For *ungrouped data*, the mode is determined by observing the value in the data set that is repeated most often. For

Table 4-1. Measures of Central Tendency by Measurement Scale

Measurement Scale	Appropriate Measure of Central Tendency		
	Mode	Median	Mean
Nominal	yes	no	no
Ordinal	yes*	yes	no
Interval	yes*	yes	yes
Ratio	yes*	yes	yes

*Modal measurements are allowed in ordinal, interval, and ratio scales, but in practice are seldom used.

Source: Reprinted with publisher's permission from *Statistical Concepts with Applications to Business and Economics* by R.W. Madsen and M.L. Moeschberger, page 226, ©1980, Prentice-Hall, Inc.

example, suppose that the past eight quarterly dividends for a certain stock, paid in cents, are as follows: 10, 12, 20, 12, 15, 17, 25, 12.

The *mode* is 12 cents per share, since this dividend was paid more frequently than any other. This amount, 12 cents, was paid in three of the eight quarters.

In another example, suppose each of 14 library staff members were asked for the number of siblings in their family, with the resulting distribution:

Number of Children	1	2	3	4	5	6	7
Frequency	1	4	2	3	2	1	1

From this data set, the mode is 2, since four of the fourteen staff members have 2 siblings. When asked the number of siblings in their families, more staff members responded with the number 2 than with any other number.

When data are grouped into classes, the mode is calculated differently. First, the *modal class* is identified. This is the class containing the highest frequency of observations. Then the mode, a single number, is estimated from the modal class. Usually, the mode is given as the midpoint of the modal class. In the sibling example, suppose we group the data into the following classes:

Number of Children	1–3	4–6	7–9
Frequency	7	6	1

Table 4-2. Type and Number of Libraries in Country X

Academic libraries	4600
Armed Forces libraries	400
Government libraries	1600
Law libraries	400
Medical libraries	1500
Public libraries (Including branches)	9000
Religious libraries	800
Special libraries	4000
Total	22,300

Source: Hypothetical data

In this grouping, the 1–3 class is the modal class. The mode is estimated by using the class limits, 1 and 3. The midpoint of this class, $(1 + 3)/2 = 2$, is the best estimate for the mode of the grouped frequency distribution.

The advantage of the mode is that it is the only measure of central tendency that can be used with nominal scale data. Table 4-2 presents categorical data on types of libraries. The data are nominal scale since they refer to a nonquantitative variable, "type of library," and there are no interval or ordinal relations among the types of libraries. The modal class is "public." The mode is often applied to everyday experience, though most may not recognize this. Colonial furniture, brunette, and type A blood are examples of modes. Example 4-1 is an additional exercise illustrating determination of the modal class.

The mode also has liabilities as a measure of central tendency. A data set may not have a mode, as in the data sets {2, 3, 4, 5, 6} or {2, 2, 2, 2}. These sets do not have a mode since all the elements occur with the same frequency. No element occurs more often than another. Or a data set may have more than one mode. Distributions with one mode are *unimodal*; distributions with two modes are *bimodal*. A distribution with three modes is *trimodal*. Distributions that have two or more modes are also *multimodal distributions*.

In a bimodal distribution, two scores or categories occur more frequently than any other. An example of a grouped data bimodal distribution is illustrated in Figure 4-1, where the graph peaks at frequencies of

7. The mode can be located in open-ended distributions. This is because it is not affected by either the quantity or numerical value of items in remote classes.
8. Multimodality indicates that two or more sets of dissimilar or heterogeneous data are part of the distribution. The common practice is to separate the subgroups, if possible, and to study them separately.

The Median

For any distribution where values are ranked from smallest to largest, the *median* is the data set value which is above one-half and below one-half of the values. In determining the median, all that is considered is whether the data values are greater than or less than this middle value. The median is an appropriate measure for ordinal, interval, and ratio scale data. It is inappropriate for nominal scale data because nominal scale data cannot be ranked.

Unlike the mode, the median is always a single value. In determining the median, the result is always expressed in the same units as the original data.

The median is represented by the symbol, $\tilde{X}$. The symbol over the X is called a *tilde* (read "til'-da"). To compute the median, data are organized into an ascending order array. The median's rank in the array can be found

$$\text{Rank} = \frac{(n+1)}{2} \qquad\qquad (4-1)$$

where n = number of items in the array. The medians of grouped and ungrouped data are arrived at in different ways.

For *ungrouped data*, the median of an odd number of scores is the middle score. Similarly, the median of an even number of scores lies between two scores.

For example, suppose a survey of the hours of service of 15 special libraries produced the following data array:

Score	8	8	10	12	12	12	14	14	14	15	15	15	16	17	18
Rank	1	2	3	4	5	6	7	8	9	10	11	12	13	14	15

When we apply Formula 4-1 with $n = 15$, an odd number, the rank of the median is $(15 + 1)/2 = 8$, or the 8th item in the array. The value of the 8th item in the data set is 14. Hence, 14 hours is the median.

If there is an even number of observations, the median lies between two of the values. For example, eight children are interviewed to determine how many hours of television they watch daily. The data are

```
Score  1  1  2  3  5  5  6  6
Rank   1  2  3  4  5  6  7  8
```

When we apply Formula 4-1 with $n = 8$, an even number, the *rank* of the median is $(8 + 1)/2$, or 4.5. In other words, the value of the median lies midway between the values of the 4th and 5th observations. The median is 4 hours. Notice that the median is not necessarily one of the values in the data set.

That the median can be a value which is not in the original data set means that the librarian must be careful when interpreting the median. Suppose a library is concerned about the availability of parking spaces in an adjacent lot. On a particular day, the number of available parking spaces is noted each hour:

```
Score  2  2  2  3  4  5  6  7  8  9  9  10
Rank   1  2  3  4  5  6  7  8  9 10 11  12
```

There is an even number of items, 12, in the array. When we apply Formula 4-1, the rank of the median is $(12 + 1)/2$, or 6.5. The median lies between the 6th and 7th values in the array, or between 5 and 6. Hence, the median is 5.5 spaces. Here the median provides a good picture of the central tendency of the data set. The empty spaces cluster around 5 or 6. The reader should not interpret the median value of 5.5 to suggest there are, literally, 5.5 parking spaces available.

Grouped data must be handled differently than ungrouped data. The following example helps to illustrate the procedure for finding the median of grouped data that are continuous. Suppose a library wishes to determine the median time required for its interlibrary loan section to fill requests. Records for requests filled since the beginning of the year are examined. A frequency distribution for the grouped data is shown in Table 4-3. Each of these 156 records contains the clerk's notation of the number of days required to fill the request. (A designation of zero days means that the request was filled on the day it was received.) It is not possible to list the actual values included in the class interval that contains the median, because the frequency distribution does not show

Table 4-3. Summary of Days Required to Fill Interlibrary Loan Requests (n = 156)

Class Interval	Frequency f	Upper Class Boundary	Cumulative Frequency
0-3	24	3.5	24
4-7	48	7.5	72
8-11	40	11.5	112
12-15	15	15.5	127
16-19	14	19.5	141
20-23	9	23.5	150
24-27	6	27.5	156
	n = 156		

the raw data values for the distribution. To determine the median, therefore, *interpolation* is required.

For grouped data, the rank of the median is

$$\text{Rank} = \frac{n}{2} \qquad\qquad (4-2)$$

Notice that this definition is different from Formula 4-1, which is the definition of the median for ungrouped data. In Table 4-3, $n = 156$, and the rank of $\tilde{X} = 156/2$, or 78. Hence the median is the 78th item in the distribution. The frequency distribution shows this score is contained in the interval whose real limits are 7.5 to 11.5. The 78th item is the 6th element in the median class, since $78 - 72 = 6$. Thus, to arrive at the desired 78th rank, 6 steps into the 7.5–11.5 interval are required. The interval contains 40 steps, $f = 40$; so the median must lie 6/40 of the way between 7.5 and 11.5. That is,

$$\tilde{X} = 7.5 + \frac{6}{40}(11.5 - 7.5)$$

$$= 7.5 + 0.15\,(4.0)$$

$$= 7.5 + 0.6$$

$$= 8.1 \text{ days}$$

Fortunately, this procedure can be shortened. Statisticians use the following formula to determine the median of grouped data.

$$\tilde{X} = L + \frac{w}{f}\left(\frac{n}{2} - F\right) \qquad\qquad (4-3)$$

where
   L = lower class boundary of the median class
   n = total number of observations in the data set
   F = cumulative frequency up to, but not including, the median class
   f = frequency of the median class
   w = size of the median class

When we apply Formula 4-3 to the example, where $L = 7.5$, $n = 156$, $F = 72$, $f = 40$, and $w = 4$

$$\tilde{X} = 7.5 + \frac{4}{40}\,[0.5\,(156) - 72]$$

$$= 7.5 + \frac{1}{10}\,(78 - 72)$$

$$= 7.5 + \frac{1}{10}\,(6)$$

$$= 7.5 + 0.6$$

$$= 8.1 \ \text{days}$$

The median can also be calculated for grouped data with open-ended classes, unless the median falls in an open-ended class. Example 4-2 illustrates the technique to find the median of grouped data with an open class interval. Data which represent the number of hours scheduled per week for student employees at a university library are summarized in Table 4-4.

The median is an excellent measure of central tendency for ordinal data. Calculating the median of ordinal scale data can be illustrated by finding the median of responses to a questionnaire. Suppose a survey form is given to 24 library clientele who use microform materials. To facilitate responses, ordinal scale categories are provided for the

Table 4-4. Student Employee Hours Per Week at XYZ University (n=73)

Number of Hours Worked	Number of Students	Class Limits	Cumulative Frequency
Less than 3	1	—	1
4.0-5.9	1	5.95	2
6.0-7.9	6	7.95	8
8.0-9.9	9	9.95	17
10.0-11.9	18	11.95	35
12.0-13.9	16	13.95	51
14.0-15.9	7	15.95	58
16.0-17.9	9	17.95	67
18.0-19.9	4	19.95	71
20.0 or more	2	—	73
	n = 73		

respondent, such as Excellent, Good, Fair, Poor, and Needs Improvement. Ordinal scale measurement is appropriate because the respondent's relative judgment is sought on questions such as quality of

---

Example 4-2. Finding the Median of Grouped Data with an Open-Ended Class

Referring to data presented in Table 4-4, the median class is the class containing the $(n+1)/2$ rank observation. From formula 3-7, with n=73, this is $(73+1)/2$ or the 37th observation. The boundaries of the interval containing the median are 11.95 and 13.95.

Applying Formula 4-8, L=11.95, n=73, F=35, f=16, w=2. Then,

$$\tilde{X} = 11.95 + \frac{2}{16} [0.5 \, (\, 73) - 35]$$

$$= 11.95 + \frac{2}{16} (\, 36.5 - 35)$$

$$= 11.95 + \frac{2}{16} (\, 1.5)$$

$$= 11.95 + 0.1875$$

$$= 12.1375 \text{ or } 12.1 \text{ hours} .$$

Notice that the result is rounded to the nearest one-tenth hour because the original values were stated in tenths.

service, usefulness of materials retrieved, and timeliness of responses (among others).

To make tabulation of the survey easier, each of the categories is assigned a numerical score. These scores are values such as Excellent = 5, Good = 4, Fair = 3, Poor = 2, and Needs Improvement = 1. Remember, the numerical designations are rankings, not exact measurements. A ranking of Good, represented by 4, is not twice as good as a ranking of Poor, represented by 2.

The tabulation of the responses to Question 1 (n = 24) is shown in Table 4-5. The frequency distribution organizes the data from low to high. Hence, it is not necessary to write the values horizontally in an array. Using Formula 4-1, with $n = 24$, we see that the rank of the median is $(24 + 1)/2 = 12.5$. Hence, the median lies between the 12th and 13th scores. In the distribution, this point is between the categories Good and Fair.

In previous examples, where the median falls between two observations, the median was reported as an intermediate value. For example, the median number of parking spaces was between 5 and 6, which is equal to 5.5. The number of parking spaces is a ratio scale measurement, because the intervals between observations are equal and because there is an absolute zero point. The observations Good, and Fair, however, are ordinal scale measurements. Further, the intervals between observations such as Good, Fair, and Poor, cannot be assumed to be equal. All that can be observed is that the median lies between 3 and 4, or between Good and Fair. No intermediate value can be calculated. Had there been an odd number of scores, the median could have been reliably identified as a single category, such as Good.

Determining the median of scores based on ordinal scale measurement, as illustrated above, is a common practice that often leads to confusion. The consumer of statistics must be alert for occasions when the discrete ordinal classes are treated as though they were continuous.

Table 4-5. Responses to Question 1	
Category	Frequency
Excellent = 5	5
Good = 4	7
Fair = 3	6
Poor = 2	4
Needs Improvement = 1	2

When this happens, the researcher has incorrectly used the ordinal rankings as though they were exact measurements.

Additional Comments and Insights on the Median*

1. The median provides information about the point in the distribution above and below which 50% of the observations fall.
2. Arraying of data is required before the median is calculated.
3. The median is less familiar or less intuitively obvious to people than either the mode or the mean. (The mean will be discussed in the next section.)
4. Every data set has a median that is unique. The median can be calculated for ordinal scale data and for grouped data with open-ended classes, unless the median falls in an open-ended class.
5. The median is *not* necessarily equal to one of the data values.
6. The median is an appropriate measure if the measurement scale is ordinal, interval, or ratio. It is not appropriate for nominal scale data.
7. The median is affected by the number but not the value of *all* the observations in a data set. It is not affected by extreme scores. This "robustness" of the median makes it a preferred statistic for describing the central tendency of distributions with extreme values.
8. The median is unreliable if the data do not cluster at the center of the distribution.

The Arithmetic Mean

The arithmetic mean, popularly referred to simply as the *mean*, is a measure familiar to almost everyone. The mean for a series of ungrouped observations is obtained by first adding all the scores in the data set. Then this sum is divided by the total number of scores. The mean is an appropriate measure if the measurement scale is interval or ratio. However, nominal and ordinal scale measurements cannot be added together, so their means cannot be determined.

If each data point is represented by X, and if there are N scores, the mean for the data set, expressed mathematically as $\overline{X}$ (read X bar), is

$$\overline{X} = \frac{X_1 + X_2 + X_3 + \ldots + X_N}{N}$$

---

* Portions of this text were derived from *Business and Economic Statistics* by W.A. Spurr, L.S. Kellogg, and J.H. Smith. ©1961, Richard D. Irwin, Inc., pages 195-196. Used by permission of the publisher.

Table 4-6. Annual Number of Days Individual Data Terminals Are Out of Sevice										
Terminal No.	1	2	3	4	5	6	7	8	9	10
Days out of service	8	9	4	9	8	4	5	3	6	4

To illustrate Formula 4-4, consider the data in Table 4-6, which shows the annual number of days that a library's computer terminals are out of service due to malfunction or regular maintenance.

To determine the mean by Formula 4-4, the values are added. The total is then divided by the number of observations:

$$\bar{X} = \frac{\sum_{i=1}^{10} X_i}{10}$$

$$= \frac{8 + 9 + 4 + 9 + 8 + 4 + 5 + 3 + 6 + 4}{10}$$

$$= \frac{60}{10}$$

$$= 6 \text{ days}$$

The interpretation of this measure is that each terminal was out of service for 6 days. This represents a total of 60 workdays in the year for the terminals as a group. This amount of time would be equivalent to a total downtime of 12 workweeks for a single terminal.

When the mean is computed, the value of each data point is a part of the total, and this total will sometimes include extreme values. If one or more of the data points is extreme, either high or low, the calculated mean may not be representative of the rest of the data. When a distribution contains extreme values, it may be best to calculate two means, one that includes the extreme value and one that is calculated without the extreme value. Alternatively, the mean can be reported along with the median and mode, which are less sensitive to extreme values.

Suppose, for example, that members of a consortium report the amount that each expended during a year on document delivery (inter-library loan) (see Table 4-7). The mean expenditure is

$$\bar{X} = \frac{\sum_{n=1}^{7} X_i}{7}$$

$$= \frac{X_1 + X_2 + X_3 + X_4 + X_5 + X_6 + X_7}{7}$$

$$= \frac{17,500 + 18,500 + 18,250 + 17,750 + 18,500 + 24,750 + 17,750}{7}$$

$$= \frac{133,000}{7}$$

$$= \$19,000$$

As can be seen, the mean of the data set exceeds all the values except for the amount reported by Institution F. Institution F's expenditure is an extreme value, not representative of the other six values. If data point F is excluded, the mean is 108,250/6, or $18,041.67. This value is representative of those in the data set. Alternatively, the median of the distribution, $18,250, is less sensitive to extreme values. It may provide the user with more helpful and more representative information.

When the amounts to compute the mean are summed, the signs of the observations must be considered. Negative data scores must be included in the tabulation, as are the positive scores. For example, suppose cash in the library's cash register(s) is compared with the register tapes at the end of each day. If no cash errors have been made, there should be no difference between the amount of cash in the drawers and the final balance shown on the cash register tape(s). The differences recorded for a sample 1-week period are as follows: $0.25, $0.50, $-1.10, $0.25, $-1.25, $-0.70, and $-0.75. The value $0.25 means the cash in the register drawer exceeds the tape by this amount. The value

Table 4-7. Annual Interlibrary Loan Expenditures by Consortium Member

Institution	Amount Expended
A	$17,500
B	18,500
C	18,250
D	17,750
E	18,500
F	24,750
G	17,750

$-1.15 means the cash drawer is short by this amount. Using Formula 4-4, we calculate the mean:

$$\overline{X} = \frac{\sum\limits_{n=1}^{7} X_i}{7}$$

$$= \frac{X_1 + X_2 + X_3 + X_4 + X_5 + X_6 + X_7}{7}$$

$$= \frac{0.25 + 0.5 + (-1.10) + 0.25 + (-1.25) + (-0.7) + (-0.75)}{7}$$

$$= \frac{0.25 + 0.5 - 1.10 + 0.25 - 1.25 - 0.7 - 0.75}{7}$$

$$= \frac{-2.80}{7}$$

$$= \$ - 0.40$$

Thus, during the 1-week period, the register(s) averaged a daily loss of 40 cents. If this loss is representative for the year, the annual loss to the library is $146.00 (i.e., 365 days x $0.40/day). This method of reporting has many implications for planning and other purposes. Organizations can, for example, often evaluate employee performance with these reports. If a measurable performance standard has been established, these reports can be an objective aspect of performance evaluation.

If data are presented by a grouped frequency distribution, the mean is determined by multiplying the class midpoint of each class interval by the frequency of observations in that class. These sums are totaled and divided by the number of observations in the distribution. In mathematical terms, the formula is

$$\overline{X} = \frac{\sum\limits_{i=1}^{k} f_i M_i}{\sum\limits_{i=1}^{k} f_i} \qquad\qquad (4-5)$$

$$= \frac{f_1 M_1 + f_2 M_2 + f_3 M_3 + \ ... \ + f_k M_k}{f_1 + f_2 + f_3 + \ ... \ + f_k}$$

where f = frequency or number of observations in each class

M = class midpoint for each class interval
k = number of classes
Formula 4-5 can be illustrated by the book copyright data in Table 4-8. These data have been grouped into a frequency distribution of 8 classes ($k = 8$). The class midpoints have been determined by using either Formula 3-1 or 3-2.

In this example, the frequency of the first interval is $f_1 = 8$. The class midpoint of the first interval is $M_1 = 56.5$. Other values are $f_2 = 13$, $M_2 = 60.5$, $f_3 = 14$, $M_3 = 64.5$, and so on. According to Formula 4-5,

$$\overline{X} = \frac{\displaystyle\sum_{i=1}^{k} f_i M_i}{\displaystyle\sum_{i=1}^{k} f_i}$$

$$= \frac{f_1 M_1 + f_2 M_2 + f_3 M_3 + \ldots + f_8 M_8}{f_1 + f_2 + f_3 + \ldots + f_8}$$

$$= \frac{8\,(56.5) + 13\,(60.5) + 14\,(64.5) + \ldots + 7\,(84.5)}{8 + 13 + 14 + \ldots + 7}$$

Table 4-8. Distribution of 20th Century Copyright Dates (n=93)

Interval	Frequency n	Midpoint M	Frequency x Midpoint n * M
55-58	8	56.5	452.0
59-62	13	60.5	786.5
63-66	14	64.5	903.0
67-70	16	68.5	1096.0
71-74	16	72.5	1160.0
75-78	10	76.5	765.0
79-82	9	80.5	724.5
83-86	7	84.5	591.5
	n=93		Sum = 6478.5

Source: Table 3-4

$$= \frac{452.0 + 786.5 + 903.0 + \ldots + 591.5}{93}$$

$$= \frac{6478.5}{93}$$

$$= 69.66, \text{ or } 70$$

Since the data are discrete, the mean is rounded to 70. This distribution statistic tells the librarian that the average copyright date of the 93 books in the study is 1970. Excluding a rare book or archive collection, this statistic confirms that the books in the study are relatively old.

In another example that illustrates computation of the arithmetic mean by using the class midpoint, suppose a tally is made of the time required for checking out library materials in a busy library. The data are given in Example 4-3.

Figures 4-2A, B, and C each illustrates a distribution with many low scores and few high scores. The center of this distribution is different for each of the three measures of central tendency. For the mode (Figure 4-2A), the center is the most frequent score. For the median (Figure 4-2B), it is that score which divides the distribution so that half the scores lies on either side of it. The median lies to the right of the mode in this distribution. For the mean (Figure 4-2C), the center of the distribution is that point which balances the many low scores with the few high scores.

*Additional Comments and Insights on the Mean**

1. The mean is among the most popularly used statistics for summarizing data. As a result, practitioners and consumers of statistics widely understand and accept it.
2. Every data set has a mean unique to that data set. The mean is always expressed in the same units as the original data.
3. The mean is not necessarily equal to one of the data values.
4. The mean is an appropriate measure if the measurement scale is interval or ratio. The mean is not appropriate for nominal or ordinal measurement scale data.
5. The mean is a useful measure for making comparisons between and among data sets.

---

* Portions of this text were derived from *Business and Economic Statistics* by W.A. Spurr, L.S. Kellogg, and J.H. Smith. ©1961, Richard D. Irwin, Inc., page 195. Used by permission of the publisher.

Example 4-3. Using Class Midpoint to Determine the Arithmetic Mean

Time (Minutes)	Clients (f)	Midpoint (X)	f*X
0 – 1.99	17	1	17
2 – 3.99	23	3	69
4 – 5.99	36	5	180
6 – 7.99	29	7	203
8 – 9.99	14	9	126
10 and over	1*	18	18
Total	120		613

*Required 18 minutes

From the data, $N = 17 + 23 + 36 + 29 + 14 + 1$, or $N = 120$. Then we apply Formula 4-4:

$$\overline{X} = \frac{\sum_{i=1}^{k} f_i M_i}{\sum_{i=1}^{k} f_i}$$

$$= \frac{f_1 M_1 + f_2 M_2 + f_3 M_3 + f_4 M_4 + f_5 M_5 + f_6 M_6}{f_1 + f_2 + f_3 + f_4 + f_5 + f_6}$$

$$= \frac{17(1) + 23(3) + 36(5) + 29(7) + 14(9) + 1(18)}{17 + 23 + 36 + 29 + 14 + 1}$$

$$= \frac{17 + 69 + 180 + 203 + 126 + 18}{17 + 23 + 36 + 29 + 14 + 1}$$

$$= \frac{613}{120}$$

$$= 5.1 \text{ minutes}$$

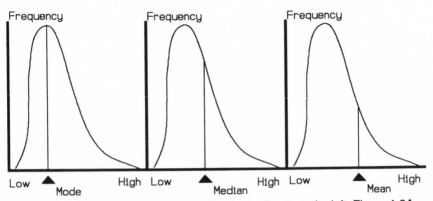

Fig 4-2. Balance point of a distribution. In the figure on the left, Figure 4-2A, the mode is the balance point. The mode is the distribution's most frequent score. In the middle figure, Figure 4-2B, the median is the balance point. One-half of the distribution's scores are on each side of the median. The last figure, Figure 4-2C, shows the mean as the balance point. It balances the distribution's many low scores with its few high scores.

6. The mean is based on *all* observations in a data set. If one or more of the values is extremely high or low, the mean may be affected too much by the extreme value(s). They make the mean unrepresentative of the rest of the data. The effect of an extreme value is particularly visible when the number of observations is small. Thus, as the size of the sample becomes larger, the impact of extreme values is reduced.

7. The mean can be computed from the original data without forming an array or frequency distribution. It can also be computed from a known total sum and the number of items that form the sum.

8. The mean of a large distribution can be tedious to calculate since each data point is included. This problem is reduced by grouping data into classes.

9. If a frequency distribution has an open interval at either its high or low end of the scale, it is *not* possible to calculate the mean. This is because no class midpoint can be determined for the interval.

10. The mean is determined by a rigid formula and, therefore, can be used in other calculations.

The Weighted Arithmetic Mean

The weighted arithmetic mean is used to give different "weights" to individual measurements. This occurs, for example, when an instructor assigns different weights to written assignments, quizzes, and the final exam when arriving at a grade. A *weighted mean* is also used when one wishes to obtain an overall mean for several data sets that are not all composed of the same number of elements.

In the weighted mean, weights $W_1, W_2, W_3, \ldots, W_k$ are associated with the data points $X_1, X_2, X_3, \ldots, X_k$. The "weight" depends on the significance or importance attached to the item of interest. The weighted mean is found by

$$\overline{X}_w = \frac{\sum\limits_{i=1}^{k} w_i x_i}{\sum\limits_{i=1}^{k} w_i} \tag{4-6}$$

$$= \frac{w_1 X_1 + w_2 X_2 + w_3 X_3 + \ldots + w_k X_k}{w_1 + w_2 + w_3 + \ldots + w_k}$$

To illustrate the weighted mean, suppose a total of $2000 in shares of a mutual fund is purchased as part of an IRA annual savings program. At various times during the year, purchases are made of 40 shares at $12.50 a share, 62 shares at $8 a share, 50 shares at $10 a share, and 56 shares at $9 a share. The total amount of money expended to obtain the 208 shares is $40(12.50) + 62(8.00) + 50(10.00) + 56(9.00) = \$2000.00$. Since 208 shares were purchased, the mean cost per share is $2000/208, or $9.62. When we apply Formula 4-6 to the IRA shares example,

$$\overline{X}_w = \frac{\sum\limits_{i=1}^{k} w_i x_i}{\sum\limits_{i=1}^{k} w_i}$$

$$= \frac{w_1 X_1 + w_2 X_2 + w_3 X_3 + w_4 X_4}{w_1 + w_2 + w_3 + w_4}$$

$$= \frac{40(12.50) + 62(8.00) + 50(10.00) + 56(9.00)}{40 + 62 + 50 + 56}$$

$$= \frac{2000}{208}$$

$$= 9.6154 \text{ or } \$9.62$$

If the four separate purchase prices are simply averaged by using Formula 4-1, ($12.50 + 8 + 10 + 9)/4, an incorrect answer of $9.88 per share is obtained. The error is caused by not considering that each purchase resulted in a different number of shares being acquired. Hence, the data sets are not composed of the same number of elements.

The following example illustrates finding the weighted mean when the weights are expressed as percents. Suppose that students in a library science class are told at the beginning of the quarter that their course grade will be a composite based on all their work. The midterm will count 30%; written assignments, 20%; term paper, 20%; and the final examination, 30%. In these four categories, student X's average is 87%, 94%, 90%, and 93%. To compute the final average, the weighted mean must be calculated. In this problem, $W_1 = 0.30$, $W_2 = 0.20$, $W_3 = 0.20$, and $W_4 = 0.30$. Also, $X_1 = 87$, $X_2 = 94$, $X_3 = 90$, and $X_4 = 93$. Then,

$$\overline{X}_w = \frac{w_1 X_1 + w_2 X_2 + w_3 X_3 + w_4 X_4}{w_1 + w_2 + w_3 + w_4}$$

$$= \frac{.30(87) + .20(94) + .20(90) + .30(93)}{.30 + .20 + .20 + .30}$$

$$= 90.8\%$$

Hence, student X's weighted average is 90.8%. Notice that weights (percents that each part of the course grade will count toward the final grade) W_1, W_2, W_3, and W_4 are relative frequencies for the student's component average, X_1, X_2, X_3, and X_4, respectively. Their sum is $W_1 + W_2 + W_3 + W_4 = 1$. When percents are used, the decimal weights must always sum to 1.

A useful example of applying the weighted mean on the business side of library administration is the problem of the village library that builds a 2-story addition of 20,000 gross square feet. As part of the project, conduit must be installed to contain wires to link spaces in the addition to the computer facility in the old building and for an internal intercom system. Six sizes of conduit, ranging between 1 inch and 4 inches, are required. Per installed foot, these varying sizes cost $6, $7.50, $9, $11, $15, and $18. Library requirements are shown in Table 4-9.

Suppose two vendors submit bids. Vendor A states that, for an average price of $11 per foot, his firm will install the conduit. For an additional $2.50 per foot, the vendor will pull the required wire pairs.

Table 4-9. Library Conduit Requirements and Cost Per Foot

Conduit Size	Cost per Foot of Conduit	Quantity Required
A	$ 6.00	620
B	7.50	475
C	9.00	500
D	11.00	350
E	15.00	225
F	18.00	200

Vendor B submits a bid of $28,375, which *includes* the cost of pulling the required wire pairs. In both bids, wire is to be supplied by the library.

In analyzing the two bids to select a vendor, we would first compute the weighted mean. Using Formula 4-6, we then compute:

$$\overline{X}_w = \frac{\displaystyle\sum_{i=1}^{k} w_i x_i}{\displaystyle\sum_{i=1}^{k} w_i}$$

$$= \frac{w_1 X_1 + w_2 X_2 + w_3 X_3 + w_4 X_4 + w_5 X + w_6 X_6}{w_1 + w_2 + w_3 + w_4 + w_5 + w_6}$$

$$= \frac{\begin{array}{l}620\,(\,6.00) + 475\,(\,7.00) + 500\,(\,9.00) + \\ 350\,(\,11.00) + 225\,(\,15.00) + 200\,(\,18.00)\end{array}}{620 + 475 + 500 + 350 + 225 + 200}$$

$$= \frac{22,370}{2370}$$

$$= 9.439 \text{ or } \$9.44$$

Vendor A seems to have arrived at his average by finding the mean of the cost per foot of the six conduits without regard to the required quantity. Since the quantities differ, however, averaging the costs using Formula 4-4, as in the mutual fund example, is inaccurate. Using the amount of $11 per foot, Vendor A's bid is $26,070 plus the cost of wire pulling. This bid represents an additional $5925, bringing the total cost to $31,995. Since the vendor has separated the price for pulling the wires, presumably this option can be declined and awarded to another party, if desired.

Vendor B's bid is less than his competitor's, but it includes pulling the wires. While the cost is lower, this bid may still be less attractive since the library's flexibility in shopping for wire pulling is reduced. If Vendor B, like the other vendor, has factored a cost of $2.50 per foot to pull the wires, the installation portion of the job is $22,450 ($28,375 - $5,925 = $22,450). This amount is very close to the cost one would expect, based on using the weighted mean.

If all other things are equal, Vendor B's bid seems to be the better choice. This judgment, of course, is subject to change. When the bids on supplying the wire are received, some of them may contain offers to pull the wires through the conduit at a more favorable price. In any event, a decision made entirely on the statistics would be unwise. Reputation for quality, timeliness, and similar factors should also be considered.

A similar example of weighted averages in library construction is computing the average cost of floor coverings when two or more types or grades of carpets are selected or when different types of tile are identified for use.

Finally, the reader's attention is called to the fact that the arithmetic mean computed from *grouped data* is a weighted mean. The weights are $f_1, f_2, \ldots, f_k$. The mean from grouped data is an average of the interval midpoints, where each interval midpoint is weighted proportionally to the frequency of its interval.

For an additional example of the use of the weighted mean, suppose that five suburban public libraries are part of a consortium. Suppose, too, that through document delivery (interlibrary loans) they share resources. Staff at the supervisory and management level meet monthly to discuss common problems, and occasionally staff are shared among the institutions to assist with in-service training. The results of a salary survey for full-time, hourly circulation personnel are shown in Example 4-4.

Example 4-4. Using the Weighted Mean

Institution	Average Salary	Base of Comparison
A	$15,125	11
B	14,725	15
C	14,515	10
D	15,500	8
E	14,250	12

To find the mean salary for the consortium, Formula 4-6 is used:

$$\bar{X}_w = \frac{w_1 X_1 + w_2 X_2 + w_3 X_3 + w_4 X_4 + w_5 X_5}{w_1 + w_2 + w_3 + w_4 + w_5}$$

$$= \frac{11\,(\,15{,}125) + 15\,(\,14{,}725) + 10\,(\,14{,}515) + 8\,(\,15{,}500) + 12\,(\,14{,}250)}{11 + 15 + 10 + 8 + 12}$$

$$= \frac{166{,}375 + 220{,}875 + 145{,}150 + 124{,}000 + 171{,}000}{56}$$

$$= \frac{837{,}400}{56}$$

$$= \$14{,}775$$

Summary of Critical Concepts

1. *Frequency distributions* provide a useful technique for organizing and displaying data. Even so, they are limited in their usefulness. They do not provide quantitative, summary statements about the data.
2. *Measures of central tendency* are summary statements which describe the center of a distribution. These measures are the mode, median, and mean.
3. The *mode* is the only measure of central tendency that may have more than one value. A distribution may not have a mode, or it may have several modes. The mode is usually not used alone as a measure of central tendency to describe a data set.

4. The *median* of a data set is the value which is above the lower one-half and below the upper one-half of the values. The median can be thought of as the most central-measure of a distribution. Every data set has a median that is unique. Even so, the median is not necessarily one of the values of the data set. The median is affected by the number of observations in the data set, but *not* by their values. Hence, the median is not affected by extreme scores.

5. The *median* is the preferred central tendency measure for distributions (such as income) which have extreme values.

6. The *mean* for a series of ungrouped observations is obtained by adding all the scores in the data set; this sum is then divided by the total number of scores.

7. The *mean* is among the most popularly used statistics for summarizing data. Although every data set has a mean that is unique, it is not necessarily one of the values of the data set. The mean is based on all the observations in a data set and is therefore sensitive to extreme scores. If a distribution has an open-ended class interval, it is not possible to compute the mean.

Key Terms

Central Tendency. The middle of a distribution of scores. Three measures of central tendency are mode, median, and mean.

Extreme Value. A score or value that falls outside the range of the other measurements in the data set. For example, in the data set {1,2,3,3,9} the value 9 is extreme.

Mean. The sum of all the values of a set of observations divided by the number of observations. For the mean, the size or "weight" of each data point defines the center of the distribution.

Median. The value of the distribution's central item when observations are arranged by size from low to high or high to low. For the median, the distribution's center is the score below or above which 50% of the observations fall.

Mode. The data value that is the most often repeated in the set. For the mode, the center point is the distribution's most often occurring observation. A distribution may have no mode. It may have a single mode (unimodal) or it may have more than one mode (multimodal).

Self-Assessment Quiz

True or False   1.   It is not possible to determine the data set's mean if the distribution contains an open-ended class interval.

True or False   2.   Extreme values affect the mean of a data set.

True or False   3.   The mean is the most central item in a data set.

True or False   4.   If 5 were subtracted from each score in a data set of 3 items, the distribution's mean would be reduced by 5.

True or False   5.   The mean is the central tendency measure most popularly used for describing an income distribution.

True or False   6.   It is possible to determine both the mean and median for any frequency distribution.

True or False   7.   If there are 100 items in a distribution, the median is the 50th item in the array.

True or False   8.   The median statistic considers the value of each data point in a distribution.

True or False   9.   For most distributions, the median is the preferred measure of central tendency.

True or False 10.   The median and mode are widely accepted central tendency measures for qualitative data.

True or False 11.   The mode is the most often occurring value in a data set.

True or False 12.   A multimodal distribution may show that a set is composed of dissimilar or heterogeneous data.

True or False 13.   The mode for a data set is unique.

True or False 14.   In a distribution with a mode, the mode is the highest point in the distribution.

True or False 15.   The mean for a data set is unique.

True or False 16.   Extreme values in a data set affect the mode to the same extent as they affect the mean.

True or False 17.   If two distributions have the same mean, the two distributions look exactly alike.

True or False 18.   Assume you are jogging and that you are passing the same number of joggers as are passing you. Based on this observation, your jogging speed is the mean speed.

Answers

1. True. The mean can only be computed for interval or ratio scale.
2. True. Extreme values can cause the mean to be substantially greater or less than the majority of data points.
3. False. The median, *not* the mean, is the "most central" item.
4. True. Convince yourself of this by working through the formula as follows:

$$\frac{\sum\limits_{i=1}^{3}(x_i - 5)}{3} = \frac{(x_1 - 5) + (x_2 - 5) + (x_3 - 5)}{3}$$

$$= \frac{x_1 - 5 + x_2 - 5 + x_3 - 5}{3}$$

$$= \frac{x_1 + x_2 + x_3 - 15}{3}$$

$$= \frac{x_1 + x_2 + x_3}{3} - \frac{15}{3}$$

$$= \overline{X} - 5$$

For any size data set, subtracting any constant from, or adding any constant to, every X_i will decrease or increase the mean by that constant.

5. False. The median is the most popularly used central tendency measure for describing income distributions. This is because income distributions usually have extreme values and medians are not affected by extreme values.
6. False. The mean cannot be determined in a distribution if it contains an open-ended class interval. The median, however, can be determined for any frequency distribution.
7. False. The median is the mean of the two middle terms of an array having an even number of scores. For an array of 100 items, the median is located midway between the 50th and 51st items.
8. False. The median considers location in the array since it is the "middle" value. The mean considers the value of each score.
9. False. The mean is more widely used as the average of a distribution.
10. True. The mode and median can be used to interpret qualitative data. The mean can only be used with quantitative data.

11. True. The mode is always located at the highest point of a frequency distribution.

12. True. An example to illustrate this is that men tend to weigh more than women. A frequency distribution of weights of men and women selected at random is bimodal. This suggests that weight data for men and women should be reported in two separate distributions, each of which would then be unimodal.

13. False. A data set may have a single mode, several modes, or no mode. The mean and median are unique measures of central tendency for a distribution.

14. True. The mode is the highest point in a distribution because it occurs with the greatest frequency.

15.True. The mean for a distribution is unique since a data set has one and only one mean.

16. False. Extreme values affect the mean but do not affect the mode.

17. False. An infinite number of frequency distributions could give the same value for the mean. Consider these three distributions, each of which has a mean of 5: {3, 5, 7}, {1, 2, 12}, or {-1, 3, 5, 7, 11}.

18. False. Your jogging speed is the median speed. Since 50% of the runners are faster than you ("score" above you in speed) and 50% are slower than you ("score" below you), your speed is the distribution's center, the median.

Discussion Questions and Problems

1. The data listing below represents the number of sick days taken by 31 library employees during the last fiscal year:

2	3	5	2	7	4	7	0
1	4	5	0	7	3	2	0
4	6	7	3	3	5	5	3
4	1	4	5	4	7	4	

   a. Organize the data into an array and create a frequency distribution (ungrouped).

   b. Without grouping the data, determine and interpret the distribution's mean, median, and mode.

   c. Discuss the implications of lost productivity due to employee absences.

2. The librarian at a corporate library recently leased several pieces of computer hardware before deciding which system to purchase. Each

piece of equipment has a different cost per hour for its use, a calculation performed by system software. At the end of 40 days, the following costs per hour had accrued for each 7.5-hour day of use:

30	26	32	36	25	14	18	31
24	15	35	10	13	24	32	19
16	37	16	18	17	12	28	13
23	15	18	29	21	35	15	17
21	31	12	16	22	13	16	35

a. Organize the data into an array and create a frequency distribution.
b. Without grouping the data, determine the mean and median operating costs.
c. Group the data and determine the mean and median operating costs. Explain any difference between the measures found by grouping and those found in (b) above.
d. Determine the total cost for the leased equipment for the 40-day period.
e. Determine the mean hourly cost.

3. A librarian conducted an informal survey to estimate the average age of library users. During a representative 2-hour period, a staff member, known to be good at guessing ages, made the following tabulation:

Age	Frequency
1 and under 10	15
10 and under 20	20
20 and under 30	26
30 and under 40	18
40 and under 50	15
50 and under 60	3
60 and under 70	2
70 and under 80	1
Total	100

a. Determine the mean and median of the distribution.
b. Plot the distribution's histogram.

4. What is the effect on the mode, median, and mean of the following:
a. adding 5 points to all scores
b. subtracting 5 points from all scores
c. increasing all scores by 5%.

5. If you conducted a study of the age distribution of users of the Childrens' Department, would you consider age to be a discrete or continuous variable? What would you choose for class boundaries?

6. Cite various types of data for which the median, rather than the mean, would be the appropriate central tendency measure.

7. Last month a librarian worked as a freelance indexer and earned $13.50 per hour for 75 hours of work, $16.25 per hour for 30 hours of work, $9.50 per hour for 7.5 hours of work, and $12 per hour for 37.5 hours of work. Determine the librarian's mean earnings per hour for the month.

8. At the end of a library's Summer Reading Program, participants were given special merit certificates and a coupon redeemable for an ice cream cone. Within the first few hours after the coupons were issued, the ice cream parlor merchant recorded the following flavor choices: vanilla, pecan, strawberry, vanilla, chocolate, mocha, strawberry, pecan, strawberry, chocolate, vanilla, chocolate, strawberry, mocha, pecan, vanilla, mocha, chocolate, strawberry, mocha, chocolate, vanilla, strawberry, strawberry, and chocolate.
   a. Identify the level of measurement represented by the data.
   b. Identify the rank order of the children's flavor preferences.
   c. Identify the level of measurement represented by the ranks in (b) above.

9. The librarian has asked you to estimate the number of titles in the library's collection. Over the past several years the library has operated under the assumption that collection size is about 47,500 volumes. The library has not yet converted to an online catalog system and does not maintain a title count of its various collections. In estimating collection size, you will be using two methods and will then compare your results. Data are provided below on the number of shelflist cards per 1-inch section of the shelflist catalog and the number of books per section of shelving. To increase the accuracy of your estimate, the counts have been repeated ten times.

Number of Titles/1 inch of Shelflist		Books/Section of Shelving	
94	103	180	156
106	97	195	170
99	104	185	169
96	98	193	160
102	101	164	178

   a. Given that the cards in the shelflist catalog measure 500 inches, what is your best estimate for the collection's size?
   b. If the library has 376 selections of shelving and if 75% of them are full, estimate the size of the collection.
   c. Using your answer from (a) as the base, determine the percent difference in estimates derived from the two methods.
   d. Estimate the number of new titles that can be accommodated on the 25% of shelving that is now unoccupied.

10. The director of technical services for a public library that serves a community of 30,000 is preparing a report requiring the calculation of certain ratios between adult and juvenile materials added to the collection. The data source for this report will be materials cataloged by area of Dewey classification over the previous two years.

Dewey	Adult Year 2	Juvenile Year 2	Adult Year 1	Juvenile Year 1
000–099 General Works	53	15	45	29
100–199 Philosophy	39	15	44	14
200–299 Religion	41	2	60	11
300–399 Social Sciences	448	76	338	68
400–499 Language	3	7	6	1
500–599 Pure Sciences	63	75	54	52
600–699 Technology	470	49	378	67
700–799 The Arts	343	54	293	47
800–899 Literature	169	38	113	29
900–999 Geography & History	290	77	262	46
Fiction	933	524	849	207
Biography	90	79	85	61

a. Calculate the percent change in the number of books cataloged by Dewey classification for both adult and juvenile materials between Year 1 and Year 2.
b. Find the mean percent change for both adult and juvenile materials cataloged.
c. For each Dewey classification, calculate the ratio of juvenile to adult materials cataloged in each year.
d. Calculate the mean ratio of juvenile to adult materials cataloged.
e. If any of the ratios differs widely from the mean, speculate on reasons.

11. The technical services director wishes to check the time lag between when a book order is received and when it is ready to be placed into the collection.

In conducting this study, your data source will be the book order cards that are kept in the permanent order files. When an order card is received, a staff member stamps it with that day's date. After the item has been verified (checked that it is not already owned by the requesting unit and that the item is in print), the item is ordered, and again the date is recorded on the card. When the invoice is received from the vendor, the date is again recorded on the card. Finally, after the book has been cataloged and is ready to be placed into the collection, the date is also recorded on the card.

To study the various lag times in the acquisitions and technical services process, a clerk collects data from completed transactions as recorded on cards in the permanent order file. For each card, the clerk computes and records the number of elapsed calendar days. Although there are 775 order records in the file, only 440 cards have all four dates and can be used in the study.

Number of Days	Days before Ordering	Days for Vendor to Fill Order	Days to Process Item
1 – 7	72	1	35
8 – 14	125	1	43
15 – 21	127	1	55
22 – 28	71	82	130
29 – 35	39	84	71
36 – 42	52	10	50
43 – 49	1	22	29
50 – 56		17	9
57 – 63		15	7
64 – 70		5	5
71 – 77		2	4
78 – 84			2

a. Next to each column in the chart, determine percents.
b. Graph the cumulative frequency distribution for each of the three columns of data. Interpret your findings.
c. Determine the mean number of days required for a book to be ordered, for the vendor to fill the order, and for the item to be processed.
d. Speculate on ways that the technical services director might reduce the lag time evidenced in each of the data columns.

12. Acquisitions librarians from a consortium of ten corporate libraries tabulated their collection size and yearly acquisitions as follows:

Library	Collection Size	Acquisitions
1	42,000	2150
2	15,000	2025
3	11,000	554
4	8000	500
5	7350	46
6	6500	500
7	5150	303
8	975	63
9	812	53
10	630	42

a. Using the above data, calculate the ratio of acquisitions to collection size for each library and express your answers as percents.

b. Find the mean percent for the ratio of acquisitions to collection size.

c. Give an explanation for the value observed for library 2. (Hint: Library 2 has been in operation for only 3 months.)

d. Give an explanation for the value observed for Library 5. (Hint: The librarian has not needed the collection for several years but will begin this activity next month.)

Chapter Five

Measures of Variability

Learning Objectives

After reading and understanding the contents of this chapter, you will be able to:

1. Identify and discuss the differences and advantages of the various measures of variability, such as the range, percentile range, interquartile range, and standard deviation.
2. Calculate the value of the range, percentile range, interquartile range, and standard deviation.
3. Explain and show how the measures of variability augment measures of central tendency.
4. Explain the usefulness of Chebyshev's Theorem as a rule of thumb for describing a distribution.
5. Determine the coefficient of variation and explain its use in analyzing the variation in two data sets.
6. Identify distributions as symmetrical or skewed.
7. Identify and give library examples of distributions that produce *J*-curves, reverse *J*-curves, and *U*-curves.
8. Explain the usefulness of Pareto's 80/20 Rule.

In Chapter Four, the mode, median, and mean as measures of central tendency were discussed and illustrated. These measures are effective for identifying the center of a distribution, but each considers the center to be a different point.

Even so, simply to consider measures of "center" for a data distribution ignores the question of how data points are grouped about the center. For sets of data with identical measures of center, the data sets may differ in how the points are spread, distributed, or dispersed about that center. These concerns are addressed by the topic of this chapter, measures of variability.

Analyzing Data Dispersion

Summary statistics can hide erratic performance. For example, suppose that a cataloger is expected to catalog 15 books per day. For each day of the month, the number of books cataloged is recorded in a log. The data are listed in Table 5-1.

Applying Formula 4-4, we discover that an average of 15 books was cataloged each day. However, this statistic does not accurately reflect daily performance, which fluctuated wildly. Some days, over 30 books were cataloged; other days, no books were cataloged. These fluctuations may be caused by irregular book shipments, or the staff member may be ill, away from the office attending a professional meeting or on vacation, or perhaps the cataloger is experiencing professional or personal problems. Whatever their cause, these fluctuations suggest that there may be a problem which the summary statistic alone would hide.

To describe a given data set accurately, measures of central tendency (mode, median, mean) are often augmented by *measures of variability*, also known as *measures of dispersion*. The purpose of these statistics is to describe how data are scattered or spread about a central point.

The idea of variability is illustrated in Figure 5-1. Each of the distributions in the figure has the same mean, and the areas under the

Table 5-1. Daily Log of Books Cataloged			
Date	Books Cataloged	Date	Books Cataloged
3	1	17	16
4	15	18	15
5	24	19	28
6	2	20	14
7	0	21	15
10	13	24	17
11	15	25	29
12	0	26	6
13	10	27	14
14	34	28	32

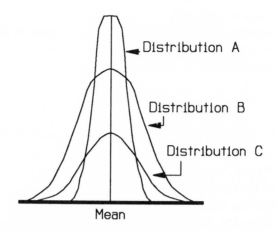

Figure 5-1. Variability of distributions that have the same mean

curves are equal. The data that form Distribution A, however, have less spread, dispersion, or variability than do the data of Distributions B and C. Similarly, Distribution B has less variability than Distribution C. Of three distributions, the mean of Distribution C is the least representative of the distribution's data as a whole, while that of Distribution A is the most representative. In other words, the data comprising Distribution A are more homogeneous than those of the other distributions. Conversely, the data of Distribution C are more heterogeneous than those in the other distributions.

Measures of variability are important in judging the *reliability* of central tendency measures. They are also useful in identifying distributions which are composed of widely dispersed data. If a distribution is to be adequately described, its variability must be characterized. Remember the cataloging example given in Table 5-1. The consumer of statistics should be wary of deception if measures of variability are not presented.

Measures of variability serve another purpose. They help a librarian to develop an intuitive sense of how a curve should look. Based on the measure of variability, the librarian is able to predict certain distribution characteristics. As the librarian's experience with data and measures of central tendency develops, it is likely that intuitive assessments will improve in accuracy.

Range

The simplest measure of variability is the *range*. For ungrouped data, range is the difference between the two extreme values of a data set. It is obtained by subtracting the smallest measurement from the largest. Hence,

Range = Highest score − Lowest score   (5 − 1)

In equation form, if X_H is the highest value in the data set and X_L is the lowest, then

Range = $X_H − X_L$ (5 − 2)

For example, the ages of five library clerks are 16, 24, 17, 32, and 38. Using Formula 5-2, where $X_H = 38$ and $X_L = 16$, we see that the range for this set of ungrouped observations is

Range = 38 − 16

= 22

For *grouped data*, the range is the difference between the value of the upper class limit of the highest class and the value of the lower class limit of the lowest class. Thus, if the highest class of grouped data is 700 - 750 and if the lowest class is 300 - 350, the range is $R = 750 - 300$, or $R = 450$. In the grouped frequency distribution of copyright dates in Table 4-7, the value of the upper class limit is 86 and the value of the lower class limit is 55. Hence, the range in copyright dates is $R = 86 - 55$, or $R = 31$. Range cannot be calculated, however, if the lowest and highest classes are open. In Table 4-4, for instance, the lowest class is "less than 3 hours" and the highest class is "20 hours or more." The range is *not* 20 - 3 = 17, since some scores are higher than 20 and some are less than 3. In this instance, *no* range can be calculated because the classes of this distribution are open.

Another limitation of the range is that it considers only the highest and lowest values of a distribution. It is not sensitive to the dispersion of data between the extreme values. This drawback is illustrated by the following three distributions, each of which has a range of 10:

Distribution 1: {12, 13, 14, 15, 16, 17, 18, 19, 20, 21, 22}
Distribution 2: {12, 13, 14, 14, 14, 14, 16, 16, 18, 19, 22}
Distribution 3: {12, 12, 12, 12, 12, 13, 14, 16, 17, 17, 22}

Visual inspection of these distributions reveals that there is substantial difference in dispersion among the three distributions. The range, however, gives no hint of this difference. An additional disadvantage with the range as a measure of dispersion is that the range tends to increase as the number of observations in the distribution increases. This is because more observations make it increasingly likely for these to be extreme values in both ends of the distribution. This lack of stability diminishes the range's usefulness. Even so, it is not unusual to find distributions described by their ranges, as in "the data scores range between 12 and 22." Weather reports and stock quotations that give the daily high and low values are examples of typical ranges that, without more information, are not descriptive of the data. The range, like the mode as a measure of central tendency, usually should *not* be used alone to describe the dispersion of data.

Additional Comments and Insights on the Range*

1. The range is an easy-to-compute, uncomplicated measure.
2. The range measures the difference between two extreme values in a distribution.
3. As the number of observations increases, the range tends to increase because of the greater chance of the distribution's including extreme values in its data set.
4. No range can be determined in open-ended distributions since open-ended classes do not have a "highest" or "lowest" value.
5. Data sets with the same range may vary widely in their distributions.

Percentiles

The range is the most general measure of variability and can be used with the mode, the median, or the mean. In contrast, percentile is a more restricted measure of variability. It is most useful in conjunction with the median. Like the median, percentiles divide a distribution into equal parts. The median divides a distribution into two equal parts; percentiles divide a distribution into 100 equal parts. Most people are familiar with percentiles from standardized tests such as the Graduate Record Examination (GRE) or the Scholastic Aptitude Test (SAT).

In any distribution, there are 99 percentiles, abbreviated $P_1, P_2, \ldots,$ P_{99}. Percentiles are most often used to describe large data sets, such as

---

* Portions of this text were derived from *Business and Economic Statistics* by W.A. Spurr, L.S. Kellogg, and J.H. Smith. ©1961, Richard D. Irwin, Inc., page 216. Used by permission of the publisher.

GRE or SAT test scores, where the data are grouped and presented by a frequency distribution. The following formula is used to determine the percentile in grouped distributions:

$$P_j = L + \frac{w}{f} (\frac{jn}{100} - F)$$ (5 – 3)

where

j = the desired percentile
L = lower class boundary of the desired percentile class
w = class interval of the desired percentile class
n = total number of observations in the data set
F = cumulative frequency less than the desired percentile class
f = actual frequency of the desired percentile class.

Table 5-2 presents a hypothetical frequency distribution of the examination scores of 200 students. The 90th percentile, P_{90}, is determined as follows: first locate the 90th percentile class by computing $(jn)/100$. This is $(90)(200)/100 = 180$. Hence, the 90th percentile class lies in the class containing the 180th item. From Table 5-2, this is the class interval "550 and under 600." Therefore, in Formula 5-3, where j = 90, L = 550, w = 50, n = 200, F = 134, and f = 47,

$$P_{90} = 550 + \frac{50}{47} (180 - 134)$$

$$= 550 + \frac{50}{47} (46)$$

$$= 550 + 48.9$$

$$= 598.9$$

The interpretation of P_{90} is that 90 percent of the students taking this examination achieved scores that are less than or equal to a score of 598.9.

Percentiles can also be estimated by graphing techniques. The data in Table 5-2 can be graphed as a less-than-cumulative percent polygon. Figure 5-2, constructed from the data in Table 5-2, shows that the median score, P_{50}, is 523.8. Other percentiles could be estimated from this graph in a similar way.

Most students who have taken nationally administered examinations are familiar with percentiles since these tests usually express students' scores in terms of percentiles. The range of possible scores on such tests is from 200 to 800. By referring to percentiles, students know where

Table 5-2. Frequency Distribution of Student Test Scores (n = 200)

Scores	Class Midpoint M	No. of Students Less than Upper Class Limits	Cumu- lative Frequency
300 and under 350	325	2	2
350 and under 400	375	8	10
400 and under 450	425	22	32
450 and under 500	475	37	69
500 and under 550	525	65	134
550 and under 600	575	47	181
600 and under 650	625	12	193
650 and under 700	675	6	199
700 and under 750	725	1	200
Total		200	

Source: Hypothetical data

they rank in the distribution in relation to other students. A score not placed in this, or another, meaningful context has little value.

Notice that Formula 5-3 is similar to Formula 4-3, the equation for the median. This is not coincidental. The median is the 50th percentile, P_{50}. While the median divides a distribution into 2 parts, percentiles divide a distribution into 100 equal parts. Related measures include the three *quartiles* (Q_1, Q_2, Q_3), which divide a distribution into 4 parts, and *deciles* ($D_1, D_2, \ldots , D_9$), which divide it into 10 parts. (The *quartiles*

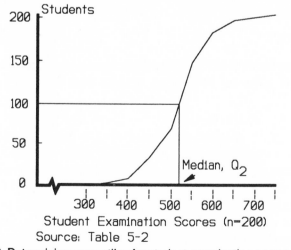

Figure 5-2. Determining percentiles for student examination scores

are discussed in greater detail below.) All these measures may be determined from Formula 5-3 by using the appropriate value for Pj.

Quartile measures may be used in many applications. For example, they may be used to assist young readers in locating words in the dictionary. In attempting to locate a word, it is helpful to know in which quartile of the dictionary the word will be found. The following mnemonic device, which conjures up an effective mental image, is a useful memory aid—Aunt *E*leanor *M*akes *S*oup or Angry *E*lephants *M*ash *S*piders.

The first letters of each of the above words approximately separate the four quartiles of words in the dictionary

A to E	the first 25% of the words in the dictionary
E to M	the second 25% of the words
M to S	the third 25% of the words
S to Z	the fourth 25% of the words.

Thus, in trying to locate the word "book" in the dictionary, the reader should target the search on the first quartile of the dictionary. If the desired word is "manuscript," the reader should refer to the third quartile of the book.

Percentile Ranges

Percentiles can be combined with ranges to yield *percentile ranges*. For instance, The *10-to-90th percentile range* is the distance between the 10th and the 90th percentiles. This measure is useful to estimate the range because it excludes high and low extreme values.

To calculate the 10-to-90th percentile range, find the 10th and 90th percentiles, then find the difference P_{90} - P_{10}. For example, P_{90} for the data in Table 5-2 is 598.9. We can determine P_{10} as follows:

$$\frac{jn}{100} = \frac{10\,(\,200\,)}{100}$$

$$\frac{jn}{100} = 20$$

This means that the 10th percentile lies in the class containing the 20th item. Table 5-2 shows that this is the class in which $L = 400$, $w = 50$, $F = 10$, and $f = 22$.

$$P_j = L + \frac{w}{f} \left(\frac{jn}{100} - F \right)$$

$$P_{10} = 400 + \frac{50}{22} (20 - 10)$$

$$= 400 + \frac{50(10)}{22}$$

$$= 400 + 22.7$$

$$= 422.7$$

Given that $P_{90} = 598.9$ and $P_{10} = 422.7$, the 10-to-90th percentile range for the data in Table 5-1 is

$$P_{90} - P_{10} = 598.9 - 422.7$$

$$= 176.2$$

The interpretation of this measure is that the middle 80 percent of the test scores lies between the test scores 422.7 and 598.9. The remaining 20 percent of the scores lies either below 422.7 or above 598.9. The percentile range is a more sophisticated and useful measurement of deviation than the simple range. This is because the percentile range excludes extreme values which may lay at either end of the array.

Interquartile Range

A variation on percentile range is *interquartile range*. Like the 10-to-90th percentile range, the interquartile range minimizes the influence of extreme observations. This is accomplished by excluding a specific proportion of data on each end of the array. The interquartile range is the distance between the first and the third quartile, Q_1 and Q_3.

Interquartile Range $= Q_3 - Q_1$ (5 – 4)

As the prefix "quar-" implies, quartiles divide a distribution into four equal parts. Accordingly, $Q_1 = P_{25}$, $Q_2 = P_{50}$, $Q_3 = P_{75}$, and $Q_4 = P_{99}$. Note that Q_2 is the median. In a grouped frequency distribution, quartiles Q_1 and Q_3 can be determined by using Formula 5-3, where $j = 25$ and $j = 75$.

$$Q_{25} = L + \frac{w}{f} \left(\frac{25n}{100} - F \right)$$

$$Q_{75} = L + \frac{w}{f} \left(\frac{75n}{100} - F \right)$$

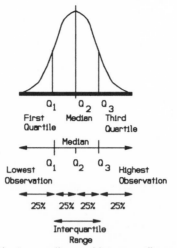

Figure 5-3. A distribution's quartiles and interquartile range

In Figure 5-3, the interquartile range refers to the observations that lie in the middle portion of the distribution between the first quartile, Q_1, and the third, Q_3. The middle one-half of distribution observations are included in this range. Because the interquartile range deals with the middle 50% of the observations, it is more stable than the simple range. Quartiles and quartile ranges can also be calculated for ungrouped data. The rank of the quartile is equal to the number of items in the data set, (N), times the percent of the data which will fall below the desired quartile (i.e., 25% for Q_1). Thus,

$$\text{Rank of } Q_1 = 0.25\,N \qquad\qquad (5-5A)$$

$$\text{Rank of } Q_3 = 0.75\,N \qquad\qquad (5-5B)$$

The use of these formulas is illustrated below. Beware, however, because quartiles can be calculated in a variety of ways. For this reason, you may find slightly different formulas in different sources.

To compare quartile ranges to simple ranges, refer to Table 5-3. This table shows data on the construction costs of public libraries. The simple range for cost per square foot is

$$\text{range} = X_H - X_L$$

$$= \$131.51/\text{sq. ft.} - \$5.36/\text{sq. ft.}$$

$$= \$126.15/\text{sq. ft.}$$

Table 5-3. Construction Costs for New Library Buildings

Community	Construction Costs	Square Feet	Cost per Sq. ft.
Carlsbad, Calif.	$ 16,350	3,050	$ 5.36
Downey, Calif.	3,700,000	68,000	54.41
Newark, Calif.	1,165,000	15,000	77.67
San Juan Cap., Calif.	2,009,000	17,000	118.18
Basalt, Colo.	146,559	1,984	73.87
Avon, Conn.	1,096,102	14,990	73.12
Middletown, Conn.	2,730,433	38,300	71.29
Ft. Lauderdale, Fla.	33,189,375	261,000	127.16
Melrose, Fla.	123,888	3,087	40.13
Pembroke Pines, Fla.	3,541,282	60,457	58.58
Sarasota, Fla.	452,286	10,000	45.23
Abbeville, Ga.	235,880	5,400	43.68
Dahlonega, Ga.	420,565	7,800	53.92
Pinehurst, Ida.	100,521	2,014	49.91
Forsyth, Ill.	256,237	6,216	41.22
Avon, Ind.	1,222,650	20,300	60.23
Bristol, Ind.	667,356	9,800	68.10
New Washington, Ind.	63,350	1,380	45.91
Rochester, Ind.	1,012,288	18,000	56.24
Mapleton, Iowa	188,000	4,000	47.00
Warsaw, Ky.	274,714	5,000	54.94
Baton Rouge, La.	383,000	6,000	63.83
Libuse, La.	135,232	3,600	37.56
Annapolis, Md.	1,131,892	11,870	95.36
Eldersburg, Md.	900,420	14,407	62.50
Reading, Mass.	813,000	30,000	27.10
West Bloomfield Twp., Mich.	812,101	16,000	50.76
Biloxi, Miss	236,916	4,500	52.65
Coffeeville, Miss	68,171	1,811	37.64
Ironton, Mo.	203,347	7,700	26.41
Washington, N. J.	506,000	7,236	69.93
Clemmons, N. C.	489,060	8,900	54.95
Williston, N. D.	1,145,690	22,300	51.38
Lake Oswego, Oreg.	1,370,400	27,100	50.57
Houston, Tex.	1,385,000	16,000	86.56
Pearland, Tex.	480,000	11,666	41.15
Bradshaw, W. Va.	18,766	480	39.10
Buffalo, W. Va.	17,876	480	37.24
Helvetia, W. Va.	19,033	480	39.65
Mt. Storm, W. Va.	21,466	480	44.72
Nutter Fort, W. Va.	48,048	1,250	38.44
Shady Spring, W. Va.	170,900	2,448	69.81
Montreal, Quebec	3,795,000	28,858	131.51
Montreal, Quebec	1,013,000	11,820	85.70

Source: Bette-Lee Fox, "Library Buildings in 1984," *Library Journal* 109(20):2224-2234; December, 1984. From the table titled "Public Library Buildings: New Buildings." Page 2229. Used by permission of the publisher.

The range for these data is large and shows that the data are widely dispersed, so much so that the sample range has little practical use.

Assume, for example, that you are the chairman of a building committee. Suppose, too, that you have collected the data in Table 5-3. From these data you can form an expectation of how much it should cost to build your new facility.

Visual inspection of Table 5-3 reveals that the data fall between $5.36 and $131.51, a range of $126.15. If this data were plotted, the distribution would be extremely wide-tailed and contain extreme values on both ends. Because of the extreme values, the median is used as the measure of central tendency because it is resistant to extreme values. The data are ranked and the median is calculated as follows:

$$\tilde{X} = \text{Observation number } \frac{(44 + 1)}{2}$$

$$= \text{Observation number } 22.5$$

$$= \frac{\text{Observation number } 22 + \text{Observation number } 23}{2}$$

$$= \frac{52.65 + 53.92}{2}$$

$$= 53.28 \text{ or } \$53.28$$

Next, you want to know how much the actual cost to build your facility might differ from the median cost. It is not helpful for you to know that the simple range of costs is $5.36/sq. ft. to $131.50/sq. ft. You cannot make cost estimates with this type of information. Instead, you decide to ignore the extreme values (i.e., $5.36, $131.50) and concentrate on the center of the data. To do this you calculate the interquartile range, which is $Q_3 - Q_1$. From Formulas 5-5A and 5-5B:

$$Q_1 = \text{Observation number } \frac{25}{100} (44)$$

$$= \text{Observation number } 11$$

$$= \$41.15 \text{ per sq. ft.}$$

$$Q_3 = \text{Observation number } \frac{75}{100} (44)$$

$$= \text{Observation number } 33$$

$$= \$69.81 \text{ per sq. ft.}$$

Interquartile range is $Q_3 - Q_1$, so

$Q_3 - Q_1$ = \$69.81 per sq. ft. - \$41.15 per sq. ft.

= \$28.66 per sq. ft.

Now you know that the median construction cost is \$ 53.29 per square foot and that the interquartile range is \$ 28.66 per square foot. By choosing to calculate the median and interquartile range you have assumed that the costs for your building will not be one of the extremes of the distribution. This assumption allows you to obtain a tighter estimate of the central tendency and variability of costs.

As chairman, you may wish to reassess the data in Table 5-2. You may be able to obtain better estimates by calculating the mean and dispersion for the subset of new libraries that are approximately the same size as the one you propose to build. Or you may wish to calculate the mean and dispersion for the subset of new libraries that are in your geographical region. Your objective is to form a good expectation of costs for the building by using *both* your professional judgment and your statistical skills.

Example 5-1 provides another illustration on the use of the interquartile range. The example, drawn from library administration, illustrates the value of the interquartile range as a quality control tool for effective decision-making.

Additional Comments and Insights on Percentile Range, Interquartile Range, and Quartile Deviation*

1. Percentiles and percentile ranges, including the quartile and inter-quartile range, are easy to calculate and understand.
2. Percentile ranges (i.e., 10th-to-90th percentile range and interquartile range) are more stable and are better indicators of variability than the simple range.
3. Measures of percentile range depend on the degree of concentration of observations at P_{10} and P_{90} or Q_1 or Q_3. They are not reliable if there are gaps in the data around these points.
4. Percentiles and quartiles may be determined in an open-ended dis-

---

* Portions of this text were derived from *Business and Economic Statistics* by W.A. Spurr, L.S. Kellogg, and J.H. Smith. ©1961, Richard D. Irwin, Inc., pages 216-217. Used by permission of the publisher.

Example 5-1. Using Quartile Ranges to Set Work Objectives

The circulation librarian at a college library employs work-study students to shelve book and journal volumes. Materials to be reshelved are picked up from the circulation desk and from tables and carrels. These items are then sorted, placed on carts, and reshelved.

The librarian has noticed that on some days the students pick up books from tables and carrels but neglect those at the circulation desk. On other days, they neglect the tables and carrels.

In an effort to establish quantitative work standards and to minimize day-to-day variation in the number of materials shelved, the librarian decides to use the interquartile range to form work goals. This is accomplished by counting the number of materials picked up from each area over a 16-day period. The data were then ranked from low to high. For example, the fewest number of books collected from all library tables on a given day was 3 and the most was 83.

	Rank Order	
Rank	Tables/Carrels	Circulation Desk
1	3	1
2	6	7
3	7	20
4	8	33
5	12	34
6	13	35
7	16	36
8	17	43
9	26	52
10	39	64
11	47	69
12	58	71
13	61	75
14	71	76
15	76	80
16	83	82

The quartiles can be easily determined since there are 16 observations (ranks). The first quartile, Q_1 occurs at rank 4 because $4/16 = 0.25$. The second quartile, Q_2, which is also the median, occurs at rank 8 because $8/16 = 0.50$. Similarly, Q_3 occurs at rank 12.

With this information, the librarian can establish work objectives, even though crude, for the student employees, such as requiring that between 12 and 58 items be cleared from the tables and 34 to 71 items from the circulation desk. Once the students become accustomed to these new work objectives, the evaluation process can be refined.

tribution or in one where the data may be ranked but not measured quantitatively (i.e., ordinal scale distribution).

Mean Deviation Measures

Unlike the various measures of dispersion that have been presented, there are two popular dispersion measures that include the value of each observation in the set. These are the *standard deviation* and the *variance.*

Each of these measures is based on the mean of the distribution and shows the absolute difference between each score in the distribution and the mean. This difference is called a *deviation.* If the data set's observations are clustered close to the distribution's mean, the mean deviation measures will be small. If there is considerable dispersion from the mean, the measures will be large.

Standard Deviation

Standard Deviation is possibly the most important measure used in dispersion analysis. Its uses and implications are far reaching. An understanding of most of the descriptive techniques discussed so far is necessary to appreciate fully the power and versatility of this statistic. Once the standard deviation for a distribution is calculated, many important facts about the distribution can be inferred.

A significant clue to the meaning of the standard deviation is present in the ordinary meanings of the words used in the term. *Standard* implies that the measurement is a uniform guideline of some kind to the nature of the distribution. The measure is, in fact, a standard because it applies uniformly to all data points in the distribution. *Deviation* accurately implies that the measure relates to the placement of data points in relation to some norm.

The standard deviation tells the investigator how far the typical data point strays from the arithmetic mean of the distribution. The standard deviation is closely related to the shape of the frequency distribution. Small standard deviations occur when data are clustered close to the mean. The corresponding frequency distribution is tall and has short tails, as in Figure 5-1, Distribution A. Large standard deviations occur when data are far from the mean. The corresponding frequency distribution is short and has long tails, as in Figure 5-1, Distribution C.

Standard deviation is the measure most often encountered in expressing how observations are scattered or dispersed about the mean. For a sample, standard deviation is commonly symbolized by lowercase s. For a population, it is symbolized by the lowercase Greek letter sigma, σ. (Please recognize that this letter differs from the Greek letter, capital sigma, Σ, that was used in summation notation.) Recognizing the statistical power of the standard deviation is made easier if you understand the algorithm underlying the construction of the measure.

Consider the data set that consists of n points, labeled as follows: $\{X_1, X_2, \ldots, X_n\}$, and assume that the mean of this data set is $\overline{X}$. The deviation of each data point from the data set's mean is given by the following:

$d_1 = X_1 - \overline{X}$ (deviation of the first data point)
$d_2 = X_2 - \overline{X}$ (deviation of second data point)
$d_n = X_n - \overline{X}$ (deviation of the nth data point)

When the individual deviations are squared, these squares can be added together. This sum is the *sum of squared deviations* from the mean, or, simply, the *sum of squares*. The standard deviation is found by dividing the sum of squares by $n - 1$, and then calculating the square root of this quotient. The algorithm is as follows:

$$s = \sqrt{\frac{\sum_{i=1}^{n} (X_i - \overline{X})^2}{n - 1}} \qquad (5-6)$$

or

$$s = \sqrt{\frac{(X_1 - \overline{X})^2 + (X_2 - \overline{X})^2 + \ldots + (X_n - \overline{X})^2}{n - 1}} \qquad (5-7)$$

To illustrate the calculation of the standard deviation, refer to Table 5-4, which is based on data first presented in Table 4-6. It lists the number of days that each of a library's 10 data terminals were out of service. The reader can verify that the mean for this data is 6. When Formula 5-6 is applied,

Table 5-4. Data Terminal Out-of-Service Days									
Terminal Number	1	2	3	4	5	6	7	8	9	10
Out-of-Service Days	8	9	4	9	8	4	5	3	6	4

$$s = \sqrt{\frac{\sum_{i=1}^{n}(X_i - \bar{X})^2}{n-1}}$$

$$= \sqrt{\frac{\begin{array}{c}(8-6)^2 + (9-6)^2 + (4-6)^2 + (9-6)^2 + (8-6)^2\\(4-6)^2 + (5-6)^2 + (3-6)^2 + (6-6)^2 + (4-6)^2\end{array}}{10-1}}$$

$$= \sqrt{\frac{\begin{array}{c}(2)^2 + (3)^2 + (2)^2 + (3)^2 + (2)^2 +\\(-2)^2 + (-1)^2 + (-3)^2 + (0)^2 + (-2)^2\end{array}}{9}}$$

$$= \sqrt{\frac{4+9+4+9+4+4+1+9+0+4}{10-1}}$$

$$= \sqrt{\frac{48}{9}}$$

$$= \frac{6.928}{3}$$

$$= 2.31 \text{ days}$$

The standard deviation can also be calculated for grouped data. If the data are grouped, and if the interval midpoints are represented by M_1, M_2, ... , M_k, each occurring with a frequency of $f_1, f_2, ... , f_k$, then the sample's standard deviation is given by

$$s = \sqrt{\frac{\sum_{i=1}^{n}(M_i - \bar{X})^2 f_i}{n-1}} \qquad (5-8)$$

where $n = f_1 + f_2 + f_3 + ... + f_n$, or $\sum f_i$. Without using the sigma notation, Formula 5-8 can be expressed as

$$s = \sqrt{\frac{(M_1 - \bar{X})^2 f_1 + (M_2 - \bar{X})^2 f_2 + ... + (M_n - \bar{X})^2 f_n}{(f_1 + f_2 + ... + f_n - 1)}} \qquad (5-9)$$

To illustrate the use of Formula 5-9, let us use data from Table 5-5,

Table 5-5. Grouped Data on Copyright Dates of Books (n = 93)

Class	Frequency f	Midpoint M
55-58	8	56.5
59-62	13	60.5
63-66	14	64.5
67-70	16	68.5
71-74	16	72.5
75-78	10	76.5
79-82	9	80.5
83-86	7	84.5
	n = 93	

which shows the copyright dates for books in a hypothetical collection. The average copyright year is 1969.7. For convenience, and with no loss in precision, we will use 69.7. The squared deviations are calculated in the table, then apply Formula 5-8:

$$s = \sqrt{\frac{\sum_{i=1}^{n} (M_i - \bar{X})^2 f_i}{n-1}}$$

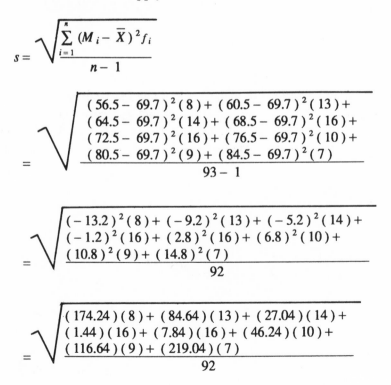

$$= \sqrt{\frac{\begin{array}{l}(56.5 - 69.7)^2(8) + (60.5 - 69.7)^2(13) + \\ (64.5 - 69.7)^2(14) + (68.5 - 69.7)^2(16) + \\ (72.5 - 69.7)^2(16) + (76.5 - 69.7)^2(10) + \\ (80.5 - 69.7)^2(9) + (84.5 - 69.7)^2(7)\end{array}}{93 - 1}}$$

$$= \sqrt{\frac{\begin{array}{l}(-13.2)^2(8) + (-9.2)^2(13) + (-5.2)^2(14) + \\ (-1.2)^2(16) + (2.8)^2(16) + (6.8)^2(10) + \\ (10.8)^2(9) + (14.8)^2(7)\end{array}}{92}}$$

$$= \sqrt{\frac{\begin{array}{l}(174.24)(8) + (84.64)(13) + (27.04)(14) + \\ (1.44)(16) + (7.84)(16) + (46.24)(10) + \\ (116.64)(9) + (219.04)(7)\end{array}}{92}}$$

$$= \sqrt{\frac{\begin{array}{l}1393.92 + 1100.32 + 378.56 + 23.04 + \\ 125.44 + 462.40 + 1049.76 + 1533.28\end{array}}{92}}$$

$$= \sqrt{\frac{6066.72}{92}}$$

$$= \sqrt{65.94}$$

$$= 8.12 \text{ years}$$

The student familiar with the standard deviation probably has seen formulas similar to 5-6 and 5-8, but with the divisor n rather than $n - 1$. This is because of the difference between calculating the standard deviation for a sample as opposed to a population. The theoretical reason for this distinction is not important in the practical use of the standard deviation. The reader needs to know that the divisor $n - 1$ produces a more accurate result in estimating the population value from a sample's standard deviation. The experienced student may also have encountered the term *variance* in conjunction with standard deviations. Variance is the square of the standard deviation, s^2, and is important in inferential statistics and other advanced applications.

Notice that the standard deviation and the variance are sensitive to the units of measurement. Refer again to Table 5-4, where the amount of time, X, each computer terminal is out of service is measured in days. If this time were measured in hours instead of days, a different value for the variance would be obtained. Table 5-6 shows the number of hours the terminals were out of service. When Formula 5-6 is applied,

$$s = \sqrt{\frac{\sum_{i=1}^{n} (X_i - \overline{X})^2}{n - 1}}$$

$$= \sqrt{\frac{\begin{array}{l}(192 - 144)^2 + (216 - 144)^2 + (96 - 144)^2 + \\ (216 - 144)^2 + (192 - 144)^2 + (96 - 144)^2 + \\ (120 - 144)^2 + (72 - 144)^2 + (144 - 144)^2 + \\ (96 - 144)^2\end{array}}{10 - 1}}$$

Table 5-6. Standard Deviation for Data Terminal Out-of-Service Hours

Terminal Number	Observation X (hours)	Mean $\overline{X}$	Deviation $X - \overline{X}$	Squared Deviation $(X - \overline{X})^2$
1	192	144	48	2304
2	216	144	72	5184
3	96	144	-48	2304
4	216	144	72	5184
5	192	144	48	2304
6	96	144	-48	2304
7	120	144	-24	576
8	72	144	-72	5184
9	144	144	0	0
10	96	144	-48	2304
				Sum: 27,648

Source: Table 4-5

$$= \sqrt{\frac{(48)^2 + (72)^2 + (-48)^2 + (92)^2 + (48)^2 + (-48)^2 + (-24)^2 + (-72)^2 + (0)^2 + (-48)^2}{9}}$$

$$= \sqrt{\frac{2304 + 5184 + 2304 + 5184 + 2304 + 2304 + 576 + 5184 + 0 + 2304}{9}}$$

$$= \sqrt{\frac{27,648}{9}}$$

$$= \sqrt{3072}$$

$$= 55.4 \text{ hours}$$

Notice that the standard deviation for downtime in hours is 24 times larger than the standard deviation for downtime in days. When every element of a data set is multiplied by a constant, the standard deviation is also multiplied by the same constant and the variance is multiplied by the square of the constant. The point to remember is the distinction between the measure of variability, s, and the actual variability of the data. The data in Table 5-4 and Table 5-6 have the same variability.

This is because they present the *same* data. However, because these data are measured in different *units*, their measures of variability, s, are different.

The reader may notice that columns have been added in Table 5-6 to show the mean, the deviation of each observation from the mean, and the square of the deviation from the mean. These additional columns facilitate computation of the standard deviation, as seen in the text.

Using the Standard Deviation to Describe Data

The standard deviation has a very definite relationship to the shape of a distribution's curve. This relationship was first described by the Russian mathematician P. L. Chebyshev.

Chebyshev's Theorem

Chebyshev's Theorem states that for any set of data, and for any selected number of standard deviations, k, the equation $1/k^2$ equals the proportion of data beyond k standard deviations of the mean. A corollary to the theorem is the equation $1 - (1/k^2)$, which yields the minimum proportion of the data that lie within k standard deviations of the mean. These relationships are true for distributions of both populations and samples.

For example, within 1.5 standard deviations from the mean lies $1 - 1/(1.5^2)$, or 0.556, which is 55.6% of the data. Therefore, in *any* distribution at least 55.6% of the data lies within 1.5 standard deviations on either side of the mean. If $k = 2$, then $1 - 1/(2^2) = 0.75$, or 75% of the data in any distribution is within 2 standard deviations of the mean. Equally important is that not more than 44.4% of the data in the first example (100% - 55.6%) and 25% in the second example (100% - 25%) of the data lie beyond 1.5 and 2 standard deviations, respectively.

For example, refer again to the data in Table 5-3. The mean for these data is 58.2, and the standard deviation is 25.2. The interested student may wish to calculate independently the mean and standard deviation. Chebyshev's Theorem states that at least 55.6% of the data will liewithin 1.5 standard deviations on either side of the mean. In other words, at least 55.6% of the data will lie in the range [58.2 ± (1.5)(25.2)], which is [20.4, 96.0] . As an aside for the student who is not familiar with the above notation, the symbol ± (read plus or minus) means that both addition and subtraction operations are to be performed with the number sets. Hence, 58.2 and 37.8 are added, to obtain 96.0, and then their difference is determined, which is 20.4.

In Table 5-3, there are 38 data points which are greater than 20.4 and less than 96.0. Since there is a total of 44 data points, 38/44 = 86.4% of the data lies within plus or minus 1.5 standard deviations. Chebyshev's Theorem is confirmed.

Chebyshev's Theorem also predicts that at least 75% of the data will lie within plus or minus 2 standard deviations. In Table 5-3 this is the range $[58.2 \pm (2)(25.2)] = (7.8, 108.6)$. There are 40 data points which are greater than 7.8 and less than 108.6. Since there is a total of 44 data points, 40/44 = 90.1% of the data lies within plus or minus 2 standard deviations. Chebyshev's Theorem is again confirmed.

Remember that Chebyshev's Theorem yields the *minimum* proportion of data within k standard deviations from the mean. As for the data in Table 5-3, the value returned by $1 - (1/k^2)$ falls on the conservative side because the theorem is designed to work with *any* set of data. It even applies to data which have very erratic or irregular curves. In more regular, mound-shaped distributions, such as those in Figure 5-1, estimates of proportions can be made with great accuracy and confidence. Distributions like those in Figure 5-1 are called *normal distributions*. In normal distribution, the interval within 1 standard deviation on either side of the mean invariably contains 68% of all data points. Within 1.5 standard deviations, 86.6% can be found. Within 2 standard deviations, 95% of the data can be found. Finally, 99.7%, or virtually all the data, can be found within 3 standard deviations.

Usually, the librarian can obtain a good estimate of the shape of a distribution by assuming that it is nearly normal. For example, the data in Table 5-3 and depicted in Figure 5-4 are irregular and wide-tailed. Nonetheless, approximately 86.6% of the data falls within 1.5 standard deviations, and approximately 95.4% of the data falls within 2 standard deviations.

Distance from Mean	Percent of Data	
	Normal Distribution	Distribution in Table 5-3
± 1.5 standard deviation	86.6%	86.4%
± 2.0 standard deviation	95.4	90.1
± 3.0 standard deviation	99.7	100.0

Often, statistical reports give only numerical values for means and standard deviations. The value of Chebyshev's Theorem and the normal distribution is that the statistical consumer can use the reported standard deviation and mean to build a mental picture of the frequency distribution.

Estimating the Standard Deviation

The standard deviation for a mound-shaped distribution can be estimated easily and accurately. This is because virtually all the data in a mound-shaped distribution are within 3 standard deviations of the mean. The heuristic is that the range of a set of data is approximately 4 to 6 times the standard deviation. The multiple of 4 provides a good estimate for a data set containing a small number of observations, while 6 is an appropriate multiple for a larger number of observations.

Assume, for example, that members of a library consortium report a mound-shaped distribution of collection sizes from a low score of 4700 volumes to a high of 153,000 volumes. Remember that 99.7% of the data will be contained within 3 standard deviations of the mean, or, mathematically, within the interval expressed by $\overline{X} - 3s$ to $\overline{X} + 3s$. The total span of this interval is $6s$. Hence,

$6s \approx 153,000 - 4700$

or

$6s \approx 148,300$

so

$$s \approx \frac{148,300}{6} \text{ or } 24,717 \text{ volumes}$$

This estimate of the standard deviation in this example reveals that considerable data are dispersed. Therefore, the arithmetic mean would not be a useful measure in describing these data.

Additional Comments and Insights on the Standard Deviation*

1. The standard deviation is a widely used measure of dispersion.
2. The standard deviation reflects the shape of the distribution.
3. The standard deviation uses the values of all scores in its computation. It is not dependent on the rankings of the scores. The measure is sensitive to extreme values, and, since all scores are used, an extreme point will inflate the standard deviation.

---

* Portions of this text were derived from *Business and Economic Statistics* by W.A. Spurr, L.S. Kellogg, and J.H. Smith. ©1961, Richard D. Irwin, Inc., page 217. Used by permisssion of the publisher.

4. The standard deviation should not be used if there are only a few data points.

5. In a normal distribution, the interval $\overline{X} - s$ to $\overline{X} + s$, which is 1 standard deviation of the mean, contains 68% of the data. Similarly, the interval $\overline{X} - 2s$ to $\overline{X} + 2s$, which is 2 standard deviations of the mean, contains 95% of the data. Finally, the interval $\overline{X} - 3s$ to $\overline{X} + 3s$, which is 3 deviations of the mean, contains 99.7% of the data.

Coefficient of Variation

It is often useful to compare the amount of variation in two distributions. For instance, a librarian may be interested in how the variation in operating expenses of his or her library compares to the variation in similar libraries. The librarian's first intuition may be to form the ratio:

$$\frac{s \text{ (operating expense Library A)}}{s \text{ (operating expense Library B)}}$$

However, a simple ratio of standard deviations is meaningless. This is because the simple ratio can be inflated or deflated simply by changing the units in which operating expenses (thousands of dollars, dollars, cents) are measured. Recall the earlier discussion about Table 5-4 and Table 5-5 data. When downtime was measured in hours rather than days, the standard deviation increased by a ratio of 24. Thus the ratio

$$\frac{s \text{ (downtime in hours)}}{s \text{ (downtime in days)}} = 24$$

even though the variability of the data, whether measured in hours or days, is constant.

To make sure that a comparison of standard deviations is not biased by differences in the magnitude of the values in the two data sets, the librarian should calculate the *coefficient of variation*, V. The coefficient of variation is the ratio of a distribution's standard deviation to its mean times 100.

$$V = \frac{100 \, s}{\overline{X}} \tag{5-10}$$

Refer again to Tables 5-3 and 5-4.

$$\frac{V \ (\text{downtime in hours})}{V \ (\text{downtime in days})} = \frac{100 \ (\frac{55.4}{144})}{100 \ (\frac{2.31}{6})}$$

$$= \frac{38.5\%}{38.5\%}$$

$$= 1$$

The ratio of coefficients of variation equals 1. This is because the distribution has the same variability whether it is measured in hours or in days.

The coefficient of variation requires only that both data sets be measured in ratio scale. That is, both distributions must be measured with scales that have absolute zero points. Accordingly, the coefficient of variation cannot be used to compare distributions of intelligence or achievement scores. This is because educational and psychological scales have no absolute zero point.

The coefficient of variation is used to adjust for size differentials and to prevent incorrect assumptions that may arise from focusing on the standard deviation alone. Suppose the standard deviation in the budget for a multibranch library has been increasing over the past three years:

Year	Mean Budget of All Branches	Standard Deviation	Coefficient of Variation
Year 3	$1,000,000	$90,000	9.0%
Year 2	893,000	85,759	9.6
Year 1	850,000	87,500	10.3

While the standard deviation shows that the disparity among the branches has grown, the coefficient of variation correctly shows that any inequity has decreased over the period. The coefficient of variation adjusts for the increase in standard deviation due to the growth in the overall mean budget for all the branches.

In the above example, the coefficient of variation can be used to measure the percent of change in variation from Year 1 through Year 3. The rate of decrease in budgetary inequity, as expressed by the coefficient of variation for Year 1 to Year 2, is (10.3% - 9.6%)/10.3% = .068, or about 7%. Inequity decrease from Year 2 to Year 3 is (9.6% - 9.0%)/9.6% = .062, or slightly over 6%.

The librarian will encounter the coefficient of variation in many areas. In financial analysis, the standard deviation of return on a stock is used to calculate a measurement of the stock's risk. In performance assessment, the standard deviation can be used to compare the production consistency of machines or people. For example, suppose two librarians each performs online literature searches. Each month, for six months, the number of searches completed is recorded. The mean and standard deviations for these data are as follows:

Librarian	Mean Number of Searches per Month	Standard Deviation	Coefficient of Variation
A	26	4.70	18.1%
B	91	11.75	12.9%

Librarian B's standard deviation shows greater absolute variation in output than does Librarian A's standard deviation: 11.75 searches vs. 4.70 searches. However, Librarian B performs substantially more searches than Librarian A. This output disparity makes the standard deviation an unreliable measure for interpreting Librarian B's output variation compared to Librarian A's. The coefficient of variation overcomes this disparity and shows that Librarian B exhibits less relative variation than does Librarian A, 12.9% vs. 18.1%.

Measure of Skewness

The purpose of descriptive statistics is to describe data with numbers and graphs and to reveal characteristics and trends in data. In a previous section, shapes of distributions were estimated with the standard deviation. In this and the following section, shapes and trends of distributions are considered in greater detail.

Symmetrical Distributions

Frequency distributions are either *symmetrical* or *skewed* (asymmetric). A *symmetrical* frequency distribution is a distribution in which the mean equals the median. Scores are concentrated at the center of the distribution on the horizontal axis. Classes that are equal distances on opposite sides of the center have equal frequencies. In a histogram or curve representing a distribution, symmetry can be demonstrated by drawing a vertical line through the peak of the curve perpendicular to the horizontal axis. This line then divides the curve into two equal parts, each of which is the mirror image of the other. A symmetrical distribution can be folded in half, perpendicular to the horizontal axis, and the

Figures 5-4A, B, and C. Common symmetrical distributions

two shapes will be identical. Figures 5-4A, B, and C illustrate a variety of symmetrical distributions often encountered.

Figure 5-4A depicts a frequency distribution that approximates the *normal* distribution. This "bell-shaped" distribution is repeatedly used in inferential statistics. Figure 5-4B is a rectangular distribution in which all the scores occur with the same frequency. Figure 5-4C is a unimodal symmetrical distribution.

Asymmetrical or Skewed Distributions

An asymmetrical distribution is skewed either to the right, called *positively skewed*, or to the left, called *negatively skewed*. In both cases, the distribution's mean does not equal its median. Figures 5-5A and 5-5B show two skewed distributions. Figure 5-5A depicts a distribution skewed to the right (positively). Figure 5-5B depicts a distribution skewed to the left (negatively).

In a skewed distribution, the mode always occurs at the highest peak of the curve. In a positively skewed distribution, the sequence of the three measures of central tendency, from left to right, is mode, median, and mean. In a negatively skewed distribution, the sequence of the three measures of central tendency from left to right, is mean, median, and mode. Notice that, in a negatively skewed distribution, the measures occur in alphabetical order. Notice also, from Figures 5-5A and 5-5B, that in a skewed distribution, the median is always closer to the mean than to the mode, just as the words *median* and *mean* are closer than the words *median* and *mode* in the dictionary. Since the mode is the highest point in the curve, the other two measures are easy to identify.

The idea of skewness is useful, because it provides additional information about the distribution that is not characterized by either the distribution's mean or standard deviation. "Skewness" means that the

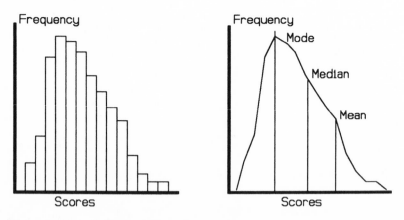

Figure 5-5A. A distribution with positive skew

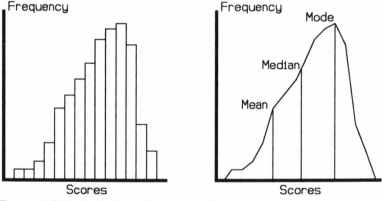

Figure 5-5B. A distribution with negative skew

data in a distribution are unevenly distributed and that the distribution tends toward either the high or the low extreme. Examples of distributions that are skewed left are seen in a distribution of students' scores for an easy examination, where most students achieved near the maximum and few obtain low scores. Left or negatively skewed distributions are also characteristic in distributions of the time required to sell slow inventory turnover items such as homes, heavy equipment, and expensive jewelry. Very few of these items sell quickly, and the majority are retained in inventory for some time. Examples of distributions that are positively skewed are those that depict products where rapid inventory turnover is characteristic, as in a distribution of the number of days required to sell fresh produce or other perishables.

J-Distributions

Highly skewed distributions are *J-distributions*, because the highest frequencies occur in the first or last category. Graphically, their curve resembles either the letter *J* or its mirror image, a *reversed-J*. Distributions of this type do not adapt well to summary descriptions. Figures 5-6A and B illustrate both of these skewed distributions.

For example, a distribution of library fund-raising contributions produces a reverse J-curve, as in Figure 5-6A. This is because most contributions are small while a few are extremely generous. Additional examples of reverse J-curves are the distribution of library card holders, categorized by the person's age, or the distribution of the value of prizes

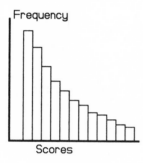 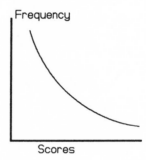

Figure 5-6A. A reverse J-distribution

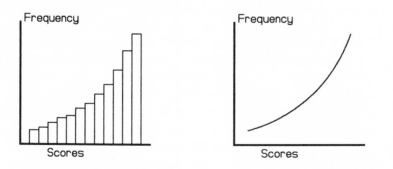

Figure 5-6B. A J-distribution

in a sweepstakes or contest, or the distribution of users of a library service, where most clientele are infrequent users and the repeat users form the distribution's tail, or a distribution of employee absences, since most employees are not absent but a few are absent many days. J-distributions, as shown in Figure 5-6B, are less often encountered in the library environment. Examples of *J*-distributions, however, are the total number of scientific and technical journals published in the United States over the past 200 years or the growth of total library resource expenditures over the past 20 years.

Pareto's 80/20 Rule

Distributions that produce J-curves or reverse J-curves tend to give credence to a general observation called the *80/20 Rule* or *Pareto's Rule*. Pareto, a nineteenth-century Italian economist, examined the distribution of wealth in Italy and discovered that 80% of it was in the ownership of only 20% of the population. Subsequently, this 80/20 Rule has been found to apply across a vast range of situations. In almost every business, 80% of turnover is due to just 20% of the product range. Similarly, 80% of transactions will come from only 20% of the customers. In bibliometric studies of journals, 80% of the citations are due to a core of 20% of the titles. A user study of videocassette circulation might yield the result that 80% of the circulation is due to 20% of those who use the service.

U-Distributions

Figure 5-7 depicts a U-distribution. In a U-distribution, a high number of frequencies occurs in the first and last categories and few in the

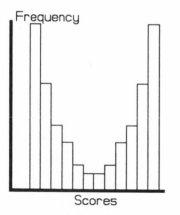
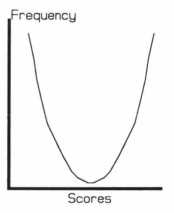

Figures 5-7. A U-distribution

middle categories. An example of a U distribution is the ages of patients admitted to a short-term acute care hospital. Children and seniors are more likely to be treated in such a facility more often than persons in the central age groupings. Cost curves for activities that are subject to economies and diseconomies of scale are U-shaped. The average cost per unit of a product or service ordinarily decreases as outputs increase. In a library, for example, staff specialization, new equipment, and simplified procedures contribute to reducing the cost per unit of service. As staff and physical plant grow to accommodate outputs, costs again begin to rise more quickly than productivity. The diseconomies of scale due to a growth in operations beyond the most favorable size result in the rise of the curve.

Economies and Diseconomies of Scale

The reference librarian assigned to conduct online literature searches, or the clerk who primarily photocopies pages and refiles books, are staff specialists in some special and large public libraries. Equipment in these libraries often includes specialized computer terminals for cataloging. These libraries also have automated systems for circulation, card catalog, word processing, statistics, budget analysis, invoicing, and other specialized library tasks. Staff specialization permits a wide variety of services, but each increases the library's "scale of plant," resulting in more complexity. More staff time is assigned to coordinate, assist, interface, and monitor operations. Hence, less staff time is available to produce services. Lines of communication become less direct, the number of meetings increases, and training for new staff becomes more difficult. The necessity for coordinating staff increases the cost of each unit of library service. This additional cost causes the library's total cost curve to incline upward. The business side of library administration must be sensitive to the trends identified by these distributions.

Summary of Critical Concepts

1. *Measures of dispersion* or *measures of variability* describe the dispersion, or spread, of data about a central point.
2. The most common *measures of dispersion* are the *range* and *standard deviation*.

3. *Range* is the difference between the largest and smallest values in a data set. Range is sensitive to extreme scores.

4. A *deviation* is the distance between any measurement in a set of data and the mean of the set. *Standard deviation* is an average of the size or magnitude of all squared deviations for a set of data. Standard deviation governs the shape of distributions. The larger the value of the group's standard deviation, the more spread out the observations.

5. The *coefficient of variation* is a relative measure of dispersion. It expresses the standard deviation as a percent of the mean. Its is used to compare distributions that reflect different time periods or that are expressed in different units, such as feet and pounds. A constraint on the use of this measure is that the variables must have a true "zero point." That is, they must be expressed in ratio scale measure.

6. *Measures of skewness* describe a data set as symmetrical or asymmetrical about a central point.

7. A *symmetrical frequency distribution* is one in which the mean equals the median. Nonsymmetrical distributions are called *asymmetrical* or *skewed*. Recognition and analysis of a distribution's skewness provides additional information about the distribution that is not characterized by its mean or standard deviation.

8. A distribution skewed to the right is *positively skewed*. One skewed to the left is *negatively skewed*. In both cases, the distribution's mean does not equal its median.

9. Highly skewed distributions are sometimes called *J-distributions* or *reverse-J distributions*. Data that produce highly skewed distributions give credence to a general observation known as the 80/20 Rule or Pareto's Rule. This rule states that 80% of total activity is due to 20% of those elements that cause the activity.

10. Cost curves for activities that are subject to *economies and diseconomies of scale* tend to be U-shaped. Such distributions suggest that the average "cost per unit" of a product or service decreases as the scale of operation increases to produce more outputs. In academic, special, and large public libraries, an increased scale of operations is achieved through staff specialization for a high division of labor, specialized equipment, and the systematic reduction of complex processes into simple repetitive operations. Each efficiency contributes to reducing library costs per unit of service. At a certain point, however, costs begin to rise more quickly than productivity. This is caused by staff and physical plant increases perceived by management as needed to accomplish production. This further growth beyond the most favorable point results in diseconomies expressed in the rising of the library's cost curve.

Key Terms

Coefficient of Variation. A relative measure of dispersion which expresses the standard deviation as a percent of the mean. It is useful for comparing the variability of two or more data sets or for comparing two data sets of widely varying magnitudes. This measure is applicable only in variables that are measured in ratio interval scale.

Deviation. The difference between a given score and the mean of the distribution to which it belongs, represented mathematically by $(X - \bar{X})$.

Dispersion (Variability). The amount of variation in a data set. Dispersion measures are range, interquartile range, standard deviation, and variance.

80/20 Rule or *Pareto's Rule.* The common observation that 80 percent of turnover can be attributed to 20 percent of products or clientele.

Interquartile Range. Measure of dispersion or variability. It is the difference between the third quartile and the first quartile. Stated mathematically, $Q_3 - Q_1$.

Quartile. One of four data points, each representing an increment of 25% of the scores in a data set.

Range. For ungrouped data, the difference between the largest and smallest numbers in a data set. For example, if the largest number in a data set is 20 and the smallest number is 5, Range = 20 - 5, or 15. The range is determined by the high and low observations in the data set and is unaffected by the total number of observations. For grouped data, the range is the difference between the upper class limit of the highest class and the value of the lower class limit of the smallest class. For example, if the highest class is \$50–\$59.99 and the smallest class is \$10–\$19.99, then the range is $R = \$60 - \$10$, or \$50. Notice that the highest class is rounded to the nearest dollar.

Skew. Lack of symmetry in a frequency distribution. Negative skew, or skew to the left, occurs in a frequency distribution whose scores are concentrated at the positive end of the distribution's tail. An example is the distribution of students' scores on an easy test. Few score low, and most score near the maximum. Positive skew, or skew to the right, occurs in a frequency distribution whose scores are concentrated at the low end of the scale. An example is the distribution of students' scores on a very difficult test, where most students score low and few score high.

Standard Deviation. Standard deviation is used to measure the dispersion or spread of data in the units of the original data. The square of the standard deviation is the variance.

Symmetrical Distribution. A distribution in which the mean and median equal each other. Geometrically, in a curve, histogram, or polygon representing a distribution, symmetry can be shown by drawing a vertical line through the peak of the curve perpendicular to the horizontal axis. This line divides the figure into two equal parts, each of which is the mirror image of the other.

Self-Assessment Quiz

True or False 1.   A dispersion measure such as the standard deviation identifies how well central tendency measures describe a data set.

True or False 2.   Range is the most popular example measure of dispersion.

True or False 3.   It is not possible to determine a distribution's range if the distribution contains an open interval.

True or False 4.   In a symmetrical distribution, the mean and median are equal.

True or False 5.   The mean lies to the right of the mode if a distribution is positively skewed.

True or False 6.   Given the data {15, 4, 26, 13, 3}, the range is 26.

True or False 7.   Percentiles divide a data set into 10 equal parts.

True or False 8.   The standard deviation is a measure that describes how far a specific observation in a data set lies from the mean.

True or False 9.   It is possible to calculate the standard deviation of a data set if it has an open-ended interval.

True or False 10.   A distribution's standard deviation considers the value of each data point.

True or False 11.   An advantage of the quartile deviation is that it is not sensitive to extreme scores.

True or False 12.   The standard deviation of {101, 102, 103} is greater than that of {1, 2, 3}.

True or False 13.   The data {1, 5, 9} shows more variability than the data {101, 106, 111}.

True or False 14.   Quartiles have the same width.

True or False 15.   If two distributions have the same mean and standard deviation, each distribution must look exactly alike.

True or False 16.   If $s = 0$ in a distribution, the distribution's scores are the same.

True or False 17.   If two distributions have identical means and medians, they still may differ.

True or False 18.   The standard deviation for a dataset is always less than the mean.

Answers

1. True. Measures of dispersion tell the statistics consumer how far data are from the measure of central tendency.

2. False. Standard deviation is the most popular dispersion measure.

3. True. When a distribution contains open intervals, no range can be calculated because X_H or X_L are not known.

4. True. In a symmetrical distribution, the average value equals the middle value.

5. True. In a positive skewed curve, the order, from left to right, is mode, median, mean.

6. False. Range is the difference between the largest value and the smallest value of the data set. Hence $R = 26 - 3$, or 23.

7. False. Percentiles ($P_1, P_2, \ldots, P_{99}$) divide a distribution into 100 equal parts.

8. True. The standard deviation tells the investigator how far the typical or average data point strays from the mean.

9. False. The midpoint of the interval cannot be determined for use in the calculation.

10. True. $s = \sqrt{\dfrac{\sum\limits_{i=1}^{n} (X_i - \bar{X})^2}{n-1}}$

11. True. The interquartile range focuses on the center 50 percent of the data.

12. False. The standard deviation of both sets is the same.

13. False. The deviations from the mean are less for the first data set than for the second.

14. False. The proportion of data in each quartile must be 25%, but the width may not be the same for each.

15. False. The two distributions could have different skewness.

16. True. When the standard deviation is equal to zero, there is no variability in the data. In such a distribution, all values are identical.

17. True. The two distributions may differ in the degree of dispersion or skew of the data.
18. False. Consider, for example, a dataset such as {0, 100} where the mean is 50 and the standard deviation is 70.7.

Discussion Questions and Problems

1. Contrast the advantages and disadvantages of the range as a measure of dispersion with the interquartile range. Give examples of numerical distributions where each is a superior measure of variability.
2. Using the set of numerals {0, 1, 2, ... , 9}, make up a data set of any seven numbers. Repetition is permitted. Calculate the mode, median, and mean. For convenience, select data values so that the various central tendency measures are whole numbers.
   a. Determine whether the deviations of each of your numbers in the set from the mean of the set sum to zero.
   b. Determine whether the deviations of each number from the median sum to zero.
   c. Determine whether the deviations of each number from the mode sum to zero.
3. The mean of a skewed distribution is 25 and the mode is 15. Estimate the median and explain your method.
4. Using the data {0, 1, 2, 3, 4, 5, 6, 7, 8, 9},
   a. construct a distribution of five elements (repeats pemitted), that has the largest variance possible.
   b. construct a distribution of five elements (repeats pemitted), that has the smallest variance possible.
5. The cataloger reviewed the work of five clerks. The errors for each was {2, 0, 0, 1, 2}. Determine and interpret the standard deviation.
6. What is the effect of the following on the range, standard deviation, and variance?
   a. Increase each score by 10 points.
   b. Increase each score by 10%.
   c. Decrease each score by 10 points.
   d. Decrease each score by 10%.
7. Cite examples of data sets (complete with numbers) where its standard deviation would tend to exaggerate the amount of variation present.
8. The median is a common measure of central tendency in skewed distributions such as income. In government reports on education levels, however, the mean is used. Explain the merits of this choice.

9. The number of sick days reported for a library's staff over a 2-year period were as follows:

First Year ($n = 26$)

3	4	10	2	7	3	1	10	0	11	11	2	7
6	5	3	10	3	7	6	8	6	5	4	3	6

Second Year (n = 31)

5	2	7	5	4	0	4	4	5	3	4	7	4
2	7	4	2	5	0	4	5	3	7	3	0	7
3	6	3	1	1								

  a. Determine the mean, standard deviation, and coefficient of variation for the First Year and Second Year data. What does the coefficient of variation reveal about the two distributions?
  b. In the Second Year, the library's trustees instituted a policy about paid sick days. Is there any evidence of its effect?
10. During 1-month the staff at an association's library returned 120 long-distance telephone calls to members seeking information.

Length of Reference Call (in Minutes)	Number of Calls
0 and under 2	49
2 and under 4	39
4 and under 6	15
6 and under 8	5
8 and under 10	4
10 and under 12	4
12 and under 14	2
14 and under 16	0
16 and under 18	1
18 and under 20	1

  a. Plot the distribution's histogram and comment on its shape.
  b. Determine the mean, the median, and the skew. Does the mean or the median better characterize the distribution's average?
  c. Determine the standard deviation and variance. Identify the units for the standard deviation and for the variance.
  d. Determine the interquartile range.
  e. Using Chebyshev's Theorem, at least how many values should lie between one and one half standard deviations of the mean? If the distribution is approximately normal, how many values should lie in this interval? Identify the points $(\overline{X} - 1.5s)$ and $(\overline{X} + 1.5s)$. What percent of observations lies within this interval?
  f. Based on your calculations in (c) through (e), is the interquartile

range or the standard deviation a better measure of the dispersion of this data set? Explain.

11. Explain why a distribution's standard deviation is always smaller than its range.

12. A library consortium recently surveyed its 50 member libraries to determine the days of downtime of each library's computer system during the previous 90 days. Member responses were as follows:

Days of Downtime	Frequency
0	6
1	7
2	10
3	14
4	7
5	3
6	2
7	1

a. Plot the distribution's histogram and comment on its shape.

b. Compute the mean and standard deviation. Are these good measures of central tendency and dispersion? Explain.

c. Your out-of-state librarian colleague told you that 12 members in his or her library's consortium reported downtimes between 0 and 12 days for a similar 90-day period. Estimate this standard deviation and discuss the variation between the two distributions.

13. For some time you have wondered if your library's 21-day loan period is ideal. You and your colleague, a librarian at a similar-size library with a 14-day circulation period, decide to examine 75 recently circulated items. Your frequency distribution is show below.

Days	Circulation Period 21-Day Loan	Circulation Period 14-Day Loan
0–2	2	3
3–5	3	5
6–8	4	8
9–11	5	16
12–14	7	19
15–17	9	12
18–20	18	7
21–23	16	2
24–26	8	2
27–29	2	1
30–32	1	0

a. Plot a histogram for each distribution. Comment on the shape of each histogram.

b. For each distribution, determine the mean, median, and standard deviation. For each distribution, do you expect the mean or the median to be a better measure of central tendency? Explain.

c. Calculate and explain each distribution's coefficient of variation.

d. Which distribution is more desirable in terms of maximizing each library's collection turnover rate? Why?

e. What is the effect on the library's inventory if books circulate for too long?

f. Discuss the effect on the library's inventory of limiting the number of items that may be checked out to a borrower on a single visit.

14. A state library association is interested in studying the hours of service for all public libraries in the state (n = 401). It surveyed all institutions and then developed the following frequency distribution that summarizes library hours of service per week:

Hours Open per Week	Frequency
1–5	3
6–10	25
11–15	31
16–20	56
21–25	64
26–30	58
31–35	33
36–40	39
41–45	21
46–50	29
51–55	17
56–60	17
61–65	8

a. Plot both a histogram and a "less than" cumulative frequency distribution. Comment on the shape of the histogram.

b. Determine the mean, median, range, and standard deviation for the distribution.

c. Determine and explain the meaning of the 80th percentile, P_{80}.

d. Determine the percentile, compared with other public libraries, for the institution that is open 50 hours per week.

15. In the hypothetical data below, 18 public libraries reported their hours of weekly service as

20	27	50	41	36	54	39	61	42
40	40	13	55	24	41	60	20	20

   a. Determine the mean, median, range, and standard deviation for this system of libraries.
   b. Characterize the variation of this system in regard to those libraries described in Problem 14, of which these libraries are a part.
16. A corporate library recently installed a new telephone system. Among its many features is software that monitors variables for each telephone such as the number dialed and the duration of each outgoing call.

   The librarian wishes to analyze telephone use since many of the library staff work in private offices and since all staff have telephone access. To accomplish this, the librarian collected data on the telephone activity of each of the 28 staff members for the first four months the new system was in operation. The 112 observations were grouped and the data are as follows

Minutes on Phone Per Month	Number of Employees
0	20
60	37
120	23
180	16
240	10
300	3
360	2
420	0
480	1

   The data range from one staff member who placed a 1-minute outgoing call during a single month to a staff member who placed calls totaling 510 minutes for a single month. The distribution's mean is 110.4 and its standard deviation is 92.73.
   a. Identify the modal class and, without calculation, estimate the distribution's median.
   b. Identify any extreme values.
   c. Identify the distribution's skew as positive or negative.
   d. Identify the number of staff whose duration of calls is greater than two standard deviations above the mean.
   e. If this library's reference services are provided principally to clientele who telephone the library, comment on the total number of hours of staff time that may be lost in "personal" telephone calls.
17. The director of a medium-size academic library asked the head of

technical services to study the costs associated with providing document delivery services. In order to determine the average costs for a journal article, the document delivery specialist made a tabulation of the length of 306 library science articles lent over a 1-week period. These data are tabulated as follows:

Pages	Frequency	Pages	Frequency	Pages	Frequency
1	0	11	12	21	1
2	8	12	17	22	4
3	19	13	9	23	1
4	20	14	10	24	3
5	35	15	11	25	1
6	31	16	6	26	2
7	29	17	4	27	1
8	31	18	2	28	0
9	26	19	2	29	0
10	18	20	2	30	1

  a. Construct an ungrouped frequency distribution. Also construct a grouped frequency distribution using 6 classes.

  b. Determine the ungrouped mean and median. Also determine the grouped mean and median.

  c. Determine the range and ungrouped standard deviation. Determine the grouped standard deviation.

  d. Compare and interpret the differences between the ungrouped and grouped statistics.

  e. Interpret the standard deviation and mean.

18. Give 2 library examples, other than those in the text, of each of the following:

  a. rectangular distribution (Figure 5-4B)

  b. unimodal symmetrical distribution (Figure 5-4C)

  c. reverse J and J-distribution (Figure 5-6)

  d. U-distribution (Figure 5-7).

Chapter Six

Regression and Correlation Analysis

Learning Objectives

After reading and understanding the contents of this chapter, you will be able to:

1. Describe what is meant by a linear relationship between two variables.
2. Understand the meaning of the slope of a line, and calculate the slope for any straight line.
3. Apply the least squares method to calculate the equation for the regression line which shows the relationship between a dependent and an independent variable.
4. Understand the meaning of correlation and be able to apply it to measure the strength of a linear relationship.
5. Calculate the value of the correlation coefficient using two different methods.
6. Calculate and interpret the coefficient of determination.

The two previous chapters discussed two types of descriptive statistics: measures of central tendency (mode, median, mean) and measures of variation (range, percentile range, interquartile range, and standard deviation). These measures can help a librarian to describe the central tendency and variation of a single data set, such as "number of days computer terminal is out of service." These measures can also help a librarian to compare the central tendency and variation of two different data sets.

This chapter describes techniques which allow the librarian to go one step further and to describe *linear relationships* between two sets of data, such as "number of days computer terminal is out of service" and "age of computer terminal."

Linear Regression Analysis

A linear relation between two sets of data is typified by the relationship between the data sets "number of miles driven" and "gallons of gas consumed." In general, when a driver drives more miles, he or she uses more gallons of gas. The gallons of gas consumed increase *linearly* with the number of miles driven. To determine the exact mathematical relationship between these two, or any two, sets of variables, the librarian uses *regression analysis*. Regression analysis allows the librarian to plot two data sets and to obtain an exact equation for a line which passes through them. It is this line that gives rise to the expression "linear relationship."

To apply regression analysis, the librarian must first collect data. The following table shows the data a librarian collected during five recent driving trips.

Trip	1	2	3	4	5
Miles driven	22	19	43	108	228
Gallons of gas consumed	1	1	2	5	10

Using the labeling methods described in Chapter 3, we label the number of miles driven, 22, 19, 43, 108, and 228, x_1, x_2, x_3, x_4, and x_5, respectively. Gallons of gas consumed, 1, 1, 2, 5, and 10, is labeled y_1, y_2, y_3, y_4, and y_5, respectively. The interpretation of this labeling is that 22 is the first observation of variable X (number of miles) and 1 is the first observation of variable y (gallons of gas consumed). Using the graphing techniques introduced and described in Chapter 3, we form and plot the ordered pairs (x_1, y_1), (x_2, y_2), (x_3, y_3), (x_4, y_4), and (x_5, y_5). It is left as an exercise for the interested reader to plot a scatter diagram of the following ordered pairs which represent these data: (22, 1), (19, 1), (43, 2), (108, 5), and (228, 10).

The meaning of linear relationship now becomes clearer. It is not difficult to imagine a straight line passing through the points on this scatter plot. This line is the *regression line*.

The regression line shows how the value of the Y variable is related to changes of the X variable. If the reader were to plot the ordered pairs from the gasoline consumption example, the data would show that about 1 gallon of gas is consumed for every 20 miles driven. Because the regression line shows how the y's are related to the x's, the student should think carefully about which set of data should be the y's and which set should be the x's. The x values in regression analysis are always the *independent variables*. The independent variable is usually the variable under the investigator's control. Here, the driver can decide how many miles to drive but cannot directly control the gallons of gas consumed. The independent variable can also be a variable which the investigator cannot control but which is easily measured. Examples are time, distance, atmospheric pressure, or outdoor temperature. Archivists, for example, might use "ambient pollution" as an uncontrolled independent variable and study its relationship to the data set, "document deterioration."

The y value in regression analysis is always called the *dependent variable*. The dependent variable is the variable that the investigator cannot directly change. Rather, the investigator observes how the dependent variable changes as the independent variable changes. In the example above, the librarian observed that the dependent variable, gallons of gas consumed, increased as the independent variable, miles driven, increased.

Often, the investigator believes that changes in the independent variable *cause* changes in the dependent variable. For example, the librarian may be tempted to say that pollution causes document loss through deterioration or that driving causes gas to be consumed. This is an appealing idea and an easy way to interpret statistical results. Strictly speaking, however, cause is a metaphysical rather than a statistical notion. Regression analysis can only show that two variables are related. Without additional evidence, causality cannot be inferred. More research must be done to isolate the actual causal agent.

The Regression Line

The line determined in regression analysis is the *regression line*, a straight line that travels through the points of a scatter diagram. The regression line, the basis for the equation that summarizes the relationship between the variables, can describe the location of the values of the dependent variable.

Derivation of a regression line requires reference to the basic rules of algebra and properties of straight lines. This is seen in Formula 6-1 and is illustrated in Figure 6-1. The equation for a straight line is

$$Y = mX + b \qquad (6-1)$$

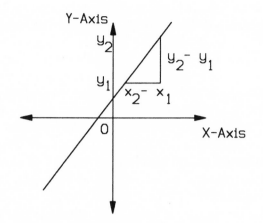

Figure 6-1. Determination of the slope of a line

In this equation, b is the *Y-axis intercept*. That is, b is that point on the Y-axis where the line intercepts or crosses the Y-axis, or where it would intercept the Y-axis if it were extended. In Formula 6-1, m is the *slope*. Every nonvertical line has a slope. In mathematics, slope means the same thing as in real life: steepness of incline or descent. The slope, m, measures the amount of a line's vertical change between coordinate pairs compared with its horizontal change. In other words, the slope of a line between two points (x_1, y_1) and (x_2, y_2) is given by the ratio of the change in the values of y to the change in the values of x. Written as an equation, this is

$$m = \frac{y_2 - y_1}{x_2 - x_1}$$ $(6-2)$

To assist in understanding the above equation, refer to Figure 6-1, where the slope may be expressed as the ratio of the change in vertical distance $(y_2 - y_1)$ to the change in horizontal distance $(x_2 - x_1)$.

The sign of m, positive or negative, identifies whether the line is ascending or descending. If m is positive $(m > 0)$, as in Figure 6-2A, then the line is ascending from left to right. If m is negative $(m < 0)$, as in Figure 6-2B, the line is descending from left to right. The absolute value of the slope, m, corresponds to the steepness of the line. The slope of $m = 1$ is less steep than the slope $m = 2$, which in turn is less steep than $m = 5$. Likewise, the slope of $m = -1$ is less steep than the slope m

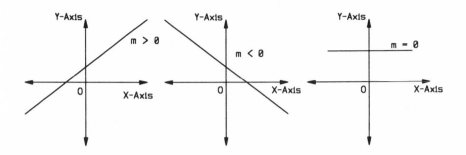

Figures 6-2A, B, and C.

= -2, which in turn is less steep than $m = -5$. A line with slope $m = 0$ is horizontal, as in Figure 6-2C.

A regression line's slope shows whether variables have *positive* or *negative relationships*. If the slope is positive, $m > 0$, the relationship between the variables is *positive* or *direct*. That is, when the relationship is positive, increases in the independent variable result in increases in the dependent variable. Hence, high scores on the dependent variable are associated with high scores on the independent variable. For example, if there is a positive relationship between the independent variable, miles driven, and the dependent variable, gallons of gas, an increase in miles driven is accompanied by an increase in gas consumed. Conversely, when miles driven decrease, gallons decrease as well. In the library, a positive relationship may exist between library hours (an independent variable) and number of items circulated (a dependent variable). If the library is open longer, more materials will be circulated.

A negative, or *inverse, relationship* is shown by $m < 0$. A negative relationship means that increases in the independent variable are associated with decreases in the dependent variable. In the library, a negative relationship may exist between the backfile age of a periodical (an independent variable) and use of that periodical (a dependent variable). As backfile age increases, use decreases.

A slope of $m = 0$ means there is no statistical relationship between the variables. The regression line is horizontal. In other words, the amount, degree, or frequency of the dependent variable is unaffected by increases or decreases in the independent variable. In the library, there is probably no relationship between library hours (an independent vari-

Table 6-1. Summations Used in Regression Calculations

Sum of the independent variables	$\Sigma X = (X_1 + X_2 + \ldots + X_n)$
Sum of the dependent variables	$\Sigma Y = (Y_1 + Y_2 + \ldots + Y_n)$
Sum of the squares of the independent variables	$\Sigma X^2 = (X_1^2 + X_2^2 + \ldots + X_n^2)$
Square of the sum of the independent variable	$(\Sigma X)^2 = (X_1 + X_2 + \ldots + X_n)^2$
Sum of the product of independent and dependent variables	$\Sigma XY = (X_1Y_1 + X_2Y_2 + \ldots + X_nY_n)$
Product of the sums of the independent and dependent variables	$\Sigma X \Sigma Y = (X_1 + X_2 + \ldots + X_n) \times (Y_1 + Y_2 + \ldots + Y_n)$

able) and collection size (a dependent variable). As library hours increase, the size of the collection will neither increase nor decrease.

The regression line can be thought of as the straight line that best passes through the middle of the data points on a scatter diagram. It is determined by the formula

$$\hat{Y} = a X + b \qquad\qquad (6-3)$$

where $b = \bar{Y} - a\bar{X}$ $\qquad\qquad$ $(6-4A)$

and $a = \dfrac{n(\sum XY) - (\sum X)(\sum Y)}{n(\sum X^2) - (\sum X)^2}$ $\qquad\qquad$ $(6-4B)$

and where n = the number of data points (number of ordered pairs). Definitions for each of the summation expressions are found in Table 6-1. For the reader's convenience, columns have been added in Tables 6-2 through 6-5 that represent these summations. This "extension of the tables" is done to clarify the calculations that are based on the data found in the tables.

Attention is drawn to the use of the symbol $\hat{Y}$ "Y-hat" which is used in the general equation for the linear regression line, Formula 6-3. This symbol distinguishes the regression equation from that of a straight line through a locus of points, and it alerts the reader that the equation is an estimation.

These formulas are often called the *least squares method*. The method is like balancing a see-saw. If two people of equal weight sit equal distances from the center of a see-saw, the see-saw will be balanced; however, if one person moves farther from the center, that person's end of the see-saw will go down and the other end of the

Table 6-2. Copy Machine Maintenance Log					
Copy Machine (n = 6)	Age (Years) X	Maintenance Cost ($ per Month) Y	X^2	XY	Y^2
1	3	15	9	45	225
2	2	10	4	20	100
3	1	11	1	11	121
4	3	12	9	36	144
5	4	20	16	80	400
6	2	13	4	26	169
Totals:	15	81	43	218	1159

see-saw will go up. The distance the ends of the see-saw move is related to the *square* of the distance the person sits from the center of the see-saw. The position of the regression line is also affected by the square of the distance of data points from the regression line. The regression line is balanced when the sum of these squared distances is minimized.

Thus, the regression line balances data pairs. In this respect, the regression line is like the mean which balances a distribution's data points. The regression line reveals the central tendency of two data sets, just as the mean reveals the central tendency of a single data set.

The following example illustrates the use of Formulas 6-3 and 6-4A in determining the equation of a regression line. Using the library's maintenance log, we determine the monthly repair costs for 6 photocopy machines. The age of each machine is noted in Table 6-2.

Substituting in Formula 6-4A to find coefficient a, we find that

$$a = \frac{6(218) - (15)(81)}{6(43) - (15)(15)}$$

$$= \frac{1308 - 1215}{258 - 225}$$

$$= \frac{93}{33}$$

$$= 2.8182$$

Substituting in Formula 6-4B to find coefficient b, we find that

$$b = (\frac{81}{6}) - (2.8182)(\frac{15}{6})$$

$$= 13.5 - (2.8182)(2.5)$$

$$= 13.5 - 7.0455$$

$$= 6.4545$$

Values for coefficients a and b are now substituted in Formula 6-3 to obtain the regression equation:

$$\hat{Y} = 2.8182\,X + 6.4545$$

Notice that the calculations are carried to 4 decimal places. This is the common practice when determining the regression equation.

This equation can now be used to describe the central tendency of monthly repair costs for different-age machines. For example, a photocopy machine that is 4 years old will tend to require

$$\hat{Y} = 2.8182\,(4) + 6.4545$$

$$= 11.2728 + 6.4545$$

$$= \$17.73 \text{ per month}$$

In other words, the repair costs for machines that are 4 years old will center on $17.73 per month. The investigator could say that the central tendency of maintenance costs (y), given age equal to 4 ($x = 4$), is $17.73 per month. Notice that the central tendency of y *given* x is different from the central tendency of y. According to Formula 4-4, the central tendency or mean of y can be shown to be

$$\bar{Y} = \frac{\sum Y_i}{n}$$

$$= \frac{81}{6}$$

$$= \$13.50 \text{ per month}$$

The actual cost for maintaining a 4-year-old machine is $20 per month. The mean of y given x, $17.73, describes this observation better than the mean of y, $13.50. Thus, regression provides more precise information about the distribution of y.

The descriptive power of regression is shown in Figure 6-3. This figure shows the age and repair costs for the 6 photocopy machines in the table above. The frequency distribution for repair costs is shown along the Y-axis. The mean of this distribution is shown by the horizon-

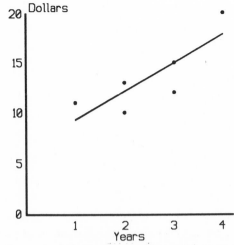

Figure 6-3. Scattergram of photocopy machine repair costs versus age

tal line. These same data points are carried to the right, where they are plotted against age, and the regression line is drawn. The regression line shows that the central tendency of repair costs is a function of age. This means that if the machines are new, mean maintenance costs are low. Similarly, if the machines are old, mean maintenance costs are high. The regression line provides more information about central tendency than the mean does.

Regression also provides more information about dispersion. Figure 6-3 shows that the cost data are widely dispersed around its mean but narrowly dispersed around its regression line. For example, repair costs for all aged machines range from $10 per month to $20 per month but the repair costs for 2-year-old machines range from $10 per month to $13 per month.

In summary, regression analysis is a quantitative method. The products of regression analysis are a scatter diagram and an equation for the line passing through the scatter diagram. Advanced techniques, not discussed in this book, allow a librarian to form and test hypotheses about relationships between two sets of data.

Sometimes the investigator has a difficult time deciding which variable is independent and which is dependent. An effective escape from this dilemma may be to plot variable *A* as the dependent variable with variable *B* as the independent variable. Then reverse these roles, "regressing" *B* on *A* instead of *A* on *B*. Reversing the variables will, without exception, produce a different regression equation. The statistical consumer should not hesitate to ask investigators to explain the basis for selecting variables as dependent or independent, and whether reversing the variables produces a more useful regression analysis.

Correlation

The librarian can use regression analysis to determine the equation of the line which passes through a scatter diagram. The technique can also be applied to determine if two sets of data are positively or negatively related. The next logical step is for the librarian to try to quantify how strong this relation is. For this, the librarian can use *correlation*, a method of determining what proportion of the variability in one set of scores can be predicted by variability in another set of scores—for example, what proportion of the variability in machine maintenance costs can be predicted or explained by differences in machine age.

This chapter explores analytical techniques which describe the degree to which one variable is linearly related to another. The analysis of the linear relationship between a dependent variable and a single independent variable is called *simple correlation analysis*. In *multiple correlation analysis*, a dependent variable is related to several independent variables. In *partial correlation analysis*, the relationship between one of the variables in a multiple correlation and the dependent variable is examined. Multiple and partial correlation analyses are not discussed.

Coefficient of Correlation

The strength of the evidence of a linear relationship between two variables is described by the *coefficient of correlation*, or *r*. This measure has no units, such as inches, minutes, or degrees. Also, it always assumes a value between -1.00 and +1.00. While there are several methods to calculate this coefficient, the usual practice is to round the result to the nearest hundredth. *Perfect correlation* is shown by a value of -1.00 or +1.00. That is, a single regression line can be drawn through all the paired data points in the scatter diagram, and all points lie on this line.

It is important to remember that a correlation coefficient of $r = -1.00$ is just as strong as a measure of a relationship as $r = +1.00$. The sign of the value of r identifies whether the correlation between the variables is positive or negative. That is, it establishes whether the relationship is direct (positive correlation) or inverse (negative correlation). A result of $r = + 0.70$ is the same strength of correlation as $r = - 0.70$. As the

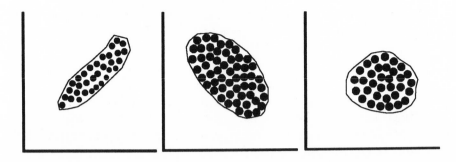

Figures 6-4A, B, and C. Scatterplots with positive, negative, and no correlation

value of *r* approaches zero from either direction on the number line, the evidence of correlation decreases. A value of *r* = 0 means there is no statistically measurable linear relationship between the variables under study. While a relationship exists between the coefficient of correlation and the size of the data set, the following approximations are helpful in interpreting the strength of either positive or negative correlation:

Value of *r*	Interpretation
0.00–0.25	little or no relationship
0.30–0.45	fair relationship
0.50–0.75	moderate to good relationship
0.80–1.00	strong relationship to perfect correlation

The correlation coefficient moves from +1 or -1 toward zero when paired data points become more dispersed around the regression line. In Figure 6-3, for example, the dispersion of data points around the regression line is low. This means that the points cluster around, or are confined near, the regression line. The correlation coefficient for Figure 6-4A is in the moderate to strong range. In Figure 6-4B the data are more scattered and the correlation coefficient is in the fair to moderate range. In Figure 6-4C, the dispersion of the points is very wide, and the correlation coefficient is in the poor to fair range.

Methods of Determining Correlation

There are several ways to calculate the coefficient of correlation. The various algorithms fall into two categories. The first category, *parametric methods*, requires parametric data—that is, data expressed in interval or ratio scale measurement. Parametric methods are powerful in determining the strength of the relationship between two variables. Parametric methods are useful in predicting the value of a dependent variable when you are given the value of the independent variable.

In contrast, *nonparametric methods*, as the name implies, use nonparametric data—that is, data that are expressed in nominal or ordinal scale measurement. Nonparametric methods are well suited to the library where the librarian frequently works with data that classify observations descriptively rather than quantitatively. Nonparametric methods are particularly useful when dealing with data that are obtained from subjective evaluation, as in assessing attitudes, perceptions, or satisfaction.

Nonparametric methods provide less information and therefore are perceived as less powerful than parametric methods. Parametric data are regarded as "hard data" while nonparametric data are often (incorrectly) regarded as "soft data." Parametric measures provide more information and precision than do nonparametric methods. Even so, the use of nonparametric methods is often more realistic due to the sometimes difficult requirement of collecting parametric data. Nonparametric methods allow managers to study variables where less information is available.

Nonparametric methods work best when the data sets are continuous, linearly related, and roughly symmetrical. When data are discontinuous, nonlinear, or irregularly shaped, parametric methods should be applied, if possible, to yield the most accurate results.

The Pearson Correlation Coefficient

The *Pearson product-moment correlation coefficient* was developed by the English mathematician Karl Pearson. It is a parametric method that uses interval- or ratio-scaled, linearly related variables. "Product," in the name of the algorithm, refers to multiplication results, and "moment" is a statistical term for deviate scores. Hence this technique, also called *Pearson's r*, involves multiplying certain scores. Application of this algorithm is simpler than deriving its proper name. The student applying this technique will appreciate the value of using a computer package for statistical analysis. Some of the more common are Minitab, SAS, and SPSS, all of which are available in personal computer versions. When the technique is performed manually, the practitioner requires a calculator that features at least 10 digits. The best way to apply the algorithm is through the table extension method introduced on page 175. Pearson's r is expressed by the formula

$$r = \frac{n\sum XY - \sum X \sum Y}{\sqrt{[n\sum X^2 - (\sum X)^2][n\sum Y^2 - (\sum Y)^2]}} \qquad (6-8)$$

The meaning of the summations in the formula are explained in Table 6-1 also. To illustrate this formula, suppose the data given in Table 6-3 have been collected about ten rural libraries and the communities they serve.

Substituting in Formula 6-8:

$$r = \frac{10(219.83) - 15.7(128.8)}{\sqrt{[10(27.29) - (15.7)^2][10(1829.46) - (128.8)^2]}}$$

$$= \frac{2198.3 - 2022.16}{\sqrt{[272.9 - 246.49][18294.6 - 16589.44]}}$$

$$= \frac{176.14}{\sqrt{(26.41)(1705.16)}}$$

$$= \frac{176.14}{\sqrt{45033.28}}$$

$$= \frac{176.14}{212.21}$$

$$= 0.83$$

Table 6-3. Expenditures for Selected Rural Community Libraries					
Library	Population (1000s) X	Expenditures ($1000s) Y	X^2	XY	Y^2
1	2.3	14.9	5.29	34.27	222.01
2	2.4	17.2	5.76	41.28	295.84
3	1.6	14.9	2.56	23.84	222.01
4	1.1	6.7	1.21	7.37	44.89
5	1.1	13.5	1.21	14.85	182.25
6	1.0	7.4	1.00	7.40	54.76
7	1.0	8.4	1.00	8.40	70.56
8	1.7	15.5	2.89	26.35	240.25
9	2.1	19.5	4.41	40.95	380.25
10	1.4	10.8	1.96	15.12	116.64

Pearson's r is 0.83. The interpretation of this measure is that a strong correlation exists between the variables' community size and operating expenditures. The information's usefulness for an administrator is that library costs for one community can be compared with those of another, similar-size community to determine whether cost differentials exist.

Coefficient of Determination

If the investigator can use a parametric measure of correlation such as Pearson's r, the investigator can calculate another parametric coefficient called the *coefficient of determination*. This coefficient tells the investigator what proportion of variation in the dependent variable is explainable by variation in the independent variable. The value of this measure varies from 0 to 1, inclusive. A value of 0 means that none of the change in the dependent variable is due to change in the independent variable. A value of 1, on the other hand, means that 100% of the change in the dependent variable is explainable by change in the independent variable.

Because the determination coefficient expresses the relationship between variables in terms of percent of accountable change, it provides a different perspective on variable relationship than does correlation. The measure is calculated by squaring the correlation coefficient, r^2. Therefore, if the correlation coefficient is -0.95, then $(-0.95)^2 = 0.90$, or 90% of the change in the dependent variable is explained by change in the independent variable. Similarly, if $r = +0.20$, then only 4% of the change in the dependent variable may be related to changes in the independent variable. The *coefficient of nondetermination*, or *coefficient of alienation*, is the quantity $1 - r^2$. In these two examples, 10% and 96%, respectively, of the change in the dependent variable are due to random factors, or error, or are otherwise unrelated to changes in the independent variable.

In the example, the coefficient of determination is $(.83)^2$, which is $(.83)(.83)$ or 0.69. This means that 69% of changes in operating expenditures can be explained by changes in community size. The coefficient of nondetermination is $1.00 - 0.69 = 0.31$. This figure is large and suggests there may be other important considerations that could explain differences in expenditures.

A problem in using the determination coefficient is in the tendency to say, "Ninety percent of the change in the dependent variable is *caused* by change in the independent variable." Neither the determination coefficient nor the correlation coefficient measures causation.

They are only ways of presenting statistical *evidence* for a relationship. The better approach is to say that the determination coefficient measures how well one variable describes changes, or "moves along" with another.

Often the correlation coefficient is confused with "determination coefficient." A correlation coefficient may sometimes be inaccurately reported as a percent. It is not uncommon to hear or read $r = 0.60$ incorrectly interpreted as "60% of the change in the dependent variable is explainable by change in the independent variable." The determination coefficient must be calculated to make this assertion. Remember, r = 0.60 simply places the relationship between variables on a scale of -1.0 to +1.0. The determination coefficient in this example is 0.60^2 = 0.36, or 36%. Moderate to good correlation is shown by the .60 coefficient. However, the coefficient of nondetermination shows that 64% of the change in the dependent variable is not accounted for by change in the independent variable. This suggests the presence of other influences of perhaps greater importance.

The Spearman Rank Order Correlation Coefficient

The *Spearman rank order correlation coefficient* is a non-parametric correlation measure. It is less precise than a parametric measure like Pearson's *r*. Spearman's coefficient is applicable where parametric data are not available or where parametric data have been rank-ordered. The measure is represented by a lowercase *r* with the Greek letter rho, ρ, as a subscript—hence, r_ρ. This algorithm uses ordinal scale data, and assumes *n* ranked data pairs, $\{(X_1, Y_1), (X_2, Y_2), \ldots , (X_N, Y_N)\}$. The coefficient is given by the formula

$$r_\rho = 1 - \frac{6 \sum D^2}{n(n^2 - 1)} \qquad\qquad (6-9)$$

or

$$r_\rho = 1 - \frac{6(D_1{}^2 + D_2{}^2 + \ldots + D_n{}^2)}{n(n^2 - 1)}$$

where D = rank A - rank B for each data pair, and n = number of data pairs.

The Spearman coefficient shows the strength and nature (positive or negative) of the linear correlation. It cannot be used to calculate the correlation of determination. An advantage of the Spearman coefficient is that it is not affected by extreme values, because it is based on

Clerk	Score Test 1	Score Test 2	Rank Test 1	Rank Test 2	Rank Difference		D^2
1	90	94	7	6	7 - 6 =	1	1
2	77	88	4	5	4 - 5 =	-1	1
3	80	84	5	4	5 - 4 =	1	1
4	62	77	2	2	2 - 2 =	0	0
5	84	96	6	7	6 - 7 =	-1	1
6	60	72	1	1	1 - 1 =	0	0
7	72	82	3	3	3 - 3 =	0	0
Totals						0	4

Table 6-4. Test Results and Rankings of Library Trainees

rankings. Extreme values in a rank correlation do not produce a large rank difference. This is not true of parametric methods, which are sensitive to extreme observations.

The Spearman coefficient can be illustrated in an example involving the training of library clerks. Seven newly hired library clerks are trained in journal shelving and retrieval procedures, then tested on each procedure. The test results are given in Table 6-4.

Substituting in Formula 6-9, we get

$$r_\rho = 1 - \frac{6[(7-6)^2 + (4-5)^2 + (5-4)^2 + (2-2)^2 + (6-7)^2 + (1-1)^2 + (3-3)^2]}{7[(7)^2 - 1]}$$

$$= 1 - \frac{6[(1)^2 + (-1)^2 + (1)^2 + (0)^2 + (-1)^2 + (0)^2 + (0)^2]}{7[49-1]}$$

$$= 1 - \frac{6[1+1+1+0+1+0+0]}{7[48]}$$

$$= 1 - \frac{6(4)}{7(48)}$$

$$= 1 - \frac{24}{376}$$

$$= 1 - .07$$

$$= 0.93$$

The interpretation of r_ρ is that a high correlation exists between performance of the first test and performance on the second test. The usefulness of this information is that there may be no need to conduct a second test. This may have an impact for conserving staff time without affecting training efficiency.

In ranking the observations, 60 is the lowest shelving test score. It is assigned rank 1. The next lowest score, 62, is given rank 2, and so on, until score 94, which is assigned rank 7. The same procedure is applied to Test 2 scores, journal retrieval. Had a score appeared more than once in the distribution, the mean of the ranks is assigned to each of the tied scores. For example, the scores 30, 32, 32, 32, 34, and 35 produce the ranking 1, 3, 3, 3, 5, and 6, because 32 occupies 2nd, 3rd, and 4th places. The mean of 2, 3, and 4 is 3.

Rank difference is determined by subtracting one set of ranks from the other. It is important to verify at this stage that the differences between the ranks sum to zero. If not, an arithmetic error has been made. The differences are then squared. The result, always positive, is recorded in column D^2, as shown.

In another example of the Spearman coefficient, assume six of the seven clerks are still employed by the library ten weeks later. The two department directors who supervise the clerks rank the skills of each from 1 = highest to 6 = lowest. An assumption is that different supervisors will rank performance by using varying mixtures of subjective and objective criteria. To learn if there is any correlation between the directors' rankings, the Spearman coefficient algorithm is applied; the results are shown in Table 6-5.

Substituting in Formula 6-9, we get

$$r_\rho = 1 - \frac{6\left[(-1)^2 + (0)^2 + (-0.5)^2 + (0)^2 + (1.5)^2 + (0)^2\right]}{6\left[36 - 1\right]}$$

$$= 1 - \frac{6\left[1 + 0 + 0.25 + 0 + 2.25 + 0\right]}{6\left[35\right]}$$

$$= 1 - \frac{6(3.5)}{6(35)}$$

$$= 1 - \frac{21}{210}$$

$$= 1 - 0.10$$

$$= 0.90$$

Despite the possibility of subjective influences in their evaluations, it

Table 6-5. Ranking of Skills of New Library Employees

Clerk	Director A Ranking	Director B Ranking	Rank Difference	D^2
1	4	5	4 - 5 = -1	1.00
2	2	2	2 - 2 = 0	0.00
3	3	3.5	3 - 3.5= -0.5	0.25
4	1	1	1 - 1 = 0	0.00
5	5	3.5	5 - 3.5= 1.5	2.25
6	6	6	6 - 6 = 0	0.00
Total			0	3.50

appears from $r_p = 0.90$ that the two department directors are measuring the same qualities or dimensions in the clerks. It may be a duplication of effort, then, to ask both directors to review each clerk. A new procedure, such as alternating reviewers, or splitting the reviews between the directors, may be more efficient. Notice in department director 2's rankings, clerks 3 and 5 were tied. This tie requires substituting the mean of the rankings determined by finding the mean $(3 + 4)/2 = 3.5$

From these examples it can be seen that the Spearman method offers many conveniences useful to the librarian. The arithmetic of the Spearman method seems easier than that in other correlation techniques, such as Pearson's r. Also, complex data can be rank ordered and the Spearman algorithm applied. Finally, the Spearman technique easily determines the degree of association between sets of ranked data. This is true even if the sources of these rankings are subjective and obtained from different people.

Summary of Critical Concepts

1. *Correlation analysis* is a statistical technique for establishing the degree of relationship between variables or among groups of variables. *Simple correlation analysis* concerns the relationship or association between two variables. A *multiple correlation analysis* concerns the degree of relationship of a dependent variable to two or more independent variables.
2. Variables can be *dependent* or *independent*. Changes in the dependent variable are said to be related to changes in the independent variable.

3. Relationships between and among variables are classified as *linear*, or *straight line*, and *nonlinear*. This chapter explores only linear relationships within the context of simple correlation techniques.

4. The relationship between two variables is shown by a *scatter diagram*. The independent variable is scaled on the horizontal axis (X-axis) and the dependent variable is scaled on the vertical axis (Y-axis). The points on the diagram are paired historical observations for the two variables.

5. The *regression line* is the "best fit" straight line drawn through the paired points on the scatter diagram. This line is determined by the *least squares method*. It expresses a mean relationship between the variables, based on the paired data points. A regression line describes the central tendency of the dependent variable, given the independent variable.

6. A *correlation coefficient* shows two things: positive or negative association between the variables and the strength of their linear relationship, if any. *Positive association* evidences a positive or direct relationship between the variables. This means that an increase in the independent variable is accompanied by a proportionate increase in the dependent variable. *Negative association* evidences an *inverse relationship* between the variables. That is, an increase in the independent variable is accompanied by a decrease in the dependent variable, and vice versa. The absolute value of the correlation coefficient is an *index* of the strength of association between the variables. In perfect correlation, either $r = -1.00$ or $r = +1.00$, the paired points fall directly on the regression line. As the points become *scattered* about the regression line, the correlation coefficient approaches zero. A value of $r = 0$ means there is no linear correlation. Correlation coefficients are expressed to the nearest hundredths.

7. The coefficient's sign describes only the nature of the relationship. That is, it identifies the relationship as direct (positive) or inverse (negative). A correlation of $r = -1.00$ is just as strong as $r = +1.00$. A coefficient of $r = -0.65$ shows the same strength or degree of association between the variables as $r = +0.65$.

8. The *coefficient of determination*, r^2, is the ratio of explained variance to total variance. This measure shows the proportion of the total variance in the dependent variable that is explained by variation in the independent variable. The *coefficient of nondetermination* is $1 - r^2$.

9. Correlation techniques are of two types, parametric and nonparametric. *Parametric methods* require parametric data—that is, data expressed in interval or ratio scale measure. *Nonparametric methods* use nonparametric data, or data expressed in nominal scale or ordinal scale measure.

10. The *Pearson product-moment correlation coefficient* is a parametric measure. The determination coefficient, r^2, is calculated from the coefficient derived from the algorithm. The *Spearman rank order correlation coefficient* is a nonparametric measure. Only rank-ordered data can be used in this technique, even if higher-order data are available. The determination coefficient is meaningless if computed from this measure.

Key Terms

Coefficient of Correlation. The square root of the coefficient of determination. Abbreviated r, the sign of this measure shows the direction of the relationship between two variables. A positive sign shows a positive or direct relationship. A negative sign shows a negative or inverse relationship. The correlation coefficient has no units such as inches or seconds. It always assumes a value between $r = -1.00$ and $r = +1.00$. A value of $r = -1.00$ shows *perfect negative (inverse) correlation,* and $r = +1.00$ shows *perfect positive (direct) correlation.* The absolute value of the coefficient shows the strength of the linear association between the variables. A correlation coefficient of $r = -0.80$ is just as strong as $r = +0.80$. The correlation coefficient is often confused with the coefficient of determination.

Coefficient of Determination. The proportion of variation in the dependent variable explained by the independent variable. This measure, abbreviated r^2, assumes a value between 0 and 1. A value of 0 means that none of the change in the dependent variable is explainable by changes in the independent variable. A value of 1 means that 100% of the change in the dependent variable is explainable by changes in the independent variable. This measure is often confused with the correlation coefficient.

Correlation Analysis. A method to determine the degree to which variables are linearly related. Variables are *positively* related when an increase in one variable is accompanied by an increase in the other. Variables are *negatively* or *inversely* related when an increase in one variable is accompanied by a decrease in the other. In *simple correlation analysis,* a dependent variable is related to a single independent variable. In *multiple correlation analysis,* a dependent variable is related to several independent variables. In *partial correlation analysis,* the relationship between one of the variables in a multiple correlation and the dependent variable is examined.

Least Squares Method. A technique for passing or "best fitting" a straight line through the approximate middle of a set of paired data points. This is done in such a way that the sum of the squared vertical distances between the line and the paired points is minimized.

Nonparametric Methods. Methods, techniques, or algorithms that use nonparametric data. Such data must be in ordinal (rank) scale and are usually drawn from a study of attitudes or subjective assessments. An example of a nonparametric method is the Spearman rank order correlation coefficient.

Regression Analysis. A method of predicting from historical data the value of a dependent variable from one or more independent variables, X_i. *Linear regression techniques* determine how much the dependent variable changes for a given change in the independent variable. They also determine the equation of the line connecting the variables. They also estimate the accuracy with which the dependent variable can be predicted from historical values.

Regression Line. The *linear regression line* is the straight line which best "fits" a set of paired data points. The linear regression line is determined by the *least squares method.* The line measures the mean relationship between the data points of the two variables.

Scatter Diagram, Scattergram, or *Scatterplot.* A graph of paired data points on the rectangular coordinate plane. The *independent variable* is plotted on the X-axis and the *dependent variable* is plotted on the Y-axis. A scatter diagram is an effective portrayal of the relationship between two variables.

Self-Assessment Quiz

True or False   1.   Simple correlation analysis is a statistical technique that establishes the degree of cause and effect between two variables.

True or False   2.   If the relationship between data points for two variables can be described by a straight line, the variables are linearly related.

True or False   3.   A scatter diagram is effective for showing the relationship or association between two variables.

True or False   4.   In correlation analysis, the data consist of paired observations of historical data of the independent variable and dependent variable.

True or False   5.   If coordinate pairs were plotted on a scatter diagram and the points outlined a circle, the correlation coefficient would be perfect, or $r = 1$.

True or False	6.	A determination coefficient of $r^2 = 0.90$ means that 90% of the dependent variable's variation is caused by changes in the independent variable.
True or False	7.	Nonparametric methods are required for dealing with data that are shaped by consumer attitudes or subjective management decisions.
True or False	8.	The sign of the slope of the regression line, like the sign of the correlation coefficient, shows the direction of the relationship between the variables.
True or False	9.	Positive linear correlation establishes statistical evidence of an inverse relationship between the variables.
True or False	10.	The Spearman correlation coefficient algorithm requires ordinal data.
True or False	11.	A rank correlation method is less sensitive to extreme observations than is a parametric method.
True or False	12.	The stronger the correlation between two variables, the closer r^2 is to 1. Conversely, the weaker the relationship, the closer r^2 is to 0.
True or False	13.	Correlation and regression analysis provide statistical evidence of cause and effect relationships between variables.
True or False	14.	As the points on a scatter diagram begin to fall away from the regression line, the correlation coefficient varies from +1.00 or -1.00.

Answers

1. False. Correlation analysis shows only how data sets are mathematically related.
2. True. In a linear relationship, data move together.
3. True. A scatter diagram shows how closely the variables are related and whether their relation is negative or positive.
4. True. The data for a correlation analysis are historical in the sense that they were collected before the time of the analysis.
5. False. Only relationships that can be described by a straight line are linear. If the scatter diagram looks like a circle, no linear relationship exists. In this case, $r = 0$.
6. False. The coefficient of determination does not show that one variable causes another. The coefficient of determination describes

the percent of the variation in the dependent variable that is explained by variation in the independent variable.
   7. True. Subjective or attitudinal data are necessarily measured on an ordinal scale. Ordinal scale data can only be analyzed with nonparametric methods.
   8. True. Negative slope means the line descends from left to right; positive slope means the line ascends from left to right.
   9. False. Positive linear correlation, just like positive slope of the regression line, shows a direct relationship between the variables. Negative linear correlation, like negative slope of the regression line, shows an inverse relationship between the variables.
  10. True. The data must either be collected in ordinal scale or translated into ordinal scale.
  11. True. No matter how extreme a score is, its rank will be limited by the number of observations in the data set.
  12. True. The coefficient of determination, r^2, is the measure of the percent of variation in the dependent variable that is explained by variation in the independent variable.
  13. False. Correlation and regression can only provide evidence of a linear relationship.
  14. True. If all the points lie on the regression line, $r = 1$. As points fall away from the line, the r value approaches zero.

Discussion Questions and Problems

   1. Explain the meaning of correlation and regression. Discuss the purpose of each and identify how they are related.
   2. Explain what is meant by positive linear and negative linear relationships. Give two examples of each from
      a. every day experience
      b. your favorite sport
      c. the library environment.
   3. Suppose each of the following pairs of variables is linearly related. For each pair, identify the independent and dependent variable and provide reasons for your choice. Explain why you expect a positive or negative correlation coefficient between the variables
      a. college entrance examination and high school grade point average
      b. college entrance examination and college grade point average
      c. electricity usage and current outdoor temperature
      d. price of a stock and its earnings per share

   e. amount of food consumed and body weight
   f. supervisor's skill and employee output
   g. ticket prices and passengers per 100 miles
   h. noise level of environment and employee morale
   i. rate of library circulation and publication date of book.
4. Distinguish between correlation coefficient and determination coefficient. Discuss any merits of the combined use of these coefficients.
5. List and discuss the advantages and disadvantages of parametric and nonparametric methods.
6. List and discuss reasons why the determination coefficient is not useful in nonparametric methods.
7. Use an encyclopedia to find background information on Sir Francis Galton, who introduced the idea of regression. Summarize his reasoning in 75–100 words.
8. Distinguish between a regression line's slope and the correlation between two variables. What overlapping information does each provide? What unique information, if any, does each provide?
9. Explain why a vertical line has no slope and a horizontal line's slope is 0.
10. Explain why the value of the correlation coefficient is not affected if the dependent and independent variables are interchanged.
11. Plot the following 10 pairs of data points on a scatter diagram: (1,2), (1,4), (2,2), (2,4), (2,5), (3,2), (3,4), (3,3), (4,4), and (6,14).
   a. Verify that the coefficient of correlation for these points is $r = 0.7616$ and that the coefficient of determination is 0.58. Interpret each measure.
   b. Verify that the equation of the regression line is
   $$\hat{Y} = 1.8010\,X - 0.4627\,.$$
   c. Exclude the coordinate pair (6,14). Using the remaining 9 data pairs, verify that the correlation coefficient is $r = 0.1118$ and that the determination coefficient is 0.0125. Interpret each measure. Explain the effect of excluding this single, extreme data pair.
12. Data on the operating expenditures for ten rural libraries are given in the text. Regress operating expense on population. Verify that the regression equation is EXPENSE = 6.6694 (POPULATION) + 2.40903. Reverse the variables. Regress population on operating expense. Verify that the regression equation is POPULATION = 0.1033 (EXPENSE) + 0.2395. Show that the correlation coefficient, r, is the same regardless of which variable is independent and which is dependent. Which variable do you think should be the independent variable?
13. Problem 3-13 outlined a leisure reading collection of paperback

books for a prison library. When the data survey was conducted to determine each book's circulation, a notation was also made of the book's copyright year. The data below identify the circulation per title of the adventure fiction books by copyright year.

1969—16.2	1980—12.0
1970—13.5	1981—14.7
1971—11.1	1982—16.4
1972—14.2	1983—17.0
1973—11.2	1984—20.2
1974—15.3	1985—18.6
1975—13.8	1986—17.1
1976—11.4	1987—15.4
1977—12.9	1988—13.7
1978—14.8	1989—10.6
1979—13.3	

a. Prepare a line graph that illustrates the data. Interpret your graph. (Hint: Plot the copyright year along the X-axis and the circulations per title along the Y-axis.)
b. Prepare a scatter diagram. Interpret your graph.
c. Determine the correlation coefficient between the copyright year and the circulation per title. Interpret your findings.
d. Perform a regression analysis, comparing the date of copyright to the frequency of circulation. Interpret your findings.
14. A variety of material formats is available in the library. In a recent study, one library ranked its formats in order of use as follows:

	Rank Order of Use in 1st Survey	Rank Order of Use in 2nd Survey
Books	2	1
Computer printouts	8	12
Films (pictorial)	13	13
Government publications	4	6.5
Manuscripts	1	3
Maps	9	10
Microcopies	10	5
Newspapers	6.5	4
Other pictorials / Photos	11	9
Periodicals	3	2
Research reports	5	8
Tape/Sound recordings	12	11
Theses/Dissertations	6.5	6.5
Videotapes	14	14

a. Use these data to calculate the Spearman's coefficient of correlation.
b. Does it appear that the two surveys are comparing the various physical formats on the same bases of use? Explain how you reached your conclusion.

15. The library's public relations officer developed several different-length commercials for broadcast over a popular radio station. The messages highlighted special reading programs and other library activities. When using library services, members of the public acknowledged that they had heard the library's commercial.

The table below shows the number of seconds in each commercial message used over a 6-week period. It also identifies the corresponding number of public responses to that message.

Number of Seconds	Number of Responses
15	7
15	9
25	10
30	9
30	11
45	13
45	10
55	13
60	12
60	14
85	17
90	14

a. Construct a scatter diagram.
b. Determine the correlation coefficient between the length of the commercial and the number of responses to it.
c. Find the regression equation and plot the regression line.
d. How many responses would you estimate would be generated by commercial messages of 40, 50, or 75 seconds?

16. At the end of fiscal year 2, the library trustees asked the librarian to report on the relationship between moneys allocated for buying new books and the circulation of books by subject category. The issue arose because some new board members believe that acquisitions ought to be driven strictly by demand, as shown by circulation.

The librarian developed the table below to begin analyzing data from this library, which serves a community of 30,000 residents. The data exclude expenditures for reference material purchases. The acquisitions budget for the materials identified is $325,000.

Do the data support the librarian's views that there is close agreement between the staff's buying decisions and the public's wants? Explain your answer, applying appropriate statistical analyses.

Dewey Class	Circulation			Acquisitions	
	Year 1	Year 2	Year 3	Year 2	Year 3
000–099	2205	2732	3564	$6785	$7785
General Works					
100–199	5297	5245	5222	7680	11,400
Philosophy					
200–299	2375	2754	2704	4030	4320
Religion					
300–399	14,083	14,677	16,917	27,160	36,940
Social Sciences					
400–499	1063	962	1061	1400	2320
Language					
500–599	4324	4214	4362	6980	9525
Pure Sciences					
600–699	13,733	10,550	9314	62,335	20,335
Technology					
700–799	17,331	18,379	16,655	33,560	36,365
The Arts					
800–899	6861	7359	7473	12,470	16,320
Literature					
900–999	14,975	16,859	18,289	39,075	39,000
Geography & History					
Biography	4364	4682	6263	7725	9675
Fiction	48,549	47,805	47,741	82,525	100,000
Mystery	13,613	12,926	14,006	26,250	30,565
Science Fiction	2096	1791	1978	7025	4500

17. For fiscal year 3 in the Problem 16, the librarian modified the manner in which acquisitions moneys were allocated. More funds were available to buy books for classifications of materials that circulated best. The acquisitions budget for the identified materials was increased by 1.25%, to $329,050.

a. When the board's policy was carried out at the end of fiscal year 2, some library staff expressed their reservations. They feared that clientele might checkout their favorite materials excessively in order to have more money appropriated to buy materials for them. Discuss whether the data show that this has happened.

    b. Construct a scatter diagram from the fiscal year 3 data. Interpret the graph.

    c. Find the regression line and plot it. Interpret the line.

    d. Based on the data, has the librarian accomplished the board's objective of linking acquisitions to circulation? Discuss whether the graph reveals the weaknesses or strengths in this approach to collection development.

18. The library's administrative assistant prepared a table that illustrates the number of sick days each staff member took over the past 12 months. Along with the number of days absent, the assistant also identified the number of years of library service for the staff member.

    a. Construct a scatter diagram from these data. Interpret your graph.

    b. Find the regression line and plot it.

    c. Find the correlation coefficient.

    d. The assistant's regression equation appears flawed since it suggests that a newly hired employee has 0.8 absences. How should the assistant respond to this criticism?

Staff Member	Years of Library Service	Number of Sick Days over Past 12 Months
1	11	5
2	6	5
3	3	2
4	5	3
5	6	4
6	1	1
7	2	3.5
8	9	5
9	11	7
10	1	1.5
11	2	0.5
12	5	2

Appendix: Answers to Selected Chapter Discussion Questions and Problems

Chapter 1

4. a. "Straw poll" for political candidates
   b. Number of books in collection that were published before 1950
   c. Value of library services to members of the community.

5. *Statistics* refers to a body of techniques used to analyze information. A *statistic* is a numerical characteristic of a sample. A *parameter* is a numerical characteristic of a population. A *variable* is a qualitative or quantitative characteristic of a population.

7. a. ordinal
   b. nominal
   c. ordinal
   d. ordinal
   e. ratio
   f. nominal
   g. interval.

8. a. discrete
   b. continuous
   c. continuous
   d. continuous
   e. discrete
   f. discrete.

Chapter 2

1. a. Not appropriate for small towns; appropriate for large cities.
   b. Appropriate and necessary; depending on size of inventory, round to nearest 100, or 1000, or even 10,000.
   c. Not applicable because inventory is small and the value of individual items is substantial.
   d. Appropriate; usually income is rounded to the nearest dollar.

6. One possibility is to make the recorder of statistics as impartial as possible. Depending on the circumstances, the recorder could be an outside consultant or a computer. Another possibility is to spot-check measurements to confirm that the reported measurements are accurate.

8. Tolerance measurement is a measurement of quantity: the number of defects. However, this quantity provides an estimate of the quality of the manufacturing process.

9. Other measures of the quality of education might include percent of students graduating or number of Nobel laureates on faculty. Ratio

measures might include the number of Nobel laureates to total faculty size.

10. When setting targets for new activities, managers may wish to consider targets used by other libraries, the historic productivity of their own staff, and that the project is new and unfamiliar, among others.

11. a. $I.I. = \dfrac{102}{246} = 0.41$

   b. The immediacy index is one measure of the currency and timeliness of articles in the journal.

   c. They may refuse good articles in subspecialties where developments are slower.

   d. Review articles contain more citations to the current year, especially if they are published toward the end of the year. The use of review articles would increase the numerator and raise the immediacy index.

   e. Publishing more, shorter articles increases both the numerator and the denominator. If the numerator increases faster than the denominator, the immediacy index rises.

12. a. $V_3 = 238, d_5 = 40$. The subscript refers to the number of the month.

   b. $\displaystyle\sum_{i=1}^{6} V_i = 1454$

   c. $\displaystyle\sum_{i=1}^{6} d_i = 237$

   d. $\dfrac{\displaystyle\sum_{i=1}^{6} V_i}{6} = \dfrac{1454}{6} = 242.33$

   e. $\dfrac{\displaystyle\sum_{i=1}^{6} d_i}{6} = \dfrac{237}{6} = 39.5$

13. a. $\displaystyle\sum_{i=1}^{8} M_i$ b. $\displaystyle\sum_{i=3}^{15} X_i$ c. $\displaystyle\sum_{i=0}^{9} X_i$

   d. $\displaystyle\sum_{i=1}^{9} f_i + 4.5$ e. $\displaystyle\sum_{n=1}^{12} n \quad (=78)$

Chapter 3

1. If there are too few classes, individual scores are lumped together and significant information is obscured.

2. A company may prepare statistical reports differently for its stockholders and the IRS. To stockholders, the company would emphasize

gains; to the IRS, the company would emphasize losses. In a public library, a report might emphasize service, deemphasizing expenditures.

3. The class widths are not equal. There should be at least 6 classes. The classes should not overlap. The classes should not be open-ended.

4.

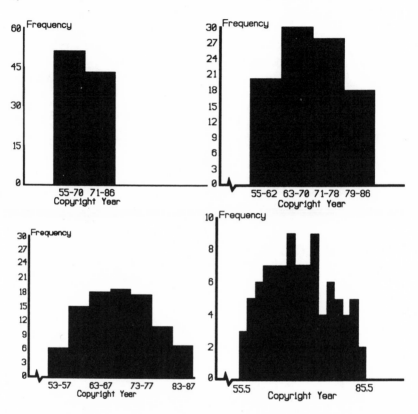

The 16-class histogram provides too much detail. The 7-class histogram provides a good visual picture of the data distribution. The 4-class histogram shows a similar bell-shaped distribution but begins to over-condense the data. The 2-class histogram provides little information.

5.

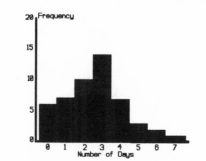

6. a. Array

18	19	19	19	20	23	23	24	25
26	28	29	30	30	32	33	35	37
39	40	44	44	44	45	46	47	47
48	48	49	50	50	50	51	51	51
52	52	52	53	53	53	54	54	55
56	59	60	60	60	61	63	65	65
65								

b. Ungrouped Frequency Distribution

18	/		42	
19	///		43	
20	/		44	///
21			45	/
22			46	/
23	//		47	//
24	/		48	//
25	/		49	/
26	/		50	///
27			51	///
28	/		52	///
29	/		53	///
30	//		54	//
31			55	/
32	/		56	/
33	/		57	
34			58	
35	/		59	/
36			60	///
37	/		61	/
38			62	
39	/		63	/
40	/		64	
41			65	///

Grouped Frequency Distribution

Class	Frequency
17–23	7
24–30	7
31–37	4
38–44	5
45–51	13
52–58	10
59–65	9
	n = 55

c.

d.

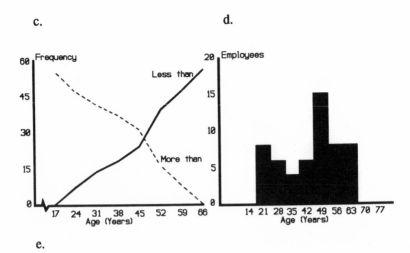

e.

f.

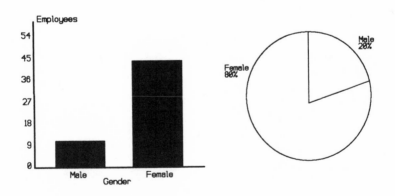

7.

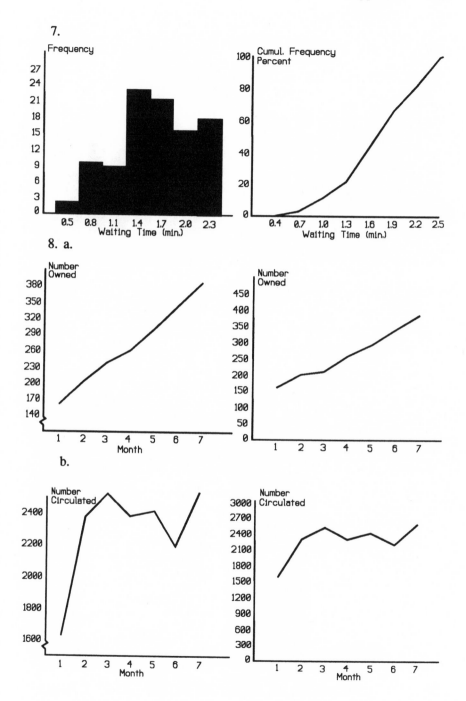

8. a.

b.

c.

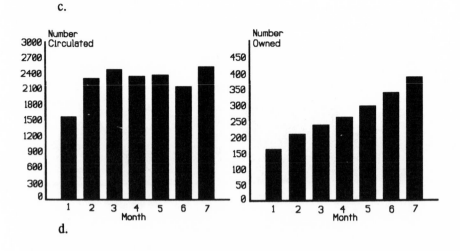

d.

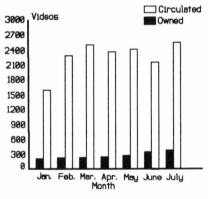

9.

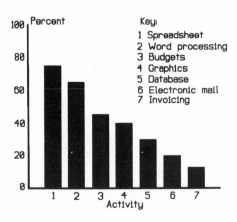

10.

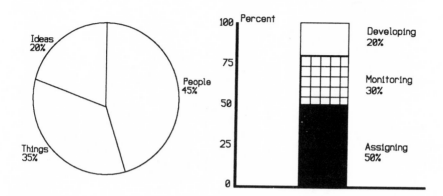

12.

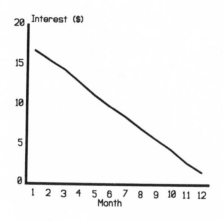

13. a. The table, when extended, shows the following columns:

Fiction	No. of Titles	Total No. of Circulations	Percent of Collection	Circulations per Title
Adventure	105	1869	8.7	17.8
Mystery	66	1958	5.5	29.7
Romance	135	5154	11.2	38.2
Science Fiction/Fantasy	132	6220	11.0	47.1
Western	91	2021	7.6	22.2
Other	138	2315	11.5	16.8
Total	667	19,537	55.5	29.3

Nonfiction

Biography	134	1392	11.2	10.4
History/Travel	255	2699	21.2	10.6
Humor	377	48	3.1	20.2
Literature	52	1247	4.3	24.0
Local interest	6	15	0.5	2.5
Self-help	35	627	2.9	17.9
Other	16	64	1.3	4.0
Total	535	6792	44.5	12.7
Grand Total	1202	26,329	100.0	21.9

b.

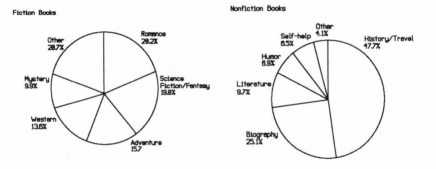

Fiction Books

Nonfiction Books

c. In this collection, the emphasis is on circulation per title. The data
   show that the most popular fiction categories are science fiction and
   fantasy, romance, and mystery. The least popular categories are the
   fiction books that do not fit the other categories, along with adventure and westerns.

   Using circulation per title as the measure, the data show that the
   most popular nonfiction categories are literature, humor, and self-
   help books. The least popular categories are books of local interest
   and titles that do not fall into the other categories.

d. To expand circulation while containing collection growth, there
   are many possibilities for the librarian to consider. Examples include reducing the number of nonfiction books and providing more
   fiction titles. Similarly, the collection can be confined to the most
   popular categories, including only a small assortment of general
   fiction titles. When selecting fiction titles, the librarian might identify older books that have been popular, despite their year of original
   publication. The librarian also might study each category in detail

to determine why certain items are popular, then include more of these in the collection.

   e. Circulation most likely would increase since there would be more available inventory (titles) from which the reader can choose when borrowing materials.

14. Percent Use

	Usually	Occasionally	Rarely
Abstracting journals	69%	23%	8%
Bibliographies/Book footnotes	51	39	10
Bibliographies/Journal footnotes	17	38	46
Colleagues	12	38	50
Librarians/Library staff	14	56	30
Subject bibliographies	14	19	67
Other	2	13	84

15. Although 56% of surveyed faculty said it would be helpful to have professional librarians help them in locating specific articles, only 14% usually consult a librarian in their search efforts. This may suggest that the library has not effectively communicated to users the services that it provides or would be willing to provide if requested. It may also mean that users perceive librarians in this library as inaccessible.

16. a. The incremental change between points is 50. That is, from 500 to 550 is +50 and from 550 to 600 is +50, etc. The graph is linear (a straight line), as in Figure 3-21, top left panel. See graph below.

   b. The incremental change between points is -25. That is, from 900 to 875 is -25 and from 875 to 850 is -25, etc. The graph is linear (a straight line) as in Figure 3-21, bottom left panel. See graph below.

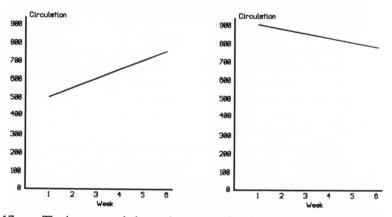

17. a. The incremental change between points increases at an increasing rate. That is, the difference between 60 and 75 is +15; between 75

and 100, it is +25; between 100 and 150, it is +50, etc. This type of change is illustrated in Figure 3-21, top center panel.

b. The incremental change between points increases at a decreasing rate. That is, the difference between 300 and 330 is +30; between 330 and 350, it is +20; between 350 and 360, it is +10, etc. The type of change is illustrated in Figure 3-21, top right panel. See graphs below.

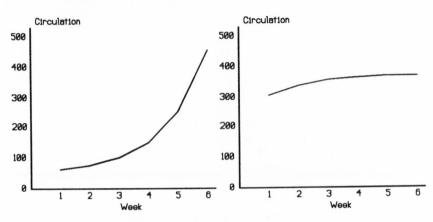

18. The incremental change between points increases at a decreasing rate. That is, the difference between 500 and 475 is -25; between 475 and 430, it is -45; between 430 and 360, it is -70, etc. This type of change is illustrated in Figure 3-21, bottom center panel. See graph below.

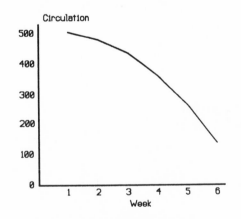

19. a. The total number of citations is 28,714 + 2955, or 31,669. The percentage of citations to books is 2955/31,669 = .09 or 9%. Citations to serials account for the remaining 28,714/31,669 = .91 or 91%.

b.

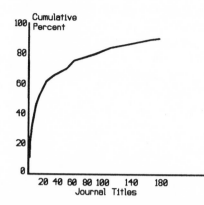

Because of the high dispersion of the literature, the number of titles required to increase collection coverage by 5% increments increases as the cumulative percent increases. A core collection of approximately 100 titles accounts for greater than 80% of all citations. The increasing number of journals required to increase the collection coverage by 5% increments reflects the diminishing marginal utility of journals as the number of journals increases. Each successive journal added to the collection makes a smaller total contribution to collection coverage than the journal which preceded it.

20. The graph illustrates that 90% of the library's circulation is accounted for by items borrowed at least once within the past 12 months. The data give no information about in-library collection use. For circulation purposes, the librarian may wish to consider items that have circulated in the last 12 months as the library's "core" collection. If space is a consideration, the librarian may want to relocate the balance of the collection to remote storage or to rely on document delivery for them if they are available through an interlibrary loan network.

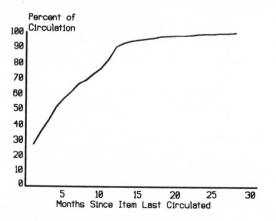

21. The distribution for the three vendors are illustrated in the graph

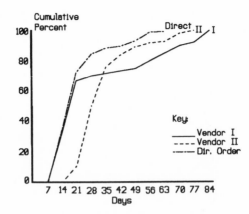

Chapter 4

1. a. Array:

0	0	0	1	1	2	2	2	3
3	3	3	3	4	4	4	4	4
4	4	5	5	5	5	5	6	7
7	7	7	7					

X	f	Tally
0	///	3
1	//	2
2	///	3
3	/////	5
4	///////	7
5	//////	6
6	/	1
7	/////	5

b. $\text{mean} = \dfrac{\sum X_i}{n} = \dfrac{0 + 0 + 0 + 1 + 1 + \ldots + 7}{31} = \dfrac{117}{31} = 3.77$

$\text{median} = \text{observation } \dfrac{(n+1)}{2} = \text{observation } \dfrac{(31+1)}{2}$

observation number 16 is 4

The mode is the most frequent observation, which is 4 for this distribution.

The mean is the average of every value in the data set; the median is the value that divides the data set in half; the mode is the most often observed value.

c. The total number of sick days is equivalent to the entire staff missing nearly 4 days.

2. a. Array:

10	12	12	13	13	13	14	15
15	15	16	16	16	16	17	17
18	18	18	19	21	21	22	23
24	24	25	26	28	29	30	31
31	32	32	35	35	35	36	37

$\underline{x}$	$\underline{f}$		$\underline{x}$	$\underline{f}$
10	/		25	/
11			26	/
12	//		27	
13	///		28	/
14	/		29	/
15	///		30	/
16	////		31	//
17	//		32	//
18	///		33	
19	/		34	
20			35	///
21	//		36	/
22	/		37	/
23	/			
24	//			

b. $\overline{X} = \dfrac{\sum X_i}{n} = \dfrac{10 + 12 + 12 + 13 + ... + 37}{40} = 22$

$\widetilde{X} =$ the value of observation number $\dfrac{(n + 1)}{2}$, which is observation number 20.5

$$= \frac{X_{20} + X_{21}}{2}$$

$$= \frac{19 + 21}{2}$$

$= 20$ Note: It is only coincidental that the value for the median, 20, approximates the observation number of the median in the data set,

20.5. Try this same application with other data sets to convince yourself.

c.

Class	Frequency
10-14	7
15-19	13
20-24	6
25-29	4
30-34	5
35-39	5

median rank = n/2 = 20

$$\tilde{X} = L + \frac{W}{f} \left(\frac{n}{2} - F \right)$$

$$= 15 + \frac{5}{13} \left(\frac{40}{2} - 7 \right) = 20$$

$$\text{mean} = \frac{\sum f_i M_i}{\sum f_i}$$

$$= \frac{7(12) + 13(17) + 6(22) + 4(27) + 5(32) + 5(37)}{7 + 13 + 6 + 4 + 5 + 5}$$

$$\frac{890}{40} = 22.25 = 890/40 = \$22.25$$

d. Total cost = $\overline{X}(40) = 22(40) = \$880$

e. Mean hourly = $\dfrac{\overline{X}}{7.5} = \$2.93$ per hour

3. a. $\overline{X} = \dfrac{\begin{array}{c} 15(5) + 20(15) + 25(26) + 35(18) + \\ 45(15) + 55(3) + 65(2) + 75(1) \end{array}}{100}$

$$= \frac{2700}{100}$$

$$= 27$$

$$\tilde{X} = L + \frac{w}{f} \left(\frac{n}{2} - F \right)$$

$$= 20 + \frac{10}{26} \left(\frac{100}{2} - 35 \right)$$

$$= 20 + \frac{10}{26} (15)$$

$$= 25.77$$

b.

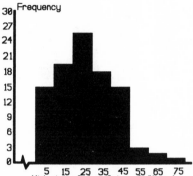

4.

Arithmetic Function Applied to Each X_i	Effect on Mean	Effect on Median	Effect on Mode
Add 5 to each term	+5	+5	+5
Subtract 5 from each term	-5	-5	-5
Increase each term by 5%	+5%	+5%	+5%

The distribution's mean is increased by 5 if 5 is added to each data point in the distribution, or it is decreased by 5 if each data point is decreased by 5, etc. Convince yourself this is true by experimenting with small data sets.

5. Time and age are infinitely divisible (years, hours, seconds, nanoseconds). However, it is easier to consider age as a discrete variable.

6. Family income, life expectancy, body weight, among others.

7. $$\overline{X}_w = \frac{13.50 (75) + 16.25 (30) + 9.50 (7.5) + 12.00 (37.5)}{75 + 30 + 7.5 + 37.5}$$

$$= \frac{2021.25}{150}$$

$$= \$13.475 \text{ per hour, or } \$13.48 \text{ per hour}$$

8. a. Nominal level

b. The rank order of flavor preferences from high to low preference is strawberry, chocolate, vanilla, mocha, and pecan.

c. Ordinal level.

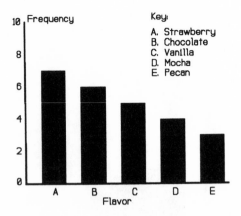

9. a. The mean number of titles/1 inch of shelflist is

$$\frac{\sum X_i}{n} = \frac{1000}{10}$$
$$= 100$$

Since there are 500 inches of cards in the shelflist, the best estimate for collection size is 500 inches x 100 titles/inch = 50,000 titles.

   b. The mean number of titles/section of shelving is

$$\frac{\sum X_i}{n} = \frac{1750}{10}$$
$$= 175$$

Since only 75% of the available shelving is filled, the best estimate for collection size is 75% x 376 sections x 175 titles/section
= .75 x 376 x 175 = 49,350 titles.

   c. The percent difference between the estimates is

$$\frac{(50,000 - 49,350)}{50,000} \ (100\%) = \frac{650}{50,000} \ (100\%) = 1.3\%$$

   d. The unoccupied shelving could hold an additional
25% x 376 x 175 = .25 x 376 x 175 = 16,450 titles

10. a. See the columns below, labeled "% Change Adult" and "% Change Juvenile."

   b. The mean adult percent change is 7.6%. The mean juvenile percent change is 66.8%.

   c. See columns labeled "Juvenile : Adult" for 1988 and 1989, below.

   d. The mean Juvenile : Adult ratio in 1988 was 0.35 and in 1989 was 0.55.

   e. The ratios for the 400–499 Dewey classification range differ widely from their means in both 1988 and 1989. Because the values from which these ratios are calculated are small, the ratios may not accurately reflect the data.

	% Change Adult	% Change Juvenile	Year 2 Juvenile:Adult	Year 1 Juvenile:Adult
000-099	17.8	-48.3	0.28	0.64
100-199	-11.4	7.1	0.38	0.32
200-299	-31.7	-81.8	0.05	0.18
300-399	32.6	11.8	0.17	0.20
400-499	-50.0	600.0	2.33	0.17
500-599	16.7	44.2	1.19	0.96
600-699	24.3	-26.9	0.10	0.18
700-799	17.1	14.9	0.16	0.16
800-899	49.6	31.0	0.22	0.26
900-999	10.7	67.4	0.27	0.18
Fiction	9.9	153.1	0.56	0.24
Biography	5.9	29.5	0.88	0.72

11. a.

Number of Days	Days before Ordering	Days for Vendor to Fill Order	Days to Process Item
1–7	16.4%	0.2%	8.0%
8–14	28.4	0.2	9.8
15–21	28.9	0.2	12.5
22–28	16.1	18.6	29.5
29–35	8.9	19.1	16.1
36–42	1.1	47.7	11.4
43–49	0.2	5.0	6.6
50–56		3.9	2.0
57–63		3.4	1.6
64–70		1.1	1.1
71–77		0.5	0.9
78–84			0.5

b.

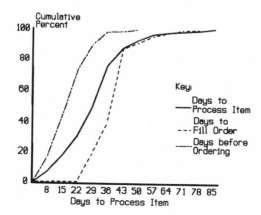

c. Mean number of days before ordering:

$$\bar{X}_w = \frac{\begin{array}{c}4(72) + 11(125) + 18(127) + \\ 25(71) + 32(39) + 39(5) + 46(1)\end{array}}{440}$$

$$= \frac{7213}{440}$$

$$= 16.4$$

Mean number of days for vendor to fill order:

$$\bar{X}_w = \frac{\begin{array}{c}4(1) + 11(1) + 18(1) + 25(82) + 32(84) + \\ 39(210) + 46(22) + 53(17) + 60(15) + 67(5) + 74(2)\end{array}}{440}$$

$$= \frac{16{,}257}{440}$$

$$= 36.9$$

Mean number of days to process item

$$\bar{X}_w = \frac{\begin{array}{c}4(35) + 11(43) + 18(55) + 25(130) + 32(71) + \\ 39(50) + 46(29) + 53(9) + 60(7) + 67(5) + 74(4) + 81(2)\end{array}}{440}$$

$$= \frac{12{,}099}{440}$$

$$= 27.5$$

12.

a.

Library	Acquisitions/Collection Size (%)
1	5.1%
2	13.5
3	5.0
4	6.2
5	0.6
6	7.7
7	5.9
8	6.5
9	6.5
10	6.7

b. $\bar{X} = \dfrac{5.1 + 13.5 + 5.0 + 6.2 + 0.6 + 7.7 + 5.9 + 6.5 + 6.5 + 6.7}{10}$

$= \dfrac{63.7}{10}$

$= 6.37$

    c. Libraries that have just begun operation might be expected to have a higher than average level of acquisitions compared to collection size. Since the collection is being developed and is growing rapidly, the number of acquisitions will be high while the total collection size is still small. Therefore, the ratio of acquisitions to collection size will be high.

    d. The low ratio suggests that the collection is becoming increasingly obsolete because of a reduced level of new acquisitions. It may also be because of a failure to weed the collection regularly, which has resulted in a large collection size, so that the denominator of the ratio overwhelms the numerator.

Chapter 5

1. The interquartile range is superior to the range if the data are wide-tailed or if the distribution has open ends. The range, however, is easier to calculate and is superior to the interquartile range if the data are narrow-tailed.

2. The sum of deviations from the mean will always equal zero, but the sum of deviations from the median and mode will only coincidentally equal zero.

3. In a skewed distribution, the median is between the mean and the mode but is closer to the mean. A good estimate of the median for this distribution would be median approximately 22.

4. a. $\{0, 0, 9, 9, 9\}$

$$\overline{X} = \frac{\sum X_i}{n} = \frac{0 + 0 + 9 + 9 + 9}{5} = 5.4$$

$$s = \sqrt{\frac{\sum (X_i - \overline{X})^2}{n}}$$

$$= \sqrt{\frac{(0 - 5.4)^2 + (0 - 5.4)^2 + (9 - 5.4)^2 + (9 - 5.4)^2 + (9 - 5.4)^2}{5}}$$

$$= \sqrt{\frac{29.16 + 29.16 + 12.96 + 12.96 + 12.96}{5}}$$

$$= 4.41$$

    b. $\{0, 0, 0, 0, 0\}$

$$\overline{X} = \frac{\sum X_i}{n} = \frac{0+0+0+0+0}{5} = 0$$

$$s = \sqrt{\frac{\sum(X_i - \overline{X})^2}{n}}$$

$$= \sqrt{\frac{(0-0)^2 + (0-0)^2 + (0-0)^2 + (0-0)^2 + (0-0)^2}{5}}$$

$$= \sqrt{\frac{0}{5}} = 0$$

5. $$\overline{X} = \frac{\sum X_i}{n} = \frac{2+0+0+1+2}{5} = 1$$

$$s = \sqrt{\frac{(2-1)^2 + (0-1)^2 + (0-1)^2 + (1-1)^2 + (2-1)^2}{5-1}}$$

$$= \sqrt{\frac{4}{4}} = 1$$

6. See solution 3-4 for hints on reading this table

	Range	S.D.	Variance
a.	Same	Same	Same
b.	Increases by 10%	Increases by 10%	Increases by 10%
c.	Same	Same	Same
d.	Decreases by 10%	Decreases by 10%	Decreases by 10%

9. a. Mean, standard deviation, and coefficient of variation: sick days Year 1

$$\overline{X} = \frac{\sum X_i}{n}$$

$$= \frac{143}{26}$$

$$= 5.50 \text{ days}$$

$$s = \sqrt{\frac{\sum(X_i - \overline{X})^2}{n-1}}$$

$$= \sqrt{\frac{\begin{array}{c}(2.5)^2 + (4.5)^2 + (3.5)^2 + (4.5)^2 + (0.5)^2 + \\ (1.5)^2 + (4.5)^2 + (1.5)^2 + (2.5)^2 + (0.5)^2 + \\ (4.5)^2 + (5.5)^2 + (0.5)^2 + (1.5)^2 + (1.5)^2 + \\ (3.5)^2 + (5.5)^2 + (0.5)^2 + (2.5)^2 + (0.5)^2 + \\ (1.5)^2 + (5.5)^2 + (2.5)^2 + (2.5)^2 + (0.5)^2 + (2.5)^2\end{array}}{25}}$$

$$= \sqrt{\frac{246.25}{25}}$$

$$= \sqrt{9.85}$$

$$= 3.14 \text{ days}$$

$$V = \frac{3.14}{5.50} \,(\,100\%\,)$$

$$= 57.1\%$$

Mean, standard deviation and coefficient of variation: sick days Year 2

$$\bar{X} = \frac{\sum X_i}{n}$$

$$= \frac{117}{31}$$

$$= 3.77 \text{ days}$$

$$s = \sqrt{\frac{\sum (X_i - \bar{X})^2}{n - 1}}$$

$$= \sqrt{\frac{\begin{array}{c}(1.23)^2 + (0.23)^2 + (1.77)^2 + (0.23)^2 + (3.23)^2 + \\ (1.77)^2 + (1.23)^2 + (3.23)^2 + (1.23)^2 + (0.77)^2 + \\ (3.23)^2 + (0.77)^2 + (0.23)^2 + (0.77)^2 + (2.23)^2 + \\ (1.23)^2 + (0.23)^2 + (1.77)^2 + (3.23)^2 + (0.77)^2 + \\ (0.23)^2 + (3.23)^2 + (1.23)^2 + (0.77)^2 + (2.77)^2 + \\ (3.77)^2 (0.23)^2 + (3.77)^2 + (3.77)^2 + (2.77)^2 + (0.23)^2\end{array}}{30}}$$

$$= \sqrt{\frac{135.42}{30}}$$

$$= 2.12 \text{ days}$$

$$V = \frac{2.12}{3.77} \, (100\%)$$

$$= 56.2\%$$

The coefficients of variance for the Year 1 and Year 2 data set are nearly equal. This implies that the two distributions have the same variability, and therefore that the difference between means is a good measure of the average difference between the two distributions.

b. The new policy appears to have had two effects. First, the average number of sick days per employee has declined by almost 2 days, from 3.77 to 2.12 days. Second, the number of employees taking sick leave has increased from 25 to 30. Nonetheless, the total number of sick days has declined from 143 to 117 days.

10. a. The data are heavily skewed to the right and leptokurtic. This suggests that the median may be a better measure of central tendency than the mean.

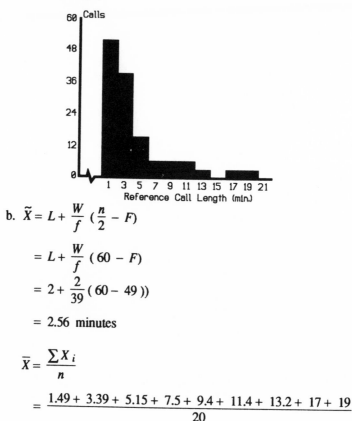

b. $\tilde{X} = L + \dfrac{W}{f} \, (\dfrac{n}{2} - F)$

$$= L + \frac{W}{f} \, (60 - F)$$

$$= 2 + \frac{2}{39} \, (60 - 49\,))$$

$$= 2.56 \text{ minutes}$$

$$\bar{X} = \frac{\sum X_i}{n}$$

$$= \frac{1.49 + 3.39 + 5.15 + 7.5 + 9.4 + 11.4 + 13.2 + 17 + 19}{20}$$

$$= \frac{418}{120}$$

$$= 3.48 \text{ minutes}$$

As shown in part a, the median is a better measure of central tendency because the mean is influenced by the skew of the distribution. The skew can be calculated as follows:

$$s(k) = \frac{3(\text{mean} - \text{median})}{\text{standard deviation}}$$

$$= \frac{3(3.48 - 2.56)}{3.38}$$

$$= 0.82$$

c. $$s = \sqrt{\frac{\sum(X_i - \bar{X})^2}{n-1}}$$

$$= \sqrt{\frac{\begin{array}{l} 49(1 - 3.48)^2 + 39(3 - 3.48)^2 + 15(5 - 3.48)^2 + \\ 5(7 - 3.48)^2 + 4(9 - 3.48)^2 + 4(11 - 3.48)^2 + \\ 2(13 - 3.48)^2 + (17 - 3.48)^2 + (19 - 3.48)^2 \end{array}}{119}}$$

$$= \sqrt{\frac{1359.94}{119}}$$

$$= 3.38 \text{ minutes}$$

The variance is found by squaring the standard deviation, that is,

$$s^2 = (3.38)(3.38)$$

$$= 11.42 \text{ minutes squared}$$

d. $$Q_3 - Q_1 = [L + \frac{w}{f}(\frac{75n}{100} - F)] - [L + \frac{w}{f}(\frac{25n}{100} - F)]$$

$$= [4 + \frac{2}{15}(90 - 88)] - [0 + \frac{2}{49}(30 - 0)]$$

$$= 4.267 - 1.224$$

$$= 3.043$$

e. Chebyshev's Theorem predicts that 55.6% of the data will fall in the range $[\bar{X} \pm 1.5s] = [3.48 \pm 1.5(3.38)] = [3.48 \pm 5.07]$.

The left endpoint of the interval is 3.48-5.07, or -1.59, and the right endpoint is 3.48+5.07, or 8.55.

All the data points in the classes 0 and under 2, 2 and under 4, 4 and under 6, 6 and under 8, are greater than -1.59 and less than 8.55. This is a total of 108 data points. In addition, there are some data points in the class 8 and under 10 which are also less than 8.55. If we spread the four data points in this range evenly over the width of the range, they would fall $X_{109} = 8$, $X_{110} = 8.5$, $X_{111} = 9.0$, and $X_{112} = 9.9$. Thus, X_{109} and X_{110} are also less than 8.55. A total of 110 data points falls in the range $\overline{X} \pm 1.5s$. In percent terms, this is equal to 110/120 = 92%. Thus the percent of data contained in the range far exceeds the percent estimated by Chebyshev's Theorem.

The actual percent of data (92%) far exceeds that which would be expected for a normal distribution (87%). The implication is that the standard deviation overestimates the amount of deviation in the distribution. The standard deviation is an overestimate because it is affected by the skew of the data.

f. As discussed in part e, the standard deviation overestimates the variation of these data. The interquartile range is the preferred measure of deviation because it accurately shows that 50% of the data is contained in the range (1.2, 4.3).

11. The range is the distance between the most extreme values of the distribution. The standard deviation is the average distance between the mean and all other values.

12. a. The distribution has a slight negative skew.

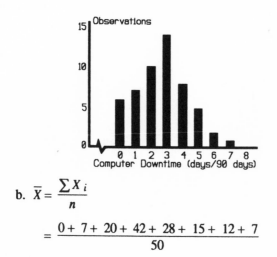

b. $\overline{X} = \dfrac{\sum X_i}{n}$

$= \dfrac{0 + 7 + 20 + 42 + 28 + 15 + 12 + 7}{50}$

$$= \frac{131}{50}$$

$$= 2.62 \text{ days}$$

$$s = \sqrt{\frac{\sum (X_i - \overline{X})^2}{n - 1}}$$

$$= \sqrt{\frac{\begin{array}{c} 6(0 - 2.62)^2 + 7(1 - 2.62)^2 + 10(2 - 2.62)^2 + \\ 14(3 - 2.62)^2 + 7(4 - 2.62)^2 + 3(5 - 2.62)^2 + \\ 2(6 - 2.62)^2 + (7 - 2.62)^2 \end{array}}{49}}$$

$$\sqrt{\frac{137.78}{49}}$$

$$= 1.677 \text{ days}$$

c. The standard deviation calculated in part b can be estimated with the equation $4s \approx$ range $\approx 7 - 0 \approx 7$ so $s \approx 1.75 \approx 1.67$
This same equation can be used to estimate the standard deviation of the out-of-state data, $4s \approx 12 - 0 \approx 12$ so $s \approx 3$.
The estimated standard deviation for the out-of-state values is larger than the standard deviation for the in-state values. However, the largest out-of-state value, 12, is larger than the largest in-state value, 7. This implies that the mean for the out-of-state values is probably higher than the mean for the in-state values. The result is that the co-efficients of variation for the two data sets will be roughly equal.

13. a.

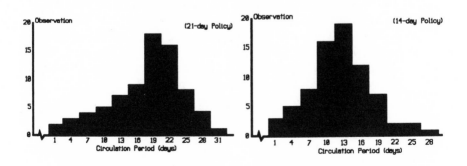

The distribution for the library with the 14-day policy is more symmetrical and has a smaller mean than the distribution for the library with the 21-day policy.

b. 21-day policy:

$$\bar{X} = \frac{1308}{75}$$

$$= 17.44 \text{ days}$$

$$\tilde{X} = 18 + 2\left(\frac{8}{18}\right)$$

$$= 18.89 \text{ days}$$

$$s = \sqrt{\frac{3192.48}{74}}$$

$$= 6.57 \text{ days}$$

14-day policy:

$$\bar{X} = \frac{933}{75}$$

$$= 12.44 \text{ days}$$

$$\tilde{X} = 12 + 2\left(\frac{6}{19}\right)$$

$$= 12.63 \text{ days}$$

$$s = \sqrt{\frac{2280.48}{74}}$$

$$= 5.55 \text{ days}$$

The mean and median for the 21-day policy differ by over 1 day while the mean and median for the 14-day policy are nearly the same. This confirms the visual observation in part a that the 21-day distribution is skewed left and the 14-day distribution is nearly symmetrical. In a skewed distribution, the median is a better measure of central tendency; in a symmetrical distribution, the mean is preferred.

c. 21-day policy:

$$V = \frac{100\,s}{\bar{X}}$$

$$= \frac{657}{17.44}$$

$$= 37.67\%$$

14-day policy:

$$V = \frac{100\,s}{\overline{X}}$$

$$= \frac{555}{12.44}$$

$$= 44.61\%$$

The 14-day distribution has a slightly higher variance than the 21-day distribution.

d. Under the 14-day policy, books are returned, on average, $\overline{X}_{21} - \overline{X}_{14} = 17.44 - 12.44 = 5$ days earlier. The 14-day policy maximizes turnover opportunity.

e. The effect of a longer circulation period is that the library's inventory (collection) is not available for check-out. This reduces the opportunity for greater collection turnover.

f. The effect of limiting the number of items each client can check out is to keep more inventory (collections) in the library available for others to borrow or use in the library. Clients who determine that the library "never has what I want when I want it" will become discouraged and not use the library. Having collections available for clientele use is a major challenge for the librarian.

14. a. The distribution is flat and skewed to the right.

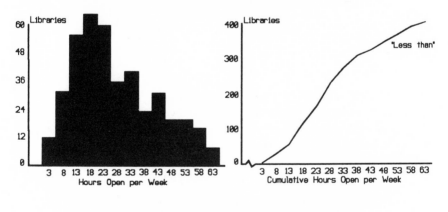

b. Mean =

$$\frac{\begin{array}{c}3\,(\,3\,)+\,8\,(\,25\,)+\,13\,(\,31\,)+\,18\,(\,56\,)+\\23\,(\,64\,)+\,28\,(\,58\,)+\,33\,(\,33\,)+\,38\,(\,39\,)+\\43\,(\,21\,)+\,48\,(\,29\,)+\,53\,(\,17\,)+\,58\,(\,17\,)+\,63\,(\,8\,)\end{array}}{401}$$

$$= \frac{11,973}{401}$$

$$= 29.86 \text{ hours}$$

$$\tilde{X} = L + \frac{W}{f} \left(\frac{n}{2} - F\right)$$

$$= L + \frac{W}{f} (200.5 - F)$$

$$= 26 + \frac{4}{58} (200.5 - 179)$$

$$= 27.48 \text{ hours}$$

$$\text{Range} = 65 - 1$$

$$= 64 \text{ hours}$$

$$s = \sqrt{\frac{\sum(X_i - \bar{X})^2}{n-1}}$$

$$= \sqrt{\frac{\begin{array}{c} 3(3 - 29.86)^2 + 25(8 - 29.86)^2 + 31(13 - 29.86)^2 + \\ 56(18 - 29.86)^2 + 64(23 - 29.86)^2 + 58(28 - 29.86)^2 + \\ 33(33 - 29.86)^2 + 39(38 - 29.86)^2 + 21(43 - 29.86)^2 + \\ 29(48 - 29.86)^2 + 17(53 - 29.86)^2 + 17(58 - 29.86)^2 + \\ 8(63 - 29.86)^2 \end{array}}{400}}$$

$$= \sqrt{\frac{81,440.90}{400}}$$

$$= 14.27 \text{ hours}$$

c. $P_{80} = L + \dfrac{W}{f} \left(\dfrac{80n}{100} - F\right)$

$$= L + \frac{W}{f} (320.8 - F)$$

$$= 41 + \frac{4}{21} (320.8 - 309)$$

43.25 hours = 43.25 hours

The interpretation of P_{80} is that 80% of all libraries in survey are open 43.25, or fewer, hours per week.

d. There is a group of libraries that are open 50 hours per week. They occur at the upper limit of the class 46–50. Because the cumulative frequency at class 46–50 is 359, there are 359 observations which are less than or equal to 50 hours per week. Thus a library which is open 50 hours per week is open as many or more hours than 359/401 = .9 or 90% of the other libraries. 50 hours = P_{90} .

15. a. First, data should be put in an ordered array:

13	20	20	20	24	27	36	39	40
40	41	41	42	50	54	55	60	61

$$\bar{X} = \frac{\begin{array}{l}13 + 20 + 20 + 20 + 24 + 27 + 36 + 39 + 40 + \\ 40 + 41 + 41 + 42 + 50 + 54 + 55 + 60 + 61\end{array}}{18}$$

$$= \frac{683}{18}$$

$$= 37.94 \text{ hours}$$

$$\tilde{X} = \text{observation number } \frac{(n+1)}{2}$$

$$= \text{observation number } \frac{19}{2}$$

$$= \text{observation number } 9.5$$

$$= \frac{\text{observation number } 9 + \text{observation number } 10}{2}$$

$$= \frac{40 + 40}{2}$$

$$= 40 \text{ hours}$$

$$s = \sqrt{\frac{\begin{array}{c}(13 - 37.94)^2 + 3(20 - 37.94)^2 + (24 - 37.94)^2 + \\ (27 - 37.94)^2 + (36 - 37.94)^2 + (39 - 37.94)^2 + \\ 2(40 - 37.94)^2 + 2(41 - 37.94)^2 + (42 - 37.94)^2 + \\ (50 - 37.94)^2 + (54 - 37.94)^2 + (55 - 37.94)^2 + \\ (60 - 37.94)^2 + (61 - 37.94)^2\end{array}}{17}}$$

$$= \sqrt{\frac{\begin{array}{c}(-24.94)^2 + 3(-17.94)^2 + (-13.94)^2 + \\ (-10.94)^2 + (-1.94)^2 + (1.06)^2 + \\ 2(2.06)^2 + 2(3.06)^2 + (4.06)^2 + \\ (12.06)^2 + (16.06)^2 + (17.06)^2 + \\ (22.06)^2 + (23.06)^2\end{array}}{17}}$$

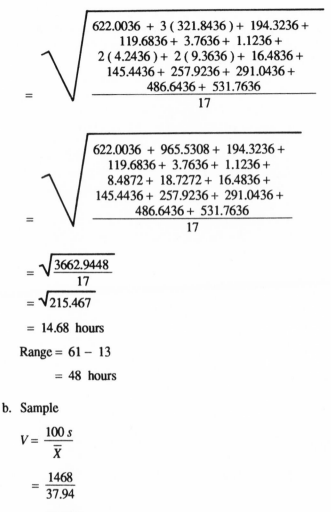

$$= \sqrt{\frac{\begin{array}{c}622.0036 + 3(321.8436) + 194.3236 + \\ 119.6836 + 3.7636 + 1.1236 + \\ 2(4.2436) + 2(9.3636) + 16.4836 + \\ 145.4436 + 257.9236 + 291.0436 + \\ 486.6436 + 531.7636\end{array}}{17}}$$

$$= \sqrt{\frac{\begin{array}{c}622.0036 + 965.5308 + 194.3236 + \\ 119.6836 + 3.7636 + 1.1236 + \\ 8.4872 + 18.7272 + 16.4836 + \\ 145.4436 + 257.9236 + 291.0436 + \\ 486.6436 + 531.7636\end{array}}{17}}$$

$$= \sqrt{\frac{3662.9448}{17}}$$

$$= \sqrt{215.467}$$

$$= 14.68 \text{ hours}$$

$$\text{Range} = 61 - 13$$

$$= 48 \text{ hours}$$

b. Sample

$$V = \frac{100\,s}{\overline{X}}$$

$$= \frac{1468}{37.94}$$

$$= 38.69\%$$

Problem 15

$$V = \frac{100\,s}{\overline{X}}$$

$$= \frac{1425}{29.86}$$

$$= 47.72\%$$

There is more variance in the large group than in the small sample.

16. a. The modal class, with a frequency of 37, is centered at 60 minutes

per month and ranges from 30 to 90 minutes per month. A good approximation for the median would be 90 minutes per month. In a skewed distribution, the median lies between the mode and the mean, but is closer to the mean.

b. The three observations centered at 300 minutes per month, the two observations centered at 360 minutes per month, and the single observation centered at 480 minutes per month are all extreme values.

c. The distribution is positively skewed since the scores are concentrated at the low end of the scale.

d. Call durations per month of $110.4 + 2(92.73) = 110.4 + 185.5 = 295.9$ minutes are greater than 2 standard deviations above the mean. Thus, the six extreme values cited in part a all lie outside 2 standard deviations above the mean.

e. The hours of staff time lost per employee per month may be estimated from the mean number of minutes of phone usage on outgoing calls. This value, 110.4 minutes per employee per month, is equivalent to 1.84 hours of staff time lost per employee per month on personal calls.

17. a. The ungrouped and grouped frequency distributions are

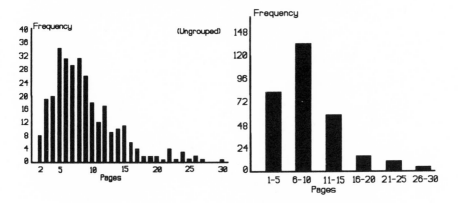

b. The ungrouped mean is calculated as follows

$$\bar{X} = \frac{\begin{array}{c} 1(0) + 2(8) + 3(19) + 4(20) + 5(35) + \\ 6(31) + 7(29) + 8(31) + 9(26) + 10(18) + \\ 11(12) + 12(17) + 13(9) + 14(10) + 15(11) + \\ 16(6) + 17(4) + 18(2) + 19(2) + 20(2) + \\ 21(1) + 22(4) + 23(1) + 24(3) + 25(1) + \\ 26(2) + 27(1) + 28(0) + 29(0) + 30(1) \end{array}}{306}$$

$$= \frac{\begin{array}{l} 0 + 16 + 57 + 80 + 175 + 186 + 203 + 248 + 234 + 180 + \\ 132 + 204 + 117 + 140 + 165 + 96 + 68 + 36 + 38 + 40 + \\ 22 + 88 + 23 + 72 + 25 + 52 + 27 + 0 + 0 + 30 \end{array}}{306}$$

$$= \frac{2753}{306}$$

$$= 8.99 \text{ or } 9.0$$

The ungrouped median is determined by locating the $(N + 1)/2$ observation in the data set. Since there are 306 observations, the median is between the 153rd and 154th observations in the set. The value for the ungrouped median, thus, is 8.

The grouped mean, derived by using the six classes above, is

$$\overline{X} = \frac{\begin{array}{l} 3 (82) + 8 (135) + 13 (59) + \\ 18 (16) + 23 (10) + 28 (4) \end{array}}{306}$$

$$= \frac{246 + 1080 + 767 + 288 + 230 + 112}{306}$$

$$= \frac{2723}{306}$$

$$= 8.90$$

The grouped median is calculated as follows

$$\tilde{X} = L + \frac{W}{f} \left(\frac{n}{2} - F \right)$$

$$= 6 + \frac{4}{135} \left(\frac{306}{2} - 82 \right)$$

$$= 6 + \frac{4}{135} (153 - 82)$$

$$= 6 + \frac{4 (71)}{135}$$

$$= 6 + 2.1$$

$$= 8.1$$

c. The range of the data is 28. The number of pages per article ranges from 2 to 30. Thus the range is calculated as 30 - 2 = 28.

The ungrouped standard deviation is calculated by using the following formula:

$$s = \sqrt{\frac{\sum(X_i - \overline{X})^2}{n - 1}}$$

$$= \sqrt{\frac{\begin{array}{l} 8(-7)^2 + 19(-6)^2 + 20(-5)^2 + 35(-4)^2 + \\ 31(-3)^2 + 29(-2)^2 + 31(-1)^2 + 18(1)^2 + \\ 12(2)^2 + 17(3)^2 + 9(4)^2 + 10(5)^2 + 11(6)^2 + \\ 6(7)^2 + 4(8)^2 + 2(9)^2 + 1(10)^2 + 2(11)^2 + \\ 1(12)^2 + 4(13)^2 + 1(14)^2 + 3(15)^2 + 1(16)^2 + \\ 2(17)^2 + 1(18)^2 + 1(21)^2 \end{array}}{306 - 1}}$$

$$= \sqrt{\frac{\begin{array}{l} 8(49)^2 + 19(36)^2 + 20(25)^2 + 35(16)^2 + \\ 31(9)^2 + 29(4)^2 + 31(1)^2 + 18(1)^2 + \\ 12(4)^2 + 17(9)^2 + 9(16)^2 + 10(25)^2 + 11(36)^2 + \\ 6(49)^2 + 4(64)^2 + 2(81)^2 + 1(100)^2 + 2(121)^2 + \\ 1(144)^2 + 4(169)^2 + 1(196)^2 + 3(225)^2 + 1(256)^2 + \\ 2(289)^2 + 1(324)^2 + 1(441)^2 \end{array}}{305}}$$

$$= \sqrt{\frac{\begin{array}{l} 392 + 684 + 500 + 560 + 279 + 116 + \\ 31 + 18 + 48 + 153 + 144 + 250 + 396 + \\ 294 + 256 + 162 + 200 + 242 + 144 + \\ 676 + 196 + 675 + 256 + 578 + 324 + 441 \end{array}}{305}}$$

$$= \sqrt{\frac{8015}{305}}$$

$$= \sqrt{26.28}$$

$$= 5.126$$

The grouped standard deviation may be calculated as follows:

$$s = \sqrt{\frac{\sum f_i(M_i - \overline{X})^2}{n - 1}}$$

$$= \sqrt{\frac{\begin{array}{l} 82(-5.9)^2 + 135(-0.9)^2 + 59(4.1)^2 + \\ 16(9.1)^2 + 10(14.1)^2 + 4(19.1)^2 \end{array}}{306 - 1}}$$

$$= \sqrt{\frac{82\,(\,34.81\,)^{2} + 135\,(\,0.81\,)^{2} + 59\,(\,16.81\,)^{2} + 16\,(\,82.81\,)^{2} + 10\,(\,198.81\,)^{2} + 4\,(\,364.81\,)^{2}}{305}}$$

$$= \sqrt{\frac{2854.4 + 109.4 + 991.8 + 1325.0 + 1988.1 + 1459.2}{305}}$$

$$= \sqrt{\frac{8727}{305}}$$

$$= \sqrt{28.62}$$

$$= 5.35$$

d. There is good agreement between the grouped and ungrouped means, medians, and standard deviations (see the table below).

	Ungrouped	Grouped
mean	8.99	8.9
median	8.1	8.0
standard deviation	5.126	5.35

e. Generally, 95% of the observations will fall between 2 standard deviations of the mean (above and below). In other words, 95% of the articles lent over a 1-week period will have between $\overline{X} \pm 2$ (standard deviation) pages. This works out to be approximately 9.0 ± 5.0 pages, or between 4.0 and 14.0 pages per article.

18. c. An example of a J-distribution is the number of articles published per year over the past 25 years.

Chapter 6

1. Regression allows the librarian to calculate the central tendency and dispersion of paired data points. The regression equation shows whether the data sets are negatively or positively related. Correlation allows the librarian to quantify the strength of the relationship and shows whether the data sets are positively or negatively related. The correlation coefficient decreases as dispersion increases.

2. In a positive linear relationship, increases in the independent variable are accompanied by increases in the dependent variable. In a negative relationship, increases in the independent variable are accompanied by decreases in the dependent variable.

Some possible examples of positive and negative relationships are

a. Positive: (time since eating, hunger)
   Negative: (miles driven, gas in tank)

b. Positive: (time since beginning of basketball game, score of basketball game)
   Negative: (rank of team, game attendance)
c. Positive: (hours library is open, number of clients)
   Negative: (years since book was published, circulation)

3.

Independent Variable	Dependent Variable	Positive or Negative
a. high school G.P.A.	college entrance exam	positive
b. college entrance exam	college G.P.A.	positive
c. current outdoor temperature	electricity usage	positive
d. earnings per share	price of stock	positive
e. food consumed	body weight	positive
f. supervisor's skill	employee output	positive
g. ticket prices	passengers/100 miles	negative
h. noise level	employee morale	negative
i. publication date of book	rate of library circulation	positive

4. The correlation coefficient shows the degree to which two variables are related and whether the relationship is positive or negative. The determination coefficient shows what percent of variation in the dependent variable can be explained by variation in the independent variable. Many consumers of statistics confuse these two coefficients. The librarian can help to avoid this confusion by using the two statistics together.

5. Nonparametric methods are well suited to the library, where much of the data that are collected is subjective. Parametric methods work well with "hard data" such as collection age and circulation.

6. The determination coefficient is not useful with nonparametric data because percents are not useful with nonparametric data. As discussed in Chapter 2, it is incorrect to say that $11F°$ is 10% warmer than $10F°$. This is because the Fahrenheit scale has no absolute zero point. Likewise, it is incorrect to say that 75% of changes in client satisfaction are explained by changes in the number of reference librarians on duty. This is because client satisfaction has no absolute zero point.

8. The regression line's slope shows the average amount of change in y for a given change in x. Correlation shows how strong this relationship is. Both the slope and the correlation show whether the relationship is negative or positive.

9. Formula 6-2 shows that the slope of a line is $(y_2-y_1)/(x_2-x_1)$. For any vertical line, $x_2-x_1 = 0$. Fractions with denominators equal to zero are undefined. For this reason, a vertical line has no slope. For any horizontal line, $y_2-y_1 = 0$. Fractions with numerators equal to 0 are 0.

10. Correlation is a measure-of degree of relatedness. Each variable has the same degree of relatedness to the other, regardless of which is considered independent and which is considered dependent. Formula 6-8 confirms this assertion. X and Y are treated equally in Formula 6-8, and the same numerical value for r will be obtained no matter which variable is labeled X and which is labeled Y. This is not true in regression since the choice of independent and dependent variable makes a difference.

11.

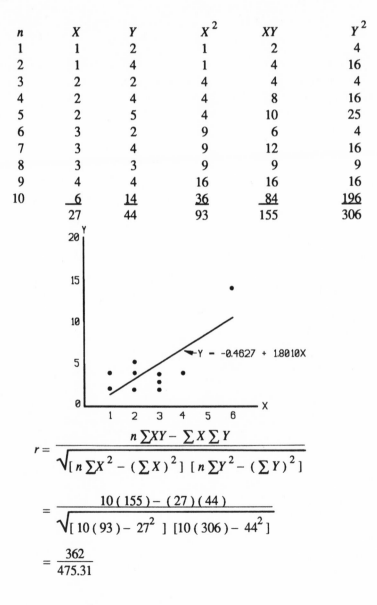

n	X	Y	X^2	XY	Y^2
1	1	2	1	2	4
2	1	4	1	4	16
3	2	2	4	4	4
4	2	4	4	8	16
5	2	5	4	10	25
6	3	2	9	6	4
7	3	4	9	12	16
8	3	3	9	9	9
9	4	4	16	16	16
10	6	14	36	84	196
	27	44	93	155	306

$$r = \frac{n \sum XY - \sum X \sum Y}{\sqrt{[n \sum X^2 - (\sum X)^2][n \sum Y^2 - (\sum Y)^2]}}$$

$$= \frac{10(155) - (27)(44)}{\sqrt{[10(93) - 27^2][10(306) - 44^2]}}$$

$$= \frac{362}{475.31}$$

= 0.7616

r^2 = coefficient of determintation

= (0.7616) (0.7616)

= 0.58

The coefficient of correlation, 0.7616, means that the x and y variables are moderately well correlated. The coefficient of determination, 0.58, means that 58% of the total variance in the dependent variable is explained by variance in the independent variable.

b. $\hat{Y} = aX + b$

$$a = \frac{n \sum XY - \sum X \sum Y}{n (\sum X^2) - (\sum X)^2}$$

$$= \frac{10 (55) - 27 (44)}{10 (93) - 27^2}$$

$$= \frac{1550 - 1188}{930 - 729}$$

= 1.801

$b = \bar{Y} - a\bar{X}$

= 4.4 − a (2.7)

= 4.4 − 1.801 (2.7)

= 4.4 − 4.8627

= − 0.4627

$\hat{Y} = − 0.4627 + 1.8 X$

c.

n	ΣX	ΣY	ΣX^2	ΣXY	ΣY^2
9	21	30	67	71	110

$$r = \frac{9 (71) - 21 (30)}{\sqrt{[9 (57) - 21^2] [9 (110) - 30^2]}}$$

$$= \frac{639 - 630}{\sqrt{(813 - 441) (990 - 900)}}$$

= 0.1118

$$r^2 = (0.1118)^2$$

$$= (0.1118)(0.1118) \text{ or } 0.0125$$

Excluding the extreme data point $(6, 14)$ decreases correlation from 0.7616 (moderate) to 0.1118 (poor). This is because the remaining data form an oval pattern, as can be seen in the figure. (The extreme point is a *point of high influence* since it increases correlation.)

12. Regression of operating expense (y) on population (x). From table in text:

ΣX	ΣY	ΣX^2	ΣXY	ΣY^2
15.7	128.8	27.29	219.83	1829.46

$$a = \frac{n \sum XY - \sum X \sum Y}{n(\sum X^2) - (\sum X)^2}$$

$$= \frac{10(219.83) - 15.7(128.8)}{10(27.29) - (15.7)^2}$$

$$= \frac{2198.30 - 2022.16}{272.90 - 246.49}$$

$$= 6.669$$

$$b = \overline{Y} - a\overline{X}$$

$$= 12.88 - (6.669)(1.57)$$

$$= 2.4097$$

$$\hat{Y} = 2.4097 + 6.669 X$$

$$\text{EXPENSE} = 6.669(\text{POPULATION}) + 2.4097$$

Regression of population (y) on operating expense (x) From Table 6-3, page 182:

ΣX	ΣY	ΣX^2	ΣXY	ΣY^2
128.8	15.7	1829.46	219.83	27.29

$$a = \frac{10(219.83) - (15.7)(128.8)}{10(1829.46) - (128.8)^2}$$

$$= \frac{176.14}{18,294.6 - 16,589.44}$$

$$= 0.1033$$

$$b = \overline{Y} - a\overline{X}$$

$$= 1.57 - (0.1033)(12.80)$$

$$= 0.2395$$

$$\hat{Y} = 0.2395 + 0.1033\,X$$

POPULATION $= 0.1033\,(\text{EXPENSE}) + 0.2395$

13.

X	Y	X^2	XY	Y^2
1969	16.2	3,876,961	31,897.8	262.44
1970	13.5	3,880,900	26,595.0	182.25
1971	11.1	3,884,841	21,878.1	123.21
1972	14.2	3,888,784	28,002.4	201.64
1973	11.2	3,892,729	22,097.6	125.44
1974	15.3	3,896,676	30,202.2	234.09
1975	13.8	3,900,625	27,255.0	190.44
1976	11.4	3,904,576	22,526.4	129.96
1977	12.9	3,908,529	25,503.3	166.41
1978	14.8	3,912,484	29,274.4	219.04
1979	13.3	3,916,441	26,320.7	176.89
1980	12.0	3,920,400	23,760.0	144.00
1981	14.7	3,924,361	29,120.7	216.09
1982	16.4	39,28,324	32,504.8	268.96
1983	17.0	3,932,289	33,711.0	289.00
1984	20.2	3,936,256	40,076.8	408.04
1985	18.6	3,940,225	36,921.0	345.96
1986	17.1	3,944,196	33,960.6	292.41
1987	15.4	3,948,169	30,599.8	237.16
1988	13.7	3,952,144	27,235.6	187.69
1989	10.6	3,956,121	21,083.4	112.36
41,559	303.4	82,246,031	600,527.0	4513.5

$(\sum X)^2 = 1,727,150,481$ $\qquad$ $(\sum Y)^2 = 92,051.6$

There does not appear to be a strong linear relationship between the number of circulations per title and the year of copyright.

c. The correlation coefficient may be calculated by using either the Pearson's product-moment or the Spearman method. The formula for the Pearson's product-moment correlation coefficient is

$$r = \frac{n \sum XY - \sum X \sum Y}{\sqrt{[\, n \sum X^2 - (\sum X)^2 \,]\, [\, n \sum Y^2 - (\sum Y)^2 \,]}}$$

$$= \frac{21\,(\,600{,}527\,) - (\,41{,}559\,)\,(\,303.4\,)}{\sqrt{[\, 21\,(\,82{,}246{,}031\,) - 1{,}727{,}150{,}481\,]\,[\,21\,(\,4513.5\,) - 92051.6\,]}}$$

$$= \frac{2066.4}{\sqrt{16{,}170\,(\,2731.9\,)}}$$

$$= \frac{2066.4}{6646.4}$$

$$= 0.31$$

Year	Circulation per Title	Year Rank	Circulation per Title Rank	D	D^2
1969	16.2	1	16	15	225
1970	13.5	2	8	6	36
1971	11.1	3	2	-1	1
1972	14.2	4	11	7	49
1973	11.2	5	3	-2	4
1974	15.3	6	14	8	64
1975	13.8	7	10	3	9
1976	11.4	8	4	-4	16
1977	12.9	9	6	-3	9
1978	14.8	10	13	3	9
1979	13.3	11	7	-4	16
1980	12.0	12	5	-7	49
1981	14.7	13	12	-1	1
1982	16.4	14	17	3	9
1983	17.0	15	18	3	9
1984	20.2	16	21	5	25
1985	18.6	17	20	3	9
1986	17.1	18	19	1	1
1987	15.4	19	15	-4	16
1988	13.7	20	9	-11	121
1989	10.6	21	1	-20	400

The correlation coefficient may also be determined by the Spearman method. Using the Spearman method requires that the data be ranked.

The Spearman correlation coefficient is calculated as follows:

$$r_\rho = 1 - \frac{6 \sum D^2}{n(n^2 - 1)}$$

$$= 1 - \frac{6(1078)}{21(441 - 1)}$$

$$= 1 - \frac{6468}{9240}$$

$$= 1 - 0.70$$

$$= 0.30$$

The values obtained by both methods are in good agreement.

d. The regression equation, $Y = aX + b$, is estimated using the following equations:

$$a = \frac{n \sum XY - \sum X \sum Y}{n(\sum X^2) - (\sum X)^2}$$

$$= \frac{21(600,527) - (41,559)(303.4)}{21(82,246,031) - (1,727,150,481)}$$

$$= \frac{12,611,067 - 12,609,000.6}{1,727,166,651 - 1,727,150,481}$$

$$= \frac{2066.4}{16,170}$$

$$= 0.128$$

$b = \bar{Y} - a\bar{X}$ Note that this can be written as $b = \dfrac{\sum Y}{n} - a\dfrac{\sum X}{n}$

$$= \frac{303.4}{21} - (0.128)(\frac{41,559}{21})$$

$$= 14.45 - 253.31$$

$$= -238.86 \text{ or } -238.9$$

When these values are used for the slope and the intercept, the equation showing the relationship between the number of circulations per title and the year of copyright is

CIRCULATIONS PER TITLE = -238.9 + 0.128 (COPYRIGHT YEAR)

14. a. $r_\rho = 1 - \dfrac{6 \sum D^2}{n(n^2 - 1)}$

	1st Rank	2nd Rank	D	D^2
Books	2.0	1.0	-1.0	1.0
Computer printouts	8.0	12.0	4.0	16.0
Films (pictorial)	13.0	13.0	0.0	0.0
Government publications	4.0	6.5	2.5	6.25
Manuscripts	1.0	3.0	2.0	4.0
Maps	9.0	10.0	1.0	1.0
Microcopies	10.0	5.0	-5.0	25.0
Newspapers	6.5	4.0	-2.5	6.25
Other pictorials (photos)	11.0	9.0	-2.0	4.0
Periodicals	3.0	2.0	-1.0	1.0
Research reports	5.0	8.0	3.0	9.0
Tape/Sound recordings	12.0	11.0	-1.0	1.0
Theses/Dissertations	6.5	6.5	0.0	0.0
Videotapes	14.0	4.0	0.0	0.0
				74.5

$= 1 - \dfrac{6(74.5)}{14(196 - 1)}$

$= 1 - \dfrac{447}{2730}$

$= 1 - 0.16$

$= 0.84$

b. The two surveys appear to be comparing the physical formats on the same bases of use. The correlation coefficient of 0.84 means there is a strong linear relationship between the two sets of variables.

15. a.

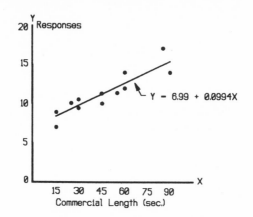

Commercial Length (sec.)

X	Y	X^2	XY	Y^2
15	7	225	105	49
15	9	225	135	81
25	10	625	250	100
30	9	900	270	81
30	11	900	330	121
45	13	2025	585	169
45	10	2025	450	100
55	13	3025	715	169
60	12	3600	720	144
60	14	3600	840	196
85	17	7225	1445	289
90	14	8100	1260	196
555	139	32,475	7105	1695

b. The correlation coefficient may determined, by using either the Pearson product-moment or the Spearman method. The Pearson product-moment is as follows:

$$r = \frac{n \sum XY - \sum X \sum Y}{\sqrt{[n \sum X^2 - (\sum X)^2][n \sum Y^2 - (\sum Y)^2]}}$$

$$= \frac{12(7105) - (555)(139)}{\sqrt{[12(32,475) - 308,025][12(1695) - 19,321]}}$$

$$= \frac{85,260 - 77,145}{\sqrt{[389,700 - 308,025][20,340 - 19,321]}}$$

$$= \frac{8115}{\sqrt{[81,675][1019]}}$$

$$= \frac{8115}{\sqrt{83,226,825}}$$

$$= \frac{8115}{9123}$$

$$= 0.890$$

The correlation coefficient may also be determined by using the Spearman algorithm. This requires that the data be ranked and the differences between the rankings then be calculated.

Seconds	Responses	Rank of Seconds	Rank of Responses	D	D^2
15	7	1.5	1.0	-0.5	0.25
15	9	1.5	2.5	1.0	1.00
25	10	3.0	4.5	1.5	2.25
30	9	4.5	2.5	-2.0	4.00
30	11	4.5	6.0	1.5	2.25
45	13	6.5	8.5	2.0	4.00
45	10	6.5	4.5	-2.0	4.00
55	13	8.0	8.5	0.5	0.25
60	12	9.5	7.0	-2.5	6.25
60	14	9.5	10.5	1.0	1.00
85	17	11.0	12.0	1.0	1.00
90	14	12.0	10.5	-1.5	2.25
					$\Sigma = 28.50$

$$r_\rho = 1 - \frac{6 \sum D^2}{n(n^2 - 1)}$$

$$= 1 - \frac{6(28.50)}{12(144 - 1)}$$

$$= 1 - \frac{171}{1716}$$

$$= 1 - 0.09965$$

$$= 0.90035 \text{ or } 0.900$$

c. The regression equation, $Y = aX + b$, is calculated using the follow-ing two equations:

$$a = \frac{n \sum XY - \sum X \sum Y}{n(\sum X^2) - (\sum X)^2}$$

$$a = \frac{12(7105) - (555)(139)}{12(32,475) - 308,025}$$

$$= \frac{85,260 - 77,145}{389,700 - 308,025}$$

$$= \frac{8115}{81,675}$$

$$= 0.0994$$

$b = \overline{Y} - a\overline{X}$

$= \dfrac{139}{12} - (0.0994)(\dfrac{555}{12})$

$= 6.99$

The regression equation is NUMBER OF RESPONSES = 6.99 + 0.0994(NUMBER OF SECONDS)

d. The regression equation can be used to estimate the response generated by commercials of length 40, 50, or 75 seconds. The values of the independent variables, number of seconds, are substituted into the regression equation and the equation is solved for the number of responses.
For a 40-second commercial,
Number of Responses = 6.99 + 0.0994 (40) = 10.97, or 11
For a 50-second commercial,
Number of Responses = 6.99 + 0.0994 (50) = 11.96, or 12
For a 75-second commercial,
Number of Responses = 6.99 + 0.0994 (75) = 14.44., or 14

The regression equation should only be used to estimate with values of the independent variable in the same range as the data used to construct the regression equation. Because we have no data on the relationship between commercial length and response for commercials longer than 90 seconds, for example, it would not be valid to use the regression equation to try to estimate the response to a 120-second radio commercial.

17. a. Whether clientele have been checking out their favorite materials excessively in order to affect the allocation of moneys for acquisitions would be apparent if the correlation between 1988 and 1989 circulation were weak. In other words, had the habits of the book-borrowing public changed so as to influence book purchases, the correlation between circulation in 1988 and 1989 would be low.

To check for the correlation between circulation in the two years, the Pearson product-moment correlation coefficient is used. The values used in solving the correlation throughout this problem were generated by the computer software package, Minitab. If you use a software package such as Minitab, SAS, or SPSS, you may get slightly different numbers than if you manually compute the sums and products. However, the final answer will be the same. The discrepancy between manual and automated calculation is that the computer converts large numbers to scientific notation.

Quantity	Value
n	14
ΣX	150,935
ΣY	155,549
ΣX^2	3,541,655,296
ΣXY	3,576,124,928
ΣY^2	3,626,602,240
$(\Sigma X)^2$	22,781,374,464
$(\Sigma Y)^2$	24,195,491,840

$$r = \frac{n\sum XY - \sum X \sum Y}{\sqrt{[n\sum X^2 - (\sum X)^2][n\sum Y^2 - (\sum Y)^2]}}$$

$$= \frac{14(3,576,124,928) - (150,935)(155,549)}{\sqrt{[14(3,541,655,296) - 22,781,374,464][14(3,626,602,240) - 24,195,491,840]}}$$

$$= \frac{50,065,747,968 - 23,477,788,672}{\sqrt{[49,583,173,632 - 22,781,374,464][50,772,434,944 - 24,195,491,840]}}$$

$$= \frac{26,587,959,296}{\sqrt{[26,801,799,168]}\sqrt{[26,576,943,104]}}$$

$$= \frac{26,587,959,296}{(163,713)(163,024)}$$

$$= \frac{26,587,959,296}{26,689,134,592}$$

$$= 0.996$$

Since the correlation between circulation in the two years is so high, there is no indication that borrowers are changing their habits to influence the acquisition of new library materials.

b.

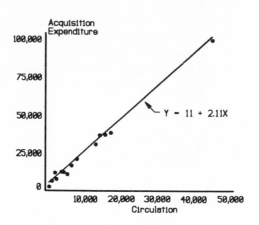

Quantity	Value
n	14
ΣX	155,549
ΣY	329,050
ΣX^2	3,626,602,240
ΣXY	7,669,859,328
ΣY^2	16,241,244,160
$(\Sigma X)^2$	24,195,491,840
$(\Sigma Y)^2$	108,273,901,568

$$r = \frac{n \sum XY - \sum X \sum Y}{\sqrt{[\, n \sum X^2 - (\sum X)^2 \,]\,[\, n \sum Y^2 - (\sum Y)^2 \,]}}$$

$$= \frac{14\,(7,669,859,328) - (155,549)(329,050)}{\sqrt{[\,14\,(3,626,602,240) - 24,195,491,840\,]\,[\,14\,(16,241,244,160) - 108,273,901,608\,]}}$$

$$= \frac{107,378,032,640 - 51,183,398,912}{\sqrt{[\,50,772,434,944 - 24,195,491,840\,]\,[\,227,377,430,528 - 108,273,901,608\,]}}$$

$$= \frac{56,194,633,728}{\sqrt{[\,26,576,943,104\,]\,[\,119,103,520,768\,]}}$$

$$= \frac{56,194,633,728}{\sqrt{[\,26,576,943,104\,]}\;\sqrt{[\,119,103,520,768\,]}}$$

$$= \frac{56,194,633,728}{[\,163,024\,]\,[\,345,114\,]}$$

$$= \frac{56,194,633,728}{56,261,951,488}$$

$= 0.999 \text{ or } 1.00$

There is a strong positive relationship between the circulation of books and the level of acquisition expenditure.

c. The regression equation can be determined by using the following two equations and the summation values given in 17a:

$$a = \frac{n \sum XY - \sum X \sum Y}{n\,(\sum X^2) - (\sum X)^2}$$

$$a = \frac{14\,(7,669,859,328) - (155,549)(329,050)}{14\,(3,626,602,240) - 24,195,491,840}$$

$$= \frac{107,378,030,500 - 51,183,398,450}{50,772,431,360 - 24,195,491,840}$$

$$= \frac{56,194,632,100}{26,576,939,520}$$

= 2.11441 Note: because the magnitude of these numbers is so great, the calculations should be carried out to five decimal places.

$b = \overline{Y} - a\overline{X}$

$$= \frac{329,050}{14} - (2.11441) (\frac{155,549}{14})$$

$$= 23,503.57 - (\frac{328,894.36}{14})$$

$$= 23,503.57 - 23,492.45$$

$$= 11.12$$

When these values are used for the slope and the intercept, the equation of the line showing the relationship between circulation and acquisition expenditures is as follows:
ACQUISITION EXPENDITURE = 11.1 + 2.11 CIRCULATION
{As can be seen, solving a problem of this type without a desktop calculator or computer is difficult and is a task left only for the most hardy.}

   d. The librarian was successful in linking acquisitions to circulation.
18. a. There is a strong positive linear relationship between the years of library service and the number of sick days taken in a 12-month period.

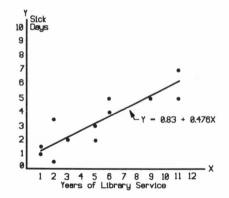

b.

Quantity	Value
n	12
ΣX	62
ΣY	39.5
ΣX^2	464
ΣXY	272.5
ΣY^2	172.75
$(\Sigma X)^2$	3844
$(\Sigma Y)^2$	1560.25

The equation for the regression line may be determined by using the following equations:

$$a = \frac{n \sum XY - \sum X \sum Y}{n (\sum X^2) - (\sum X)^2}$$

$$= \frac{12 (272.5) - (62) (39.5)}{12 (464) - (3844)}$$

$$= \frac{3270 - 2449}{5568 - 3844}$$

$$= \frac{821}{1724}$$

$$= 0.476$$

$b = \bar{Y} - a\bar{X}$ Note that this can be written as $b = \dfrac{\sum Y}{n} - a \dfrac{\sum X}{n}$

$$= \frac{39.5}{12} - (0.476) (\frac{62}{12})$$

$$= \frac{39.5}{12} - (\frac{29.512}{12})$$

$$= 3.29 - 2.46$$

$$= 0.83$$

When these values are used for the slope and the intercept, the equation showing the relationship between the years of library service and the number of sick days is

NUMBER OF SICK DAYS = 0.83 + 0.476 (YEARS OF LIBRARY SERVICE)

c.

$$r = \frac{n \sum XY - \sum X \sum Y}{\sqrt{[n \sum X^2 - (\sum X)^2][n \sum Y^2 - (\sum Y)^2]}}$$

$$= \frac{12(272.5) - (62)(39.5)}{\sqrt{[12(464) - 3844][12(172.75) - 1560.25]}}$$

$$= \frac{3270 - 2449}{\sqrt{[5568 - 3844][2073 - 1560.25]}}$$

$$= \frac{821}{\sqrt{[1724][512.75]}}$$

$$= \frac{821}{\sqrt{883,981}}$$

$$= \frac{821}{940.2}$$

$$= 0.873$$

d. Since the data consider only employees who have been employed for more than 1 year, predictions about how the equation would look for a new hire are not valid. Regression equations should only be used to predict for independent variables which fall in the same range as the data used to generate the regression equation.

Bibliography

Ben-Horim, Moshe. *Statistics, Decisions and Applications in Business and Economics*. 2nd ed. New York: Random House, 1984.

Busha, Charles H., and Harter, Stephen P. *Research Methods in Librarianship: Techniques and Interpretation*. New York: Academic Press, 1980.

Campbell, Stephen K. *Flaws and Fallacies in Statistical Thinking*. Englewood Cliffs, N. J.: Prentice-Hall, 1974.

Madsen, Richard W., and Moeschberger, Melvin L. *Statistical Concepts with Applications to Business and Economics*. Englewood Cliffs, N.J.: Prentice-Hall, 1980.

Phillips, John L. *Statistical Thinking*. 2nd ed. San Francisco: W. H. Freeman, 1982.

Rodger, Eleanor Jo, and Palmour, Vernon E. *Growth Without Expansion*. Baltimore County Public Library Long Range Plan II, 1983-1988. Chicago: American Library Association, 1983.

Rowntree, Derek. *Statistics Without Tears: A Primer for Non-mathematicians*. New York: Scribner, 1981.

Runyon, Richard P. *Winning with Statistics: A Painless First Look at Numbers, Ratios, Percentages, Means, and Inferences*. Reading, Mass.: Addison-Wesley, 1977.

Schmid, Calvin F. *Statistical Graphics Design Principles and Practices*. New York: John Wiley, 1983.

Seisel, H. *Say It with Figures*. 5th ed. New York: Harper & Row, 1968.

Spurr, William A., Kellogg, Lester S., and Smith, John H. *Business and Economic Statistics*. Homewood, Ill.: Richard D. Irwin, 1961.

Swisher, Robert, and McClure, Charles R. *Research for Decision Making: Methods for Librarians*. Chicago: American Library Association, 1984.

Zelazny, Gene. *Say It with Charts: The Executive's Guide to Successful Presentations*. Homewood, Ill.: Dow Jones-Irwin, 1985.

Zweizig, Douglas, and Rodger, Eleanor Jo. *Output Measures for Public Libraries*. Chicago: American Library Association, 1982.

Index

Arthur W. Hafner, Ph. D., is the Director of the Division of Library and Information Management for the American Medical Association, Chicago. Prior to working for AMA, Hafner was the Director of Library Services and Associate Professor of Library Science for the Chicago College of Osteopathic Medicine. He received his Ph.D. in library science and his M.S. in mathematics from the University of Minnesota.